D1539164

When Death Is Sought

Assisted Suicide and Euthanasia in the Medical Context

May 1994

**The New York State Task Force
on Life and the Law**

Members of the Task Force

Mark R. Chassin, M.D., M.P.P., M.P.H.
Chairman
Commissioner of Health
State of New York

Karl Adler, M.D.
Dean, New York Medical College

Rev. Msgr. John A. Alesandro
Chancellor
Roman Catholic Diocese of Rockville Centre

John Arras, Ph.D.
Associate Professor of Bioethics
Albert Einstein College of Medicine
Montefiore Medical Center

Mario L. Baeza, Esq.
Debevoise & Plimpton

The Right Rev. David Ball
Bishop, Episcopal Diocese of Albany

Rabbi J. David Bleich
Professor of Talmud, Yeshiva University
Professor of Jewish Law and Ethics
Benjamin Cardozo School of Law

Evan Calkins, M.D.
Professor of Medicine, Emeritus
SUNY-Buffalo

Richard J. Concannon, Esq.
Kelley, Drye & Warren

Myron W. Conovitz, M.D.
Attending Physician
North Shore University Hospital
Clinical Associate Professor of Medicine
Cornell University Medical College

Saul J. Farber, M.D.
Dean and Provost
Chairman, Department of Medicine
New York University School of Medicine

Alan R. Fleischman, M.D.
Director, Division of Neonatology
Albert Einstein College of Medicine

Samuel Gorovitz, Ph.D.
Professor of Philosophy
Syracuse University

Jane Greenlaw, J.D., R.N.
Director, Division of the Medical Humanities
University of Rochester School of Medicine and Dentistry

Beatrix A. Hamburg, M.D.
President, W.T. Grant Foundation

Denise Hanlon, R.N., M.S.
Assistant Clinical Professor
SUNY Buffalo School of Nursing

Rev. Donald W. McKinney
Chairman Emeritus, Choice in Dying

Maria I. New, M.D.
Chief, Department of Pediatrics
New York Hospital-Cornell Medical Center

John J. Regan, J.S.D.
Professor of Law
Hofstra University School of Law

Rabbi A. James Rudin
National Director of Interreligious Affairs
The American Jewish Committee

Rev. Betty Bone Schiess
Episcopal Diocese of Central New York

Barbara Shack
The New York Civil Liberties Union

Rev. Robert S. Smith
Director, Institute for Medicine in Contemporary Society
SUNY Health Science Center at Stony Brook

Elizabeth W. Stack
Commissioner
New York State Commission on
Quality of Care for the Mentally Disabled

Task Force Staff

Tracy E. Miller, J.D.
Executive Director

Carl H. Coleman, J.D.
Associate Counsel

Anna Maria Cugliari, M.S.
Health Policy Analyst

Aaron L. Mackler, Ph.D.
Staff Ethicist

Elizabeth Peppe
Administrative Assistant

Jean Pohoryles
Administrative Secretary

Consultants to the Task Force Committee on Suicide and Professional Responsibility

Nessa M. Coyle, R.N., M.S.
Director of Supportive Care Program
Pain Service, Department of Neurology
Memorial Sloan-Kettering Cancer Center

Jimmie C. Holland, M.D.
Chief, Psychiatry Service
Memorial Sloan-Kettering Cancer Center
Professor of Psychiatry, Cornell University Medical College

Diane E. Meier, M.D.
Associate Professor
Department of Geriatrics and Adult Development
Mt. Sinai School of Medicine

Norton Spritz, M.D.
Chief, Medical Service
Department of Veterans Affairs Medical Center
Professor of Medicine
New York University School of Medicine

Contents

Preface

Governor Mario M. Cuomo convened the Task Force on Life and the Law in 1985, giving it a broad mandate to recommend public policy on issues raised by medical advances. That mandate included decisions about life-sustaining treatment. Assisted suicide and euthanasia were not on the agenda initially presented to the Task Force. Nor was the prospect of legalizing the practices even remotely part of public consideration at that time.

Recently, however, public debate about the practices has intensified. Although no major efforts to legalize assisted suicide and euthanasia have been launched in New York State, we chose to examine the practices and to release this report in order to contribute to the debate unfolding in New York and nationally.

Since the Task Force's inception, we have proposed four laws to promote the right to decide about medical treatment, including life-sustaining measures. Three of those proposals, establishing procedures for do-not-resuscitate orders in health care facilities and in community settings, and authorizing individuals to create health care proxies, are now law. Our fourth proposal for legislation is pending before the New York State Legislature. It would grant family members and others close to the patient the authority to decide about treatment, including life-sustaining measures, for individuals who are too young or too ill to decide for themselves and who have not left advance treatment instructions or signed a health care proxy.

In this report, we unanimously recommend that New York laws prohibiting assisted suicide and euthanasia should not be changed. In essence, we propose a clear line for public policies and medical practice between forgoing medical interventions and assistance to commit suicide or euthanasia. Decisions to forgo treatment are an integral part of medical practice; the use of many treatments would be inconceivable without the ability to withhold or to stop the treatments in appropriate cases. We have identified the wishes and interests of patients as the primary guideposts for those decisions.

Assisted suicide and euthanasia would carry us into new terrain — American society has never sanctioned assisted suicide or mercy killing. We believe that the practices would be profoundly dangerous for large segments of the population, especially in light of the widespread

vii

failure of American medicine to treat pain adequately or to diagnose and treat depression in many cases. The risks would extend to all individuals who are ill. They would be most severe for those whose autonomy and well-being are already compromised by poverty, lack of access to good medical care, or membership in a stigmatized social group. The risks of legalizing assisted suicide and euthanasia for these individuals, in a health care system and society that cannot effectively protect against the impact of inadequate resources and ingrained social disadvantage, are likely to be extraordinary.

The distinction between the refusal of medical treatment and assisted suicide or euthanasia has not been well-articulated in the broader public debate. In fact, the often-used rubric of the "right to die" obscures the distinction. The media's coverage of individual cases as a way of presenting the issues to the public also blurs the difference between a private act and public policy; between what individuals might find desirable or feasible in a particular case and what would actually occur in doctors' offices, clinics, and hospitals, if assisted suicide and euthanasia became a standard part of medical practice. Public opinion polls, focusing on whether individuals think they might want these options for themselves one day, also offer little insight about what it would mean for society to make assisted suicide or direct killing practices sanctioned and regulated by the state or supervised by the medical profession itself.

We hope that this report will highlight certain critical distinctions and questions for public consideration. We also hope that the report and our recommendations will improve access to pain relief and the palliation of symptoms, not only for those who are terminally ill or contemplating suicide, but for all patients.

We sought the opinions and expertise of many individuals while developing our recommendations. We extend our gratitude to all those who generously lent their time and perspective to our discussion. Four individuals served as consultants in our deliberations: Nessa Coyle, R.N., Jimmie Holland, M.D., Diane Meier, M.D., and Norton Spritz, M.D. The report does not necessarily reflect their personal views about assisted suicide and euthanasia, but it does reflect their experience and insight in caring for those who are severely and terminally ill. We benefitted greatly from their expertise and their participation with us as we explored these difficult questions. We also extend our gratitude to Chris Hyman and Peter Millock who provided invaluable guidance throughout our deliberations.

The Members of the Task Force on Life and the Law

Executive Summary

Over the past two decades, the right to decide about medical treatment, including the right to refuse life-sustaining measures, has become a fundamental tenet of American law. The Task Force has sought to make this right a reality for the citizens of New York State, recommending legislation on do-not-resuscitate orders, health care proxies, and, most recently, surrogate decision making for patients without capacity. The Task Force's legislative proposals reflect a deep respect for individual autonomy as well as concern for the welfare of individuals nearing the end of life.

Recent proposals to legalize assisted suicide and euthanasia in some states would transform the right to decide about medical treatment into a far broader right to control the timing and manner of death. After lengthy deliberations, the Task Force unanimously concluded that the dangers of such a dramatic change in public policy would far outweigh any possible benefits. In light of the pervasive failure of our health care system to treat pain and diagnose and treat depression, legalizing assisted suicide and euthanasia would be profoundly dangerous for many individuals who are ill and vulnerable. The risks would be most severe for those who are elderly, poor, socially disadvantaged, or without access to good medical care.

In the course of their research, many Task Force members were particularly struck by the degree to which requests for suicide assistance by terminally ill patients are correlated with clinical depression or unmanaged pain, both of which can ordinarily be treated effectively with current medical techniques. As a society, we can do far more to benefit these patients by improving pain relief and palliative care than by changing the law to make it easier to commit suicide or to obtain a lethal injection.

In General

- This report, like much of the current debate, focuses solely on assisted suicide and euthanasia by physicians, nurses, or other health care professionals.

- In this report, "assisted suicide" refers to actions by one person to contribute to the death of another, by providing medication or a prescription or taking other steps. With assisted suicide, the person who dies directly takes his or her own life. In contrast, "euthanasia" refers to direct measures, such as a lethal injection, by one person to end another person's life for benevolent motives. Both practices are distinct from the withdrawal or withholding of life-sustaining treatment in accord with accepted ethical and medical standards.

The Clinical Background

- Contrary to what many believe, the vast majority of individuals who are terminally ill or facing severe pain or disability are not suicidal. Moreover, terminally ill patients who do desire suicide or euthanasia often suffer from a treatable mental disorder, most commonly depression. When these patients receive appropriate treatment for depression, they usually abandon the wish to commit suicide.

- Depression is distinct from the normal feelings of sadness generally experienced by terminally ill patients. It is a myth that major clinical depression ordinarily accompanies terminal illness.

- While thoughts about suicide ("suicidal ideation") are a significant risk factor for suicide, many individuals experience suicidal ideation but never commit or attempt suicide. These thoughts can be an important and normal component of coping with terminal illness.

- Uncontrolled pain, particularly when accompanied by feelings of hopelessness and untreated depression, is a significant contributing factor for suicide and suicidal ideation. Medications and pain relief techniques now make it possible to treat pain effectively for most patients.

- Despite the fact that effective treatments are available, severely and terminally ill patients generally do not receive adequate relief from pain. Studies report that over 50 percent of cancer patients suffer from unrelieved pain, even though patients with cancer are more likely than other patients to receive pain treatment.

- Numerous barriers contribute to the pervasive inadequacy of pain relief and palliative care in current clinical practice, including a lack of professional knowledge and training, unjustified fears about physical and psychological dependence, poor pain assessment, pharmacy practices, and the reluctance of patients and their families to seek pain relief.

Existing Law

- Under New York law, competent adults have a firmly established right to accept or reject medical treatment, including life-sustaining measures. Competent adults also have the right to create advance directives for treatment decisions, such as a living will or health care proxy, to be used in the event they lose the capacity to make medical decisions for themselves.

- New York is one of two states in the nation that does not currently permit the withdrawal or withholding of life-sustaining treatment from an incapacitated adult patient who has not signed a health care proxy or provided clear and convincing evidence of his or her treatment wishes. Legislation proposed by the Task Force, under consideration by the New York State Legislature, would permit family members and others close to the patient to decide about life-sustaining treatment in these circumstances.

- Neither suicide nor attempted suicide is a criminal offense in any state. Like most other states, New York prohibits assisting a suicide. Euthanasia is barred by law in every state, including New York.

- Suicide assistance generally constitutes a form of second-degree manslaughter under New York law. Euthanasia falls under the definition of second-degree murder, regardless of whether the person consents to being killed.

- The provision of pain medication is legally acceptable even if it may hasten the patient's death, if the medication is intended to alleviate pain or severe discomfort, not to cause death, and is provided in accord with accepted medical standards.

- Neither the United States nor the New York State Constitution grants individuals a "right" to suicide assistance or euthanasia. Although the right to refuse life-sustaining treatment is constitutionally protected, the courts have consistently distinguished the right to refuse treatment from a right to commit suicide. In affirming the right to forgo treatment, the courts have recognized the state's legitimate interest in preventing suicide.

Ethical Issues

- Three general positions about assisted suicide and euthanasia have emerged in the ethical and medical literature. First, some believe that both practices are morally wrong and should not be performed. Others hold that assisted suicide or euthanasia are legitimate in rare and exceptional cases, but that professional standards and the law should not be changed to authorize either practice. Finally, some argue that assisted suicide, or both assisted suicide and euthanasia, should be recognized as legally and morally acceptable options in the care of dying or severely ill patients.

- While many individuals do not distinguish between assisted suicide and euthanasia on ethical or policy grounds, some find assisted suicide more acceptable than euthanasia, either intrinsically or because of differences in the social impact and potential harm of the two practices.

The Task Force's Recommendations: Crafting Public Policy

The Ethics of Assisted Suicide and Euthanasia

- The members of the Task Force hold different views about the ethical acceptability of assisted suicide and euthanasia. Despite these differences, the Task Force members unanimously recommend that existing law should not be changed to permit these practices.

- Some of the Task Force members believe that assisted suicide and euthanasia are inherently wrong, because the practices violate society's long-standing prohibition against ending human life. These members believe that one person should not assist another's death or kill another person, even for benevolent motives.

- Other Task Force members are most troubled by the prospect of medicalizing the practices. They believe that physician-assisted suicide and euthanasia violate values that are fundamental to the practice of medicine and the patient-physician relationship.

- Some Task Force members do not believe that assisted suicide is inherently unethical or incompatible with medical practice. On the contrary, they believe that providing a quick, less prolonged death for some patients can respect the autonomy of patients and demonstrate care and commitment on the part of physicians or other health care professionals. Nonetheless, these members have concluded that legalizing assisted suicide would be unwise and dangerous public policy.

The Social Risks of Legalization

- The Task Force members unanimously concluded that legalizing assisted suicide and euthanasia would pose profound risks to many patients. For purposes of public debate, one can describe cases of assisted suicide in which all the recommended safeguards would be satisfied. But positing an "ideal" or "good" case is not sufficient for public policy, if it bears little relation to prevalent social and medical practices.

- No matter how carefully any guidelines are framed, assisted suicide and euthanasia will be practiced through the prism of social inequality and bias that characterizes the delivery of services in all segments of our society, including health care. The practices will pose the greatest risks to those who are poor, elderly, members of a minority group, or without access to good medical care.

- The growing concern about health care costs increases the risks presented by legalizing assisted suicide and euthanasia. This cost consciousness will not be diminished, and may well be exacerbated, by health care reform.

- The clinical safeguards that have been proposed to prevent abuse and errors would not be realized in many cases. For example, most doctors do not have a long-standing relationship with their patients or information about the complex personal factors relevant to evaluating a request for suicide assistance or a lethal injection. In addition, neither treatment for pain nor the diagnosis of and treatment for depression is widely available in clinical practice.

- In debating public policies, our society often focuses on dramatic individual cases. With assisted suicide and euthanasia, this approach obscures the impact of what it would mean for the state to sanction assisted suicide or direct killing under the auspices of the medical community.

- From the perspective of good health, many individuals may believe that they would opt for suicide or euthanasia rather than endure a vastly diminished quality of life. Yet, once patients are confronted with illness, continued life often becomes more precious; given access to appropriate relief from pain and other debilitating symptoms, many of those who consider suicide during the course of a terminal illness abandon their desire for a quicker death in favor of a longer life made more tolerable with effective treatment.

- The Task Force members feel deep compassion for patients in those rare cases when pain cannot be alleviated even with aggressive palliative care. They also recognize that the desire for control at life's end is widely shared and deeply felt. As a society, however, we have better ways to give people greater control and relief from suffering than by legalizing assisted suicide and euthanasia.

- Depression accompanied by feelings of hopelessness is the strongest predictor of suicide for both individuals who are terminally ill and those who are not. Most doctors, however, are not trained to diagnose depression, especially in complex cases such as patients who are terminally ill. Even if diagnosed, depression is often not treated. In elderly patients as well as the terminally and chronically ill, depression is grossly underdiagnosed and undertreated.

- The presence of unrelieved pain also increases susceptibility to suicide. The undertreatment of pain is a widespread failure of current medical practice, with far-reaching implications for proposals to legalize assisted suicide and euthanasia.

- If assisted suicide and euthanasia are legalized, it will blunt our perception of what it means for one individual to assist another to commit suicide or to take another person's life. Over time, as the practices are incorporated into the standard arsenal of medical treatments, the sense of gravity about the practices would dissipate.

- The criteria and safeguards that have been proposed for assisted suicide and euthanasia would prove elastic in clinical practice and in law. Policies limiting suicide to the terminally ill, for example, would be inconsistent with the notion that suicide is a compassionate choice for patients who are in pain or suffering. As long as the policies hinge on notions of pain or suffering, they are uncontainable; neither pain nor suffering can be gauged objectively, nor are they subject to the kind of judgments needed to fashion coherent public policy. Euthanasia to cover those who are incapable of consenting would also be a likely, if not inevitable, extension of any policy permitting the practice for those who can consent.

- These concerns are heightened by experience in the Netherlands, where the practices have been legally sanctioned. Although Dutch law requires an explicit request for euthanasia by the patient, a national study in the Netherlands found that of approximately 3300 deaths annually resulting from mercy killing, 1,000 deaths from euthanasia occurred without an explicit request. Moreover, in some cases, doctors have provided assisted suicide in response to suffering caused solely by psychiatric illness, including severe depression.

Caring for Severely Ill Patients

- Professional medical standards should recognize the provision of effective pain relief and palliative care, including treatment for depression or referral for treatment, as a basic obligation all physicians owe to their patients. The legal prohibition against assisted suicide and euthanasia should also guide professional standards of conduct.

- Physicians should seek their patients' participation in decisions about withdrawing or withholding life-sustaining treatment early enough in the course of illness to give patients a meaningful opportunity to have their wishes and values respected.

- Health care professionals have a duty to offer effective pain relief and symptom palliation to patients when necessary, in accord with sound medical judgment and the most advanced approaches available.

- New York State statutes and regulations should be modified to increase the availability of medically necessary analgesic medications, including opioids. This should be done in a balanced manner that acknowledges the importance of avoiding drug diversion. Chapter 8 sets forth specific recommendations for legal reform.

- Physicians, nurses, and patients must be aware that psychological and physical dependence on pain medication are distinct phenomena. Contrary to a widely shared misunderstanding, psychological dependence on pain medication rarely occurs in terminally ill patients. While physical dependence is more common, proper adjustment of medication can minimize negative effects.

- The provision of appropriate pain relief rarely poses a serious risk of respiratory depression. Moreover, the provision of pain medication is ethically and professionally acceptable even when such treatment may hasten the patient's death, if the medication is intended to alleviate pain and severe discomfort, not to cause death, and is provided in accord with accepted medical practice.

- The education of health care professionals about pain relief and palliative care must be improved. Training in pain relief and palliative care should be included in the curriculum of nursing schools, medical schools, residencies, and continuing education for health care professionals.

- Hospitals and other health care institutions should explore ways to promote effective pain relief and palliative care, and to remove existing barriers to such care.

- Public education is crucial to enhance pain relief practices. Like many health care professionals, patients and families often have an exaggerated sense of the risks of pain medication, and are reluctant to seek treatment for pain. Nurses and physicians should create an atmosphere that will encourage patients to seek relief of pain. Strategies for pain relief should also maximize patients' sense of control.

- Insurance companies and others responsible for health care financing should promote effective pain and symptom management and address barriers that exist for some patients.

- Health care professionals should be familiar with the characteristics of major depression and other common psychiatric illnesses, as well as the possibility for treatment. Major clinical depression is generally treatable, and can be treated effectively even in the absence of improvement in the underlying disease. Patients should also receive appropriate treatment for less severe depression that often accompanies terminal illness.

- Physicians should create an atmosphere within which patients feel comfortable expressing suicidal thoughts. Discussion with a physician or other health care professional about suicide can identify the need for treatment and make the patient feel less isolated. This discussion does not prompt suicide; on the contrary, talking with health care professionals often decreases the risk of suicide.

- When a patient requests assisted suicide or euthanasia, a health care professional should explore the significance of the request, recognize the patient's suffering, and seek to discover the factors leading to the request. These factors may include insufficient symptom control, clinical depression, inadequate social support, concern about burdening family or others, hopelessness, loss of self-esteem, or fear of abandonment.

Introduction

Respect for individual choice and self-determination has served as a touchstone for public policies about medical decisions over the past two decades. Designed to promote these values, legal reform has wrought many gains, including clear recognition of a right to refuse life-sustaining measures. Social and clinical practices, however, have changed more slowly, often leaving patients and those close to them without a sense of control over the course of treatment. As a result, the public's fear of a painful death prolonged by medical advances has not abated. This growing public concern about control at life's end and the emphasis on individual self-determination have brought us to a new crossroads in the realm of medical practice and ethics. For the first time in the United States, assisted suicide and euthanasia are issues of serious and widespread public consideration.

Assisted suicide occurs when one person assists another to take his or her own life, either by providing the means to commit suicide or by taking other necessary steps. Euthanasia entails direct measures, such as a lethal injection, by one person to end another person's life. Euthanasia may be voluntary, performed with the explicit consent of a competent adult, or it can be performed without consent, in which case it is usually called "nonvoluntary" euthanasia. Euthanasia provided over the patient's objection is generally referred to as "involuntary" euthanasia. Both assisted suicide and euthanasia are distinct from the withdrawal or withholding of life-sustaining treatment.[1]

While assisted suicide and euthanasia can be offered outside the medical context by family members or others, recent debate has focused on these practices by physicians and other health care professionals. Assisted suicide in the medical context is usually provided by giving a prescription or medications to a patient seeking to end his or her life. A lethal injection would be the most common form of euthanasia provided by doctors.

---

[1]Some use the term "euthanasia" or "passive euthanasia" to include the wrongful or inappropriate withholding or withdrawal of life-sustaining treatment. This report, like much of the current debate, uses the term "euthanasia" more narrowly, referring only to active measures, such as a lethal injection, to end the patient's life. The Task Force recognizes that defining the term in this way clarifies its own intentions, but does not address the complex relationship between action, omission and moral culpability. For a discussion of this issue, see chapter 5, pp. 82-83.

Several prominent cases have spurred debate about physician-assisted suicide and euthanasia. In 1988, in an anonymous article in the *Journal of the American Medical Association*, a physician described how he had given a lethal injection to a young woman dying of ovarian cancer.[2] The physician had no prior relationship with the patient and had not discussed the decision with her. Instead, he decided to provide the lethal injection based on her mumbled words, "Let's get this over with."

On June 4, 1993, Dr. Jack Kevorkian helped Janet Adkins commit suicide in a Volkswagen van in a Michigan park. Janet Adkins was 54 years old and still physically active but was experiencing the early symptoms of Alzheimer's disease. Kevorkian used a machine he developed that delivered a fatal dose of potassium chloride when Janet Adkins pushed a button. Nineteen other highly publicized deaths have followed with Kevorkian's assistance. Kevorkian has had little previous contact with the patients he assists, many of whom, like Janet Adkins, were not terminally ill. A retired pathologist, it is likely that he has little or no experience in diagnosing depression or treating terminally ill patients. Although some regard Kevorkian as a champion for human rights, he has crystalized the doubts of many about the potential for abuse and the dangers of physician-assisted suicide.

In contrast to Kevorkian, Dr. Timothy Quill had a long-standing relationship with the patient whose death he assisted. Writing about the case in the *New England Journal of Medicine* in March 1991, Quill explained that he had offered all available medical alternatives to his patient, encouraged her to accept treatment for her condition, and spoke with her at length about her decision before prescribing the barbiturates that would enable her to take her own life.[3]

In February 1993, the Netherlands became the first nation to establish policies permitting doctors to assist a suicide or to perform voluntary euthanasia. Under Dutch law, physicians cannot be prosecuted for either practice if they follow specified guidelines and report their actions to the coroner in each case. Although assisted suicide and voluntary euthanasia are both legally sanctioned, 85 percent of these cases have been instances of euthanasia. Policies in the Netherlands emerged from growing acceptance of the practice by physicians, and

---

[2]"It's Over, Debbie," *Journal of the American Medical Association* 259 (1988): 272. It remains unclear whether this anonymous article described a fictitious or an actual case.

[3]T. E. Quill, "Death and Dignity: A Case of Individualized Decision Making," *New England Journal of Medicine* 324 (1991): 691-94.

the long-standing reluctance of prosecutors to enforce the law prohibiting assisted suicide and euthanasia.

In the United States, legislative referenda to legalize the practices have been considered in several states. In November 1991, Washington State voted on a referendum to legalize "physician aid-in-dying" — defined to include both assisted suicide and euthanasia. The referendum failed with 54 percent of the public voting against it. If it had passed, Washington would have become the first state in the nation to legalize these activities by physicians or others. In November 1992, voters in California defeated a similar referendum by the same narrow margin. These votes will no doubt encourage attempts to legalize assisted suicide and euthanasia in other states. At the same time, publicity about Kevorkian and public debate about the practices have prompted other states to strengthen or clarify their laws prohibiting assisted suicide. Four states, including Michigan, enacted laws in 1993 to achieve this goal.[4]

Like the referenda in Washington and California, public opinion polls suggest that the public in the United States is divided on the question of legalizing assisted suicide and euthanasia. The widespread success of the book *Final Exit*, a how-to on committing suicide, left no doubt, however, that some segment of the public is deeply concerned about the dying process.[5] A best seller for many months, the book tapped into a well-spring of anxiety about the loss of control at life's end. The book's popularity is a clarion call, signaling that existing social and clinical practices do not give Americans the sense of control they desire.

The need to make decisions about the dying process and the failure to manage technological advances more wisely has also profoundly influenced some segments of the medical profession. For physicians,

---

[4]Under the Michigan law, the statutory prohibition on assisted suicide will expire no later than December 31, 1994. The law established a commission to study the issue and recommend whether the prohibition should be continued, modified, or abandoned.

[5]The full title of the book is *Final Exit: The Practicalities of Self-Deliverance and Assisted Suicide for the Dying*. It was written by Derek Humphrey, the founder of the Hemlock Society. A study reported in the *New England Journal of Medicine* about the book's impact concluded that, although the overall suicide rate in New York City had not changed following the book's publication, suicide by asphyxiation using a plastic bag, one of the methods recommended in the book, had increased. Of the 15 individuals reported to have used the book to commit suicide, most were not terminally ill and six had no history of medical illness or diagnosed illness at autopsy. P. M. Marzuk et al., "Increase in Suicide by Asphyxiation in New York City After the Publication of *Final Exit,*" *New England Journal of Medicine* 329 (1993): 1508-10.

decisions to withhold or to stop treatment, calling for their intervention in the timing and manner of death, have become routine. While earlier generations of physicians were trained to stave off death whenever possible and had few available means at their disposal to do so, physicians today, especially those who are younger, have grown accustomed to the idea that life inappropriately prolonged can also be a defeat for them and for their patients.

The medical community, like the broader society, has therefore reached a crossroads, with some physicians advocating legal change that would permit them to assist their patients to commit suicide under certain circumstances. Despite the fact that assisted suicide is illegal in most states and euthanasia is prohibited throughout the United States, press reports and polls suggest that some physicians already respond to their patients' requests for help by prescribing medication or providing a lethal injection. The practice occurs in the private relationship between doctor and patient, yielding little public information about the frequency or circumstances of medically assisted suicide or euthanasia.

In New York State, no serious effort to legalize assisted suicide or euthanasia is underway. New York's criminal law prohibits both practices.[6] The health care proxy law, enacted in 1990 to give adults an effective way to exercise the right to decide about treatment, including life-sustaining measures, explicitly states that it is not designed to permit or promote assisted suicide or euthanasia.[7] Pending legislation proposed by the Task Force, which would allow family members and others close to the patient to decide about treatment for incapacitated patients who have not signed health care proxies, contains a similar statement.[8] Hence, like the law in states across the country, New York law to date has consistently distinguished decisions to forgo life-sustaining treatment from assisted suicide and euthanasia.

The issue of assisted suicide has been posed most directly in New York State by the case involving Dr. Timothy Quill. A resident of Rochester, New York, Quill faced potential criminal and professional sanctions following publication of his article in the *New England Journal of Medicine*. A grand jury was convened in Rochester and decided not to indict him. Likewise, the State Board for Professional

---

[6]N.Y. Penal Law §§ 120.30, 120.35, 125.15(3), 125.25(1) (McKinney 1987). See chapter 4 for discussion of New York law.

[7]N.Y. Public Health Law, § 2989(3) (McKinney 1993).

[8]New York State Assembly Bill No. 7166, § 2995-q(3) (1994).

Medical Conduct considered the case and chose not to pursue professional misconduct charges. Writing for the board, a three member panel concluded that Quill could not have known with certainty that his patient would use the medication he prescribed for insomnia to kill herself. In its opinion in the Quill case, the board recognized the important moral and social issues presented by the case and asked the Task Force on Life and the Law to provide guidance for policies in New York State. The Task Force agreed to deliberate about assisted suicide and euthanasia not because of the Quill case itself, but because the case struck a public nerve, echoing broad public concern about the practices.

This report reflects the Task Force's exploration of medically assisted suicide and euthanasia. It examines the clinical, legal, and social context for the current debate about the practices. Presented in the first half of the report, that information includes important insight about the problem of suicide generally, the reasons that people commit suicide, the capacity of medicine to respond to some of those underlying reasons, and its widespread failure to do so. Chapter Four examines in-depth the law on assisted suicide and euthanasia and the relationship of that body of law to prevailing medical standards. The chapter also discusses whether there is a constitutional right to suicide assistance and euthanasia. Chapter Five sketches the current debate about assisted suicide and euthanasia, exploring the ethical arguments set forth by those who advocate legalizing assisted suicide and euthanasia as well as by those who firmly oppose any such legal change.

The second half of the report presents the Task Force's recommendations for public policy. Those recommendations first address whether the law should be changed to permit assisted suicide and euthanasia. The report also describes the principles that should animate professional medical standards. In the final chapter, the report proposes policies to enhance the treatment provided to dying and incurably ill patients. The debate about assisted suicide and euthanasia has forced a reexamination of the care provided to terminally and chronically ill individuals; it has highlighted pervasive shortcomings in the clinical response to pain, to suffering arising from treatable causes such as clinical depression, and to requests for suicide assistance. The final chapter of the report proposes specific statutory and regulatory steps to improve access to pain relief, and provides recommendations for clinical practice.

Part I

The Clinical, Legal, and Ethical Context

1

The Epidemiology of Suicide

The psychoanalytic theories of suicide prove, perhaps, only what was already obvious: that the processes which lead a man to take his own life are at least as complex and difficult as those by which he continues to live. The theories help untangle the intricacy of motive and define the deep ambiguity of the wish to die but say little about what it means to be suicidal, and how it feels.

— A. Alvarez, *The Savage God*

Suicide is the eighth leading cause of death in the United States.[1] Based on the assumption that suicide is not a rational choice, society has long sought to prevent or discourage the practice. In fact, society has generally regarded a suicide attempt as a plea for help or an indication of a need for psychiatric treatment. The debate about legalizing assisted suicide and euthanasia has challenged these assumptions, suggesting that for at least some individuals, society should shift from prevention to toleration or assistance.

Central to the current discussion of assisted suicide and euthanasia is a need to understand the nature of suicide, the motivation of individuals who commit suicide, and the specific risk factors. Suicide outside the context of terminal or chronic illness has been the subject of extensive study by sociologists, psychiatrists, and epidemiologists. Their findings shed light on the phenomenon of suicide overall, and on the motivations of those who request suicide when facing a terminal or severe illness. According to available data, only a small percentage of terminally ill or severely ill patients attempt or commit suicide. What distinguishes their life circumstances, medical conditions, or outlook from those who are also severely ill and do not attempt suicide? What

---

[1]G. Winokur and D. W. Black, "Suicide — What Can Be Done," *New England Journal of Medicine* 327 (1992): 490-91.

do they have in common with individuals who do not face physical illness and attempt or commit suicide?

Data about the desire for and incidence of suicide are not available for all patient populations. However, important studies have been conducted of acquired immunodeficiency syndrome (AIDS) and cancer patients as well as the elderly.[2] In many respects, these conditions epitomize for the public the circumstances under which suicide might be considered a rational choice.

Suicide in the General Population

Overall, 2.9 percent of the adult population attempts suicide,[3] and the suicide rate in the general population over a lifetime of 70 years is approximately one percent.[4] Studies of suicide attempters suggest that one percent to two percent complete suicide within a year after the initial attempt, with another one percent committing suicide in each following year.[5] Suicide is especially prevalent among the young and the elderly. It is the third leading cause of death for individuals 15 to 24 years of age. Over the last 30 years, the suicide rate in this age group has increased dramatically.[6] Among younger people who attempt suicide, between 0.1 percent and 10 percent will eventually commit suicide. Yet it is the elderly who have the highest rates of suicide — overall suicide rates for individuals over 65 were approximately 22 per 100,000 in 1986.[7]

Suicide is generally described as the intentional taking of one's own life. For the individual who commits suicide, the act usually represents

---

[2]See chapter 2 for a discussion of suicide and special patient populations.

[3]D. C. Clark, "Rational Suicide and People with Terminal Conditions or Disabilities," *Issues in Law and Medicine* 8 (1992): 147-66.

[4]Depression Guideline Panel, *Depression in Primary Care*, vol. 1, *Detection and Diagnosis, Clinical Practice Guideline*, no. 5, AHCPR pub. no. 93-0550 (Rockville, Md.: U. S. Department of Health and Human Services, Public Health Service, Agency for Health Care Policy and Research, April 1993), 36.

[5]G. M. Asnis et al., "Suicidal Behaviors in Adult Psychiatric Outpatients, I: Description and Prevalence," *American Journal of Psychiatry* 150 (1993): 108-12.

[6]In 1950 the rate for adolescent suicides was 2.7 per 100,000; in 1980 the rate increased to 8.5 per 100,000. C. Runyan and E. A. Gerken, "Epidemiology and Prevention of Adolescent Injury: A Review and Research Agenda," *Journal of the American Medical Association* 262 (1989): 2273-79.

[7]P. J. Meehan, L. E. Saltzman, and R. W. Sattin, "Suicide Among Older United States Residents: Epidemiologic Characteristics and Trends," *American Journal of Public Health* 81 (1991): 1198-1200.

a solution to a problem or life circumstance that the individual fears will only become worse.[8] Believing that their suffering will continue or intensify, suicidal individuals can envision no option but death. As articulated by a prominent suicidologist, the common stimulus to suicide is intolerable psychological pain. Suicide represents an escape or release from that pain.[9]

Contrary to popular opinion, suicide is not usually a reaction to an acute problem or crisis in one's life or even to a terminal illness. Single events do not cause someone to commit suicide. Instead, certain personal characteristics are associated with a higher risk of attempting or committing suicide. The way in which an individual copes with problems over the course of his or her life usually indicates whether the person is emotionally predisposed to suicide. Studies that examine the psychological background of individuals who kill themselves show that 95 percent have a diagnosable mental disorder at the time of death. Depression, accompanied by symptoms of hopelessness and helplessness, is the most prevalent condition among individuals who commit suicide. This is especially true of the elderly, who are more likely than the young to commit suicide during an acute depressive episode.

In general, individuals who attempt suicide differ from those who complete suicide. Suicide attempters are likely to be female and generally attempt suicide by taking an overdose of medication. Suicide completers, by contrast, are more often male and tend to use more lethal means.[10] Approximately 40 percent of patients who commit suicide have made previous suicide attempts.[11] Thoughts about suicide, referred to as "suicidal ideation," are an important risk factor for suicide. However, many individuals experience suicidal ideation but never commit or attempt suicide. This is especially true for patients with advanced terminal illness or debilitating chronic illness.

---

[8] A. Alvarez describes how it feels to be suicidal as follows: "The logic of suicide is different. It is like the unanswerable logic of a nightmare, or like the science-fiction fantasy of being projected suddenly into another dimension: everything makes sense and follows its own strict rules; yet at the same time, everything is also different, perverted, upside down. Once a man decides to take his own life he enters a shut-off, impregnable but wholly convincing world where every detail fits and each incident reinforces his decision." A. Alvarez, *The Savage God: A Study of Suicide* (New York: Random House, 1970), 121.

[9] E. S. Shneidman, "Some Essentials for Suicide and Some Implications for Response," in *Suicide*, ed. A. Roy (Baltimore: Williams and Wilkins, 1986), 1-16.

[10] S. B. Sorenson, "Suicide Among the Elderly: Issues Facing Public Health," *American Journal of Public Health* 81 (1991): 1109-10.

[11] Asnis et al.

The highest rates of suicide occur among patients with major affect or mood disorders (including depression), alcoholics, and schizophrenics. Individuals with clinical, or major, depression have a 15 percent rate of suicide. Ten percent of schizophrenics commit suicide, while alcoholism carries a four percent to six percent risk.[12] The elderly are also at increased risk for suicide and depression,[13] especially elderly white males, who have a suicide rate five times that of the general population.[14]

Individuals who commit suicide generally have no history of mental health treatment, although they often evidence a major psychiatric illness at the time of death. The primary risk factors for completed suicides are major depression, substance abuse, severe personality disorders, male gender, older age, living alone, physical illness, and previous suicide attempts. For terminally ill patients with cancer and AIDS, several additional risk factors are also present.[15]

Another significant predictor of suicide is a feeling of hopelessness or helplessness, a principal symptom of depression. Hopelessness is the common factor that links depression and suicide in the general population. In fact, hopelessness is a better predictor of completed suicide than depression alone.[16] Feelings of hopelessness and helplessness interact with the perception of psychological pain and the individual's sense that his or her current suffering is inescapable.

Individuals who are terminally ill constitute only a small portion of the total number of suicides. In fact, most people who kill themselves are in good physical health. Among all suicides, only two percent to four percent are terminally ill.[17] One study of adults over 50 years of age showed that more individuals committed suicide in the mistaken belief that they were dying of cancer than those who actually had a terminal illness and committed suicide. The study supports the es-

---

[12]Clark.

[13]H. Hendin and G. Klerman, "Commentary: Physician-Assisted Suicide: The Dangers of Legalization," *American Journal of Psychiatry* 150 (1993): 143-45.

[14]Y. Conwell and E. D. Caine, "Rational Suicide and the Right to Die: Reality and Myth," *New England Journal of Medicine* 325 (1991): 1100-1103.

[15]See chapter 2 for discussion.

[16]W. Breitbart, "Suicide Risk and Pain in Cancer and AIDS Patients," in *Current and Emerging Issues in Cancer Pain: Research and Practice*, ed. C. R. Chapman and K. M. Foley (New York: Raven Press, 1993), 49-65.

[17]Clark.

timate that two thirds of older persons who die by suicide are in relatively good physical health.[18]

Individuals with serious chronic and terminal illness face an increased risk of suicide — some studies suggest that the risk for cancer patients is about twice that of the general population. Some experts, however, have observed that many terminally ill patients experience a phenomenon called "cancer cures psychoneuroses." This phenomenon occurs when patients become aware that they have cancer or another progressive terminal illness, and the process of facing and mastering their fear of death dissolves many other anxieties or neuroses. As explained by one psychiatrist, "As one's focus turns from the trivial diversions of life, a fuller appreciation of the elemental factors in existence may emerge."[19]

Thus, some terminally ill patients may exhibit lower psychological stress than might be expected. Apart from circumstances where patients are depressed, terminally ill individuals are often resilient, and fight for life throughout their illness. Studies indicate that for many patients with severe pain, disfigurement, or disability, the vast majority do not desire suicide. In one study of terminally ill patients, of those who expressed a wish to die, all met diagnostic criteria for major depression.[20] Like other suicidal individuals, patients who desire suicide or an early death during a terminal illness are usually suffering from a treatable mental illness, most commonly depression.[21]

Risk Factors for Suicide

Depression

Depression, including major depression and depressive symptoms, is a critical risk factor for completed suicides.[22] Depression is present

---

[18]Ibid.

[19]F. P. McKegney and M. A. O'Dowd, "Clinical and Research Reports: Suicidality and HIV Status," *American Journal of Psychiatry* 149 (1992): 396-98.

[20]J. H. Brown et al., "Is It Normal for Terminally Ill Patients to Desire Death?" *American Journal of Psychiatry* 143 (1986): 208-11.

[21]Ibid.

[22]As early as the 17th century, writers identified a link between depression or melancholy and suicide. The *Anatomy of Melancholy*, written in 1621 by Richard Burton, identified melancholy as a medical and psychological phenomenon. The author argued that suicide "is the result of melancholy that desires self-destruction: 'In other diseases there is some hope likely, but these unhappy men are born to misery, past all hope of recovery, invariably sick, the longer they live the worse they

in 50 percent of all suicides, and those suffering from depression are at 25 times greater risk for suicide than the general population.[23] In addition, older persons with depression are more likely to commit suicide than younger persons who are depressed.[24]

The prevalence of major depressive disorder in western industrialized nations is 2.3 percent to 3.2 percent for men and 4.5 percent to 9.3 percent for women. An individual's lifetime risk of depression ranges from seven percent to 12 percent for men and 20 percent to 25 percent for women. Studies indicate that the risk of depression is not related to race, education, or income.[25]

The general population. Depressive disorders should clearly be distinguished from realistically depressed or sad moods that may accompany specific losses or disappointments in life. Clinical depression is a syndrome described as an abnormal reaction to life's difficulties. In addition to sadness, clinical depression encompasses a variety of symptoms: pervasive despair or irritability, hopelessness, loss of interest in activities that are usually considered enjoyable, trouble sleeping or excessive sleeping, appetite loss or weight change, fatigue, and preoccupation with death or suicide.

The *Diagnostic and Statistical Manual of Mental Disorders*, third edition, revised (DSM-III-R), published in 1987 by the American Psychiatric Association, lists criteria for major depression.[26] At least five of the following symptoms must be present during the same period, one of which must be depressed mood or loss of interest or pleasure, to satisfy these criteria for depression. Symptoms must be evident most of the day, on a daily basis for at least two weeks:

1. depressed mood
2. markedly diminished interest or pleasure in almost all activities
3. significant weight loss/gain
4. insomnia/hypersomnia
5. psychomotor agitation/retardation
6. fatigue

---

are, and death alone must ease them.'" T. L. Beauchamp, "Suicide in the Age of Reason," in *Suicide and Euthanasia: Historical and Contemporary Themes*, ed. B. A. Brody (Dordrecht: Kluwer Academic Publishers, 1989), 172.

[23]W. Breitbart, "Cancer Pain and Suicide," in *Advances in Pain Research and Therapy*, ed. K. M. Foley et al., vol. 16 (New York: Raven Press, 1990), 399-412.

[24]Clark.

[25]Depression Guideline Panel, 23.

[26]Ibid., 18.

7. feelings of worthlessness (guilt)
8. impaired concentration (indecisiveness)
9. recurrent thoughts of death or suicide.

Unfortunately, because a common symptom of depression is a loss of insight and a feeling of hopelessness, depressed people usually have little understanding of the severity of their illness. They are often the last to recognize their problem and seek help. It is therefore critical that primary care physicians develop the skills to recognize depression in patients, particularly the terminally ill and elderly, whose depressive symptoms may be masked by coexisting medical conditions such as dementia or coronary artery disease.

Risk factors for major depressive disorder. Overall, women have higher rates of depression than men. Individuals with a history of depressive illness in first-degree relatives are also more prone to depression. Prior suicide attempts and prior episodes of major depression also place individuals at risk. Other important risk factors for major depression include onset of depression under age 40, postpartum period, lack of social support, stressful life events, and current alcohol or substance abuse. In addition, other general medical conditions are risk factors for major depression. Depressive symptoms are detectable in approximately 12 percent to 16 percent of patients with another non-psychiatric medical condition.[27] When major depression is present, it should be treated as an independent condition.

Depression may coincide with other medical conditions for several reasons. First, the medical condition may biologically cause depression. Second, the condition may trigger depression in patients who are genetically predisposed to depression. Third, the presence of illness or disease can psychologically cause depression, as is often observed in patients with cancer. Finally, especially for cancer patients, some treatments or medications have side effects that cause depressive moods or symptoms.

A wide range of chronic illnesses are associated with an increased risk of depression. Studies indicate that patients with dementia illnesses such as Parkinson's, Huntington's, and Alzheimer's diseases have higher rates of major depression. Diabetes patients are three times as likely as the general population to develop major depression.[28]

---

[27]Ibid., 5.

[28]Ibid., 55-65. This source discusses the incidence of depression in several other chronic conditions — coronary artery disease, chronic fatigue syndrome, fibromyalgia, and stroke.

Treatment for depression in patients with chronic illness may offer patients the ability to adjust to the complex circumstances they face in coping with illnesses that are frequently debilitating and progressive.

Patients with advanced disease or terminal illness frequently experience many psychological symptoms, including anxiety, fatigue, and lack of concentration. Terminally ill patients may also develop major depression or severe depressive symptoms. Although it is normal and expected that terminally ill patients "feel sadness for the anticipated loss of health, life and all it means, and loss of a future with all that it might hold," most patients call upon their coping mechanisms to manage these feelings.[29] It is a myth, however, that severe clinical depression is a normal and expected component of terminal illness.

Healthy individuals, including health care professionals, often believe that it is normal for terminally ill patients to experience major depression. They understand feelings of hopelessness as expected and rational given the patient's condition and prognosis. As one psychiatrist explains:

> Expressions like "I'd want to die if I were in that situation" or "I'd be depressed too" are common, even among health care professionals. This misunderstanding may contribute to the poor diagnosis and treatment of depression in patients with chronic or terminal illness. The presence of physical symptoms that are associated with both the illness and depression make the diagnosis even more difficult. Terminal illness as well as depression may cause a patient to experience physical symptoms of fatigue, apathy, insomnia, weakness and loss of libido.[30]

For this reason, psychological symptoms of depression, such as hopelessness and helplessness, are often more reliable markers than physical symptoms in the assessment and treatment of major depression among individuals with chronic and terminal illness.

Pain and Suffering

For some patients, uncontrolled pain is an important contributing factor for suicide and suicidal ideation. Patients with uncontrolled pain

---

[29]Jimmie C. Holland, Chief, Psychiatry Services, Memorial Sloan-Kettering Cancer Center, "Letter to the Task Force on Life and the Law," August 16, 1993.

[30]Ibid.

may see death as the only escape from the pain they are experiencing. However, pain is usually not an independent risk factor. The significant variable in the relationship between pain and suicide is the interaction between pain and feelings of hopelessness and depression. As stated by one psychiatrist: "Pain plays an important role in vulnerability to suicide; however, associated psychological distress and mood disturbance seem to be essential co-factors in raising the risk of cancer suicide."[31]

Suffering represents a more global phenomenon of psychic distress. While suffering is often associated with pain, it also occurs independently. Different kinds of physical symptoms, such as difficulty breathing, can lead to suffering. Suffering may also arise from diverse social factors such as isolation, loss, and despair.

Pain. The International Association for the Study of Pain defines pain as follows:

> An unpleasant sensory and emotional experience associated with actual or potential tissue damage, or described in terms of such damage. ... Pain is always subjective. ... It is unquestionably a sensation in a part or parts of the body but it is also always unpleasant and therefore an emotional experience.[32]

This definition reflects a distinction between pain and nociception.[33] Nociception refers to activity produced in the nervous system in response to potentially damaging ("noxious") stimuli. Pain is the patient's perception of nociception. A patient's pain reflects both the activity of his or her nervous system, and psychological, personal, and physiological factors.[34]

Different types of pain vary both in the way they affect patients and in their responsiveness to treatment. Acute pain, which is of limited duration, may arise from injury or as a result of a surgical procedure. Chronic pain is pain that persists well beyond the normal course of healing of a disease or injury or, most typically, is associated with

---

[31]Breitbart, "Suicide Risk and Pain," 54.

[32]International Association for the Study of Pain, "Pain Terms: A Current List with Definitions and Notes on Usage," *Pain* (1986), suppl. 3, S217.

[33]"Activity induced in the nociceptor and nociceptive pathways by a noxious stimulus is not pain, which is always a psychological state, even though we may well appreciate that pain most often has a proximate physical cause." Ibid.

[34]Portenoy, 3; International Association for the Study of Pain; World Health Organization, *Cancer Pain Relief* (Geneva: World Health Organization, 1986), 9-10.

chronic or progressive diseases. Some types of pain are responsive to treatment while others, such as neuropathic pain or pain arising from chronic illness, are harder to treat. Pain may be constant, or it may occur as a result of activity. The characteristics of pain such as severity, quality (e.g., burning or stabbing), time course (continuous or inter-mittent), and location are important in assessing the nature of the pain.[35] Severity of pain may be less important than the patient's per-ception of pain and the fear of anticipated pain.

Pain may be characterized in terms of its mechanism or cause. Somatic pain, which may be caused by injury to a bone or damage to tissue, is generally localized and may be described as aching, stabbing, or pressure-like. Visceral pain, such as that arising from obstruction of the intestine or ureter, is more poorly localized, and may be felt as aching or cramping. Neuropathic pain results from damage to the nervous system.[36]

Pain is terribly real and immediately present for the person in pain, but can be less apparent to observers. This divergence can lead to a sense of isolation on the part of the patient, and to inadequate respon-ses by others in alleviating pain.

> For the person in pain, so incontestably and un-negotiably present is it that "having pain" may come to be thought of as the most vibrant example of what it is to "have certainty," while for the other person it is so elusive that "hearing about pain" may exist as the primary model of what it is "to have doubt." Thus pain comes unsharably into our midst as at once that which cannot be denied and that which cannot be confirmed.[37]

---

[35]R. K. Portenoy, "Pain Assessment in Adults and Children," in *Why Do We Care?*, Syllabus of the Postgraduate Course, Memorial Sloan-Kettering Cancer Center, New York City, April 2-4, 1992, 4-5; Acute Pain Management Guideline Panel, *Acute Pain Management: Operative or Medical Procedures and Trauma, Clinical Practice Guideline*, AHCPR pub. no. 92-0032 (Rockville, Md.: U. S. Department of Health and Human Services, Public Health Service, Agency for Health Care Policy and Research, February 1992), 7-14; E. Scarry, *The Body in Pain: The Making and Unmaking of the World* (New York: Oxford University Press, 1985), 7-8.

[36]Portenoy, 4-5; Acute Pain Management Guideline Panel, 7-14; N. Coyle et al., "Character of Terminal Illness in the Advanced Cancer Patient: Pain and Other Symptoms During the Last Four Weeks of Life," *Journal of Pain and Symptom Management* 5 (1990): 84. While pain may arise primarily from psychological causes, this is understood to occur only in rare cases.

[37]Scarry, 4.

In recent decades, new approaches have been developed to assess and report pain. Self-reporting of pain by patients is central to pain assessment. While self-reporting can be supplemented by physiological and behavioral observation, it is widely recognized that patients' behavior and physiological characteristics do not always correlate with the level of pain experienced by the patient.[38] Assessing and reporting pain is critical to effective pain relief.[39] It can also lead to important information about other aspects of the patient's medical condition, alerting the patient to disease and preventing further injury.[40]

Different types of pain impose different burdens for patients and present distinct challenges to health care professionals. Acute pain and chronic pain differ both physiologically and in the difficulties they entail. Acute pain has a well-defined temporal pattern of onset, and generally results from potentially damaging stimuli associated with injury or disease. It usually is associated with observable physical signs and responses of the autonomic nervous system. Acute pain usually does not persist beyond days or weeks.[41]

Chronic pain has been defined as "pain that persists a month beyond the usual course of an acute disease or a reasonable time for an injury to heal or that is associated with a chronic pathological process that causes continuous pain or pain [that] recurs at intervals for months or years."[42] Chronic pain may be caused by a patient's chronic or progressive disease, or by prolonged dysfunction of the nervous system. Although chronic pain may be severe and debilitating, a patient in chronic pain may not display the objective signs associated with acute pain. Chronic pain may therefore be less visible, adding to the burden

---

[38] Acute Pain Management Guideline Panel, 7-14; International Association for the Study of Pain, Task Force on Professional Education, *Core Curriculum for Professional Education in Pain* (Seattle: IASP Publications, 1991), 4-7, 14-17.

[39] The American Pain Society reports that "the most common reason for unrelieved pain in U.S. hospitals is the failure of staff to routinely assess pain and pain relief." *Principles of Analgesic Use in the Treatment of Acute Pain and Cancer Pain*, 3d ed. (Skokie, Ill.: American Pain Society, 1992), 2. A similar view was shared by 76% of respondents in a survey of cancer specialists. J. H. Von Roenn et al., "Physician Attitudes and Practice in Cancer Pain Management: A Survey from the Eastern Cooperative Oncology Group," *Annals of Internal Medicine* 119 (1993): 121-26.

[40] Portenoy, 5; Acute Pain Management Guideline Panel.

[41] K. M. Foley, "The Treatment of Cancer Pain," *New England Journal of Medicine* 3 (1985): 85; J. J. Bonica, "Definitions and Taxonomy of Pain," in *The Management of Pain*, ed. J. J. Bonica, 2d ed. (Philadelphia: Lea and Febiger, 1990), 19.

[42] Bonica, 19.

individuals face in coping with the pain in their daily activities and relationships with others.

Millions of patients in the United States experience significant or severe chronic pain. Among the most common conditions are recurrent severe headaches, back disorders, and arthritis. Pain may also arise from other chronic illnesses such as sickle cell disease, nerve injury, and sinusitis.

Chronic pain often entails serious physical, emotional, and financial burdens for the patient and those closest to him or her. The physical symptoms arising from chronic pain are distressing: loss of sleep, a decline in physical activity, fatigue, and progressive physical deterioration. It can lead to changes in the patient's personality and life-style, affecting the ability to carry out even the simplest daily tasks.[43] As described by one physician, chronic illness also entails mourning over the loss of good health and a constant struggle to avoid the next episode of illness:

> Each time the cycle of symptoms begins, the sufferer loses faith in the dependability and adaptability of basic bodily processes that the rest of us rely on as part of our general sense of well-being. This loss of confidence becomes grim expectation of the worst, and, in some, demoralization and hopelessness. …The fidelity of our bodies is so basic that we never think of it — it is the certain grounds of our daily experience. Chronic illness is a betrayal of that fundamental trust.[44]

Physical symptoms. Many patients who are terminally or chronically ill undergo distressing physical symptoms in addition to pain. These symptoms may include dyspnea (difficulty in breathing), nausea, diarrhea, constipation, and fatigue. Multiple symptoms may be present simultaneously. In advanced cancer patients, for instance, "pain, dyspnea and other symptoms do not occur in isolation: they interact so as to produce a 'crescendo' effect. The dyspneic patient will experience increasing anxiety and rapid breathing, which may then exacerbate pain arising from metastases in the ribs and spine."[45] Both pain and

---

[43]Foley, 85; Bonica, "Definitions and Taxonomy of Pain," 19; Bonica, *Management of Pain*, 189-95.

[44]A. Kleinman, *The Illness Narratives: Suffering, Healing, and the Human Condition* (New York: Basic Books, 1988), 45.

[45]World Health Organization, *Cancer Pain Relief and Palliative Care: Report of a*

other physical symptoms directly diminish a patient's quality of life. Apart from the experience of pain or discomfort itself, pain and other symptoms of serious illness may severely limit a patient's activities, denying some patients the capacity to engage in the activities of daily living most important to their sense of well-being and self.[46]

Severe or chronic pain can be associated with mild or severe disability as well as psychological conditions, such as major depression.[47] Patients with terminal illness and those with a nonterminal condition may suffer from chronic pain. To date, medicine has less experience treating chronic pain for nonterminal patients. While most pain arising from terminal illness responds to treatment, the alleviation of pain caused by nonterminal, chronic illness is less certain.[48]

Suffering. Suffering is a more global experience of impaired quality of life.[49] As defined by one physician, suffering is "the state of severe distress associated with events that threaten the intactness of the person."[50] The threat might be to the person's existence or integrity, to maintaining his or her role in the family or in society, or to his or her sense of self and identity. While pain and suffering are often associated, minor pain can occur without causing suffering, and suffering can occur in the absence of physical pain. Distressing physical symptoms and disabilities can lead to intense suffering for patients with degenerative disorders such as amyotrophic lateral sclerosis (ALS), or those who are quadriplegic as the result of a spinal cord injury. Moreover, suffering is not limited to medical patients. Suffering may arise from many causes, including physical incapacity, social isolation, fear, the death of a loved one, or frustration of a cherished goal.[51]

WHO Expert Committee, WHO Technical Report Series 804 (Geneva: World Health Organization, 1990), 41.

[46] Coyle et al.

[47] M. J. Massie and J. C. Holland, "The Cancer Patient with Pain: Psychiatric Complications and Their Management," *Journal of Pain and Symptom Management* 7 (1992): 100-101; Breitbart, "Cancer Pain and Suicide," 404; R. K. Portenoy, "Overview of Symptom Prevalence and Assessment," in *Why Do We Care?*, Syllabus of the Postgraduate Course, Memorial Sloan-Kettering Cancer Center, New York City, April 2-4, 1992, 183-89.

[48] World Health Organization, *Cancer Pain Relief*, 10. On the treatment of chronic pain, see chapter 3.

[49] Portenoy, 3.

[50] E. J. Cassell, "The Nature of Suffering and the Goals of Medicine," *New England Journal of Medicine* 306 (1982): 640.

[51] Ibid., 641-44.

Even more so than with pain, an individual's experience of suffering reflects his or her unique psychological and personal characteristics. Suffering is in effect the experience of severe psychological pain, arising from medical or personal causes. Because the experience of suffering is subjective, people are often unaware of the causes or extent of another person's suffering. Ultimately, suffering is a distinctly human, not a medical, condition.

2

Suicide and Special
Patient Populations

Of all medical conditions, cancer and acquired immunodeficiency syndrome (AIDS) are associated with the highest rates of suicide and suicide requests.[1] In general, the elderly are also at increased risk of depression and suicide. Requests for assisted suicide and euthanasia by these patients and others with serious illnesses have fueled the debate about the physician's role in responding to these requests.

The debate about legalizing assisted suicide and euthanasia has also focused attention on the treatment available for patients who are suffering from both physical and psychological pain. Available data and research on suicidal ideation and suicide attempts by patients with cancer and AIDS provide critical insight about the relationship between terminal illness, the availability of adequate palliative care, and suicide. The majority of AIDS and cancer patients who express suicidal thoughts or commit suicide suffer from unrecognized and untreated psychiatric conditions, such as depression or confusional states, and poorly controlled pain.

Patients with other chronic and seriously disabling diseases, such as degenerative neurological disorders, also experience emotional and physical suffering. Chronic, nonterminal pain often cannot be treated in the same manner as terminal pain. Some severely debilitating illnesses cause suffering that differs from the suffering experienced by AIDS and cancer patients. Unfortunately, few data are available about suicide rates, pain, and depression for patients with chronic illness.

---

[1]W. Breitbart, "Suicide Risk and Pain," in *Current and Emerging Issues in Cancer Pain: Research and Practice.*, ed. C. R. Chapman and K. M. Foley (New York: Raven Press, 1993), 49-65.

Patients with Cancer

Cancer patients face approximately twice the risk of suicide than the general population does, although few commit suicide. To date, three major studies confirm the low incidence of suicide among cancer patients. One study of cancer deaths in Finland, conducted in 1979, found that only 63 out of 28,257 cancer patients who died committed suicide.[2] In another study conducted in the United States in 1982, researchers estimated that 192 of 144,530 cancer deaths were the result of suicide. Finally, a 1985 Swedish study reports that of 19,000 cancer deaths, only 22 were suicides.[3]

The risk of suicide is greatest for patients in the later stages of the disease; 16 percent to 20 percent of these patients experience suicidal ideation. In contrast, studies have found that few ambulatory cancer patients express thoughts of suicide. Despite the low rates of suicidal ideation reported by studies, health care professionals who care for cancer patients believe that suicidal thinking is prevalent among these patients.

> Almost all patients who receive a cancer diagnosis, even when the prognosis is good, carry a "secret," rarely acknowledged, thought that says "I won't die in pain with advanced cancer — I'll kill myself first." They often have a hidden supply of drugs which is usually kept for this purpose. For most patients, the time never comes to take the pills and life becomes dearer as death approaches.[4]

Some psychiatrists urge that these feelings should be acknowledged as an important and normal component of dealing with cancer. These experts suggest that suicidal thinking is common among patients as an option to enable them to retain a sense of control or to avoid feeling overwhelmed by cancer.[5] Physicians must be skilled at assessing when

---

[2] Suicide risk relative to the general population was 1.3 for men and 1.9 for women. K. A. Louhivuori and M. Hakama, "Risk of Suicide Among Cancer Patients," *American Journal of Epidemiology* 109 (1979): 59-65.

[3] The U.S. study found the suicide risk relative to the general population to be 2.3 for men; however, women were not at increased risk (only 0.9). W. Breitbart, "Cancer Pain and Suicide," in *Advances in Pain Research and Therapy*, ed. K. M. Foley et al., vol. 16 (New York: Raven Press, 1990), 402.

[4] Jimmie C. Holland, Chief, Psychiatry Services, Memorial Sloan-Kettering Cancer Center, "Letter to the Task Force on Life and the Law," August 16, 1993.

[5] W. Breitbart, "Psychiatric Management of Cancer Pain," *Cancer* 63 (1989): 2336-42.

the thoughts are serious and whether the patient suffers from major depression — especially for those with a good prognosis or for whom the disease is in remission.

Several personal and medical factors increase the cancer patient's vulnerability to suicide and suicidal ideation. Personal factors that contribute to a wish for hastened death include a prior history of suicide (personal or family), prior psychiatric disorder, prior alcohol or drug abuse, depression and hopelessness, and recent loss or bereavement. The medical risk factors are pain, delirium, advanced illness, debilitation, and exhaustion or fatigue.[6] Psychiatric disorders are frequently present in suicidal cancer patients. A study at Memorial Sloan-Kettering Hospital in New York City showed that one third of suicidal cancer patients suffered from major depression, approximately 20 percent had delirium, and more than 50 percent had an adjustment disorder.[7]

Loss of control and feelings of helplessness may be the most significant factors for cancer patients who desire an early death.[8] Cancer or cancer treatments often cause symptoms that add to a patient's feelings of helplessness. These symptoms may include loss of mobility, paraplegia, loss of bowel and bladder function, amputation, sensory loss, and an inability to eat or swallow. Most distressing to many cancer patients is the sense that they are losing control of their mental functions, especially when confused or sedated by medications.

Cancer patients with delirium, even mild delirium, are at increased risk of suicide. Confusional states contribute to impulsive suicide attempts because the patient experiences a loss of impulse control when delirious. Patients in a state of delirium may therefore be more likely to act on a suicidal thought. In addition, the delirium may add to the patient's sense of helplessness and increase the likelihood of a suicide attempt.

Fatigue and exhaustion also contribute to a higher risk of suicide. Cancer patients become not only physically exhausted by the illness and treatments but also emotionally fatigued. Because of the chronic nature of the illness and the drawn-out disease process, the patient's or family's financial resources may also be diminished. Otherwise

---

[6]Holland, "Letter to Task Force"; Breitbart, "Psychiatric Management of Cancer Pain."

[7]W. Breitbart, "Suicide in Cancer Patients," *Oncology* 1 (1987): 49-53.

[8]W. Breitbart, "Cancer Pain and Suicide," 399-412.

committed and supportive family members and health care professionals may also tire and abandon the patient.

Studies suggest that 20 percent to 25 percent of cancer patients suffer major depression at some point during their illness. Among patients with advanced cancer and progressively impaired physical function, the presence of severe depressive symptoms rises to 77 percent.[9] While these rates of depression may be high relative to the general population, they are similar to those found among patients suffering other physical illness.[10]

For cancer patients, pain, depression, and psychiatric disorders are closely linked. Uncontrolled or poorly controlled pain can increase a patient's feelings of hopelessness and helplessness. One study of cancer patients showed that 47 percent of patients had a psychiatric disorder (of whom 68 percent had reactive anxiety or depression). The incidence of psychiatric disorders — in particular anxiety and depression — was higher in patients with pain.[11]

Treating cancer patients for depression and pain reduces levels of suicidal ideation. Allowing patients to discuss suicidal thoughts may also decrease the risk of suicide. A discussion can help patients feel a sense of control over their death. Treatment for depression can also eliminate a patient's wish to die. One study of cancer patients at a major hospital found that nine percent of psychiatric consultations concerned acutely suicidal patients. Virtually all these patients had a previously undiagnosed psychiatric disorder. Treatment for depression resulted in the cessation of suicidal ideation for 90 percent of these patients. Like the common myth that it is reasonable for terminally ill patients to be suicidal, these data argue against the common misperception that cancer patients appropriately suffer from severe clinical depression.

Depression may be difficult to diagnose in cancer patients because the standard criteria for diagnosing depression do not consider special symptoms of cancer patients. For example, severe pain may mask feelings of sadness. Somatic signs such as disturbance of sleep or appetite may be produced by medications or the illness. Physicians

[9]Ibid.

[10]Depression Guideline Panel, *Depression in Primary Care*: vol. 1, *Detection and Diagnosis, Clinical Practice Guideline*, no. 5, AHCPR pub. no. 93-0550 (Rockville, Md.: U. S. Department of Health and Human Services, Public Health Service, Agency for Health Care Policy and Research, April 1993), 63-64.

[11]W. Breitbart and J. C. Holland, "Psychiatric Aspects of Cancer Pain," *Advances in Pain Research and Therapy*, ed. K. M. Foley et al. vol. 16 (New York: Raven Press, 1990), 73-87.

must be sensitive to the special risk factors for depressive symptoms in cancer patients, especially the medications that can cause such symptoms.

While the experience of each patient is unique, certain types of pain and suffering are commonly associated with particular diseases. Studies show that 15 percent of patients with nonmetastatic cancer have significant pain, and 60 percent to 90 percent of patients with advanced cancer have moderate to severe pain, which impairs their functioning or mood.[12] Pain may arise from multiple causes. Tumor growth can lead to tissue damage, and can affect the nervous system, causing neuropathic pain. Treatments for cancer, especially radiation and chemotherapy, can carry significant side effects, including severe nausea and fatigue, loss of appetite, disfigurement, loss of libido, and infertility. Pain and other distressing symptoms are also caused by the disease itself.[13]

The variety of symptoms experienced by advanced cancer patients is illustrated by a study of 90 patients treated by a supportive care program during the last four weeks of life. The patients as a group reported 44 symptoms distressing enough to interfere with activity. The most prevalent symptoms (spontaneously identified by at least 10 percent of patients) were fatigue, pain, weakness, sleepiness, confusion, anxiety, weakness of legs, shortness of breath, and nausea. Other symptoms reported by at least five percent of patients included decreased hearing, inability to sleep, constipation, difficulty swallowing, and difficulty speaking. Many patients reported multiple symptoms, most commonly listing between two and four, but in one case as many as nine. The simultaneous presence of multiple distressing symptoms adds to the patient's suffering and poses special challenges for pain and symptom management.[14]

---

[12]K. M. Foley, "The Treatment of Cancer Pain," *New England Journal of Medicine* 313 (1985): 84-85; W. Breitbart, "Suicide Risk and Pain in Cancer and AIDS Patient," in *Current and Emerging Issues in Cancer Pain: Research and Practice*, ed. C. R. Chapman and K. M. Foley (New York: Raven Press, 1993), 49-65; N. Coyle et al. "Character of Terminal Illness in the Advanced Cancer Patient: Pain and Other Symptoms During the Last Four Weeks of Life," *Journal of Pain and Symptom Management* 5 (1990): 83.

[13]Foley, "Treatment of Cancer Pain," 85-86; R. K. Portenoy, "Pain Assessment in Adults and Children," in *Why Do We Care?* Syllabus of the Postgraduate Course, Memorial Sloan-Kettering Cancer Center, New York City, April 2-4, 1992, 5.

[14]Coyle et al.

Patients with AIDS

Individuals with AIDS are far more likely to be suicidal than the general population. One 1988 study conducted a postmortem review of AIDS deaths in New York City and estimated that the relative risk of suicide in men with AIDS aged 20 to 59 was 36 times that of the general population.[15] In this study, most patients with AIDS who committed suicide had a preexisting psychiatric disorder. Another study found that the suicide rates for males with AIDS were 7.4-fold higher than those among demographically similar men in the general population.[16] Suicide reports indicate that AIDS patients who commit suicide tend to act within nine months of receiving a diagnosis of AIDS.[17]

Studies have also detected elevated rates of suicidal ideation among groups at risk for human imunodeficency virus (HIV) infection, such as gay men and intravenous (IV) drug users. Surprisingly, within these groups, suicidal ideation among those who are HIV-positive is not higher than among those in the at-risk group who have not been identified as HIV-positive. A recent study of HIV-positive and HIV-negative individuals in the same population showed that prior to notification of HIV status, the two groups exhibited similar rates of suicidal ideation. Two months after notification, no difference in frequency of suicidal thoughts or attempts existed between those notified of a positive HIV test and individuals informed of a negative result.[18] The rate of suicidal ideation remained at over 15 percent for both groups. Researchers have concluded therefore that HIV status alone may not account for the high rates of suicidal ideation among AIDS patients. Instead, preexisting psychological characteristics may place individuals in the at-risk population for AIDS at a higher risk for suicidal ideation. In fact, the study population had a higher rate of

[15]P. M. Marzuk et al., "Increased Risk of Suicide in Persons with AIDS," *Journal of the American Medical Association* 259 (1988): 1333-37.

[16]T. R. Cote, R. J. Biggar, and A. L. Dannenberg, "Risk of Suicide Among Persons with AIDS: A National Assessment," *Journal of the American Medical Association* 268 (1992): 2066-68.

[17]Breitbart, "Suicide Risk and Pain," 55.

[18]Immediately after notification, the rate of suicidal ideation among those who were HIV-positive remained stable at 27% (individuals did not become more suicidal upon notification) and the rate of suicidal ideation among the HIV-negative group dropped to 17%. However, after two months, the HIV-positive group's rate fell to 16% — a level comparable to the rate for HIV-negative individuals. S. Perry, L. Jacobsberg, B. Fishman, "Suicidal Ideation and HIV Testing," *Journal of the American Medical Association* 263 (1990): 679-82.

current and lifetime depressive disorders and of substance abuse than the general population.

Suicidal ideation may also be influenced by the patient's perception of pain, stage of illness, and the patient's psychological state. One study of ambulatory HIV-infected patients discovered that suicidal ideation is highly correlated with the presence of pain, depressed mood, and low T4 lymphocyte counts.[19] The study also found a strong connection between pain and emotional distress. Twenty percent of HIV-infected patients without pain reported suicidal ideation, compared to 40 percent of patients with pain. Of the 110 patients in the study, only two reported serious suicidal intent. However, the intent did not correlate with the intensity of pain or extent of relief, but with mood disturbances such as depression.

Organic mental disorders such as delirium and dementia are important risk factors for suicide as AIDS progresses. Clinicians have had success in treating delirium and reducing the levels of suicidal ideation among AIDS patients. Depression is also a key factor. In one study in New York City of 12 patients with AIDS who committed suicide, 50 percent were significantly depressed. Preexisting personality disorders and history of suicidal attempts or expression of suicidal thoughts can also heighten the risk of suicide. Given the relatively recent appearance of AIDS and the changing population of individuals with AIDS (most of the earliest studies focused primarily on gay men), continued research must be conducted to understand more fully the nature of suicide within this patient population.

Patients with AIDS exhibit a range of pain symptoms similar to that of patients with cancer. Studies have found that more than half of patients with advanced AIDS experience significant pain. Pain may arise from AIDS and related infections. AIDS therapy, including antiviral agents, also causes side effects and discomfort. Common types of pain arising from the disease and treatment include abdominal pain, headache, joint pain, and peripheral neuropathy, which may produce sensations of burning, numbness, or pins and needles. Other physical symptoms include gastrointestinal manifestations such as oral infections, difficulty swallowing, and diarrhea.[20]

---

[19]Breitbart, "Suicide Risk and Pain."

[20]Ibid., 58-59; W. N. O'Neill and J. S. Sherrard, "Pain in Human Immunodefiency Virus Disease: A Review," *Pain* 54 (1993): 3-14.

The Elderly

Older age and physical illness are two risk factors for suicide. Facing deteriorating health and increasing age, the elderly are at a greater risk of suicide than any other age group. Although the rates of suicide declined between 1950 and 1980 for individuals over age 65, between 1980 and 1986, the rates increased by approximately 21 percent.[21] Men accounted for 80 percent of all deaths, and white males over 85 had the highest suicide rates for all age groups.[22] The most common means of suicide among the elderly was a gun (73 percent of the men, 29 percent of the women). An overdose of drugs or poison was more common among women. According to current estimates, the level of suicide among the elderly will double over the next 40 years.[23]

The distinction between suicide attempters and completers that is prominent for other age groups dissipates among the elderly population. Unlike younger individuals, whose suicide attempt is often a plea for help or indication of a need for a change in life circumstances, older individuals who attempt suicide are generally more likely to succeed. They also often use methods that are more violent or lethal. In addition, suicide attempts by the elderly are more clearly planned or premeditated.[24]

Risk factors for suicide, such as depression, alcoholism, physical illness, and organic mental dysfunction, which impair judgment and the ability to generate alternative options,[25] contribute to the increased rates of suicide among the elderly. Unlike younger suicidal individuals for whom a history of suicide attempts, substance abuse, and mental illness play a major role, for the elderly social isolation and physical disability are more important variables.[26] Some data suggest that when older individuals commit suicide, they are more likely to suffer from a

---

[21]P. J. Meechan, L. E. Saltzman, and R. W. Sattin, "Suicides Among Older U.S. Residents: Epidemiologic Characteristics and Trends," *American Journal of Public Health* 18 (1991): 1198-1200.

[22]Y. Conwell, M. Rotenberg, and E. D. Caine, "Completed Suicide at Age 50 and Over," *Journal of the American Geriatrics Society* 38 (1990): 640-44.

[23]G. L. Kennedy, "Depression in the Elderly," in *Psychiatry 1993*, ed. R. Michaels et al., vol. 2 (Philadelphia: J. P. Lippincott, 1993), 1-11.

[24]S. B. Sorenson, "Suicide Among the Elderly: Issues Facing Public Health," *American Journal of Public Health* 81 (1991): 1109-10.

[25]Ibid.

[26]Kennedy.

mood disorder than are younger individuals who commit suicide.[27] Available clinical data estimate that a majority of elderly persons who commit suicide suffer from depressive episodes.[28]

Few studies have examined later-life suicides. Consequently, researchers hold differing views about whether medical or psychiatric disorders cause suicidal behavior among elderly individuals, or whether factors such as social isolation or inadequate social support are more significant.[29] In addition, some argue that advances in medical care, which have prolonged the lives of persons with chronic illness, have resulted in higher suicide rates for elderly, chronically ill persons.[30]

While the prevalence of depressive symptoms increases with age, the rate of major depressive disorders declines.[31] The presence of depressive symptoms among the elderly ranges from a low of 9 percent to a high of 19 percent.[32] One study found that as many as 25 percent of elderly living in the community had depressive symptoms.[33] Rates of clinical depression among elderly community residents are similar to those for other age groups (under 3 percent).[34]

In contrast to rates of depression for elderly community residents, the prevalence of major depression is high among elderly nursing home residents, with estimates ranging from 6 percent to 25 percent. Approximately 30 percent to 50 percent of older residents experience depressive symptoms.[35] Each year approximately 13 percent of residents develop a new episode of major depression and another 18 percent develop new depressive symptoms. In addition, half of nursing home residents suffer from dementing illnesses such as Alzheimer's or

---

[27]Conwell, Rotenberg, and Caine, 640-44.

[28]Kennedy, 8.

[29]G. L. Kennedy, "Suicide, Depression, and the Elderly," Presentation to the New York State Task Force on Life and the Law, May 13, 1992.

[30]Meechan, Saltzman, and Sattin.

[31]D. G. Blazer, "Depression in the Elderly," *New England Journal of Medicine* 320 (1989): 164-66.

[32]Kennedy, "Depression in the Elderly," 3.

[33]D. Blazer, D. C. Hughes, and L. K. George, "The Epidemiology of Depression in an Elderly Community Population," *Gerontologist* 27 (1987): 281-87.

[34]National Institutes of Health Consensus Conference, "Depression in Late Life," *Journal of the American Medical Association* 268 (1992): 1018-24.

[35]Blazer, Hughes, and George, "Epidemiology of Depression."

vascular dementia and require treatment for psychological symptoms, including depression.[36] The high rates of depression among nursing home residents may be due in part to social circumstances such as separation from family and home and in part to illness and medications.

Social and medical risk factors for depression in the elderly are similar to other age groups. Some experts have also found that older individuals are more likely than younger individuals to become depressed following the death of a loved one.[37] Women are also at increased risk for depression as they age. The presence of symptoms necessary for a diagnosis of depression are also much the same as for other age groups. The elderly may differ in that they are more likely to lose weight and less likely to express feelings of guilt or worthlessness.[38]

Depression is widely underdiagnosed and undertreated among the elderly. This occurs in part because depression and other psychiatric disorders are often difficult to recognize among elderly individuals. Typical symptoms such as depressed mood may be less prominent, and other medical problems also cause symptoms associated with depression, such as disturbed sleeping patterns and loss of appetite. Health care professionals often mistake depressive symptoms for normal signs of the aging process or for dementia. A 1992 National Institutes of Health (NIH) Consensus Development Panel on Depression in Late Life recognized this confusion as a serious problem:

> Because of the many physical illnesses and social and economic problems of the elderly, individual health care providers often conclude that depression is a normal consequence of these problems, an attitude often shared by the patients themselves. All of these factors conspire to make the illness underdiagnosed and, more important, undertreated.[39]

A recent study of the treatment of depressed elderly nursing home residents confirmed that inadequate diagnosis and treatment for depression was pervasive. In one study that involved independent evaluation of residents by a research psychiatrist, fewer than 15 percent of depressed residents had correctly been diagnosed by the nursing

---

[36]Psychotherapeutic Medication in the Nursing Home: Position Statement," *Journal of the American Geriatrics Society* 40 (1992): 946-49.

[37]Kennedy, "Depression in the Elerly."

[38]Blazer, "Depression in the Elderly," 164-66.

[39]NIH Consensus Development Panel on Depression in Late Life, 1018-24.

home physician and fewer than 25 percent of those residents had been treated for depression.[40] Other studies have also reported underdiagnosis and undertreatment of depression; one study noted that only 15 percent of the alert and oriented patients with depression received treatment.[41]

The elderly are also at risk for both the undertreatment and overtreatment of pain. Cognitive impairment can make it difficult for elderly patients to express their feelings of pain adequately. Thus, pain is often overlooked by health care providers. Elderly patients may also be overtreated for pain resulting from the physiological changes that take place as individuals age. Because the elderly have a decreased ability to metabolize certain medications, they are more sensitive to analgesic effects of opioid drugs. As a result, they experience higher peaks and a longer duration of pain relief from the medication than younger patients. Finally, side effects of pain medication, such as constipation, urinary retention and respiratory depression, are also more common among elderly patients.[42]

---

[40]B. W. Rovner et al., "Depression and Mortality in Nursing Homes," *Journal of the American Medical Association* 265 (1991): 993-96.

[41]L. L. Heston et al., "Inadequate Treatment of Depressed Nursing Home Elderly," *Journal of the American Geriatrics Society* 40 (1992): 1117-22.

[42]J. Addison, "Management of Pain in the Elderly," in *Pain Management and Care of the Terminally Ill*, Washington State Medical Association, Washington State Physicians Insurance, Washington State Cancer Pain Initiative (Seattle: Washington State Medical Association, 1992), 205-14.

3

Clinical Responses to Pain and Suffering

In recent decades, important advances have been made in the field of "palliative care" — the management of pain and symptoms caused by severe illness. While the term has often been used to describe care provided near the end of life for patients who are no longer receiving curative treatments, increasingly the term refers to the palliation of symptoms and care throughout the course of a patient's illness. Medications and pain relief techniques now make it possible to treat pain effectively for most patients. Personal support and counseling can contribute to the management of pain and other symptoms caused by severe illness and the side effects of treatment. Overall, palliative care seeks to alleviate the personal suffering experienced by patients.

Unfortunately, a serious gap exists between what medicine can achieve and the palliative care routinely provided to most patients. In many cases, patients do not receive adequate relief from pain, even when effective treatments are available. Numerous barriers hamper the delivery of pain relief and palliative care, including a lack of professional knowledge and training, unjustified fears about addiction among both patients and health care professionals, inattention to pain assessment, and pharmacy practices. For many patients, pain and suffering could be alleviated using medications and techniques that have been widely publicized and require only modest resources. In some cases, palliative care requires intensive efforts by physicians and nurses, drawing upon their professional commitment as well as their expertise and careful clinical evaluation of each patient's needs.

Approaches in pain and symptom management have been most fully developed for two groups of patients: patients with cancer, and patients with acute pain, such as pain experienced following surgery. Many of the general approaches and specific treatments developed for these patients are also used to treat other patients. For example, patients with human immunodeficiency virus (HIV) disease have symptoms similar to those of cancer patients and can benefit from the same palliative treatments.[1]

Responding to chronic pain involves distinctive challenges. Many aspects of palliative care for patients with chronic pain are less well developed than the management of acute pain and cancer pain; they have received far less attention in medical training, research, and practice. Nevertheless, some advances in the assessment and treatment of chronic pain have occurred in recent years. Notable among these is the development of multidisciplinary approaches to chronic pain and the growth of multidisciplinary pain centers.[2]

Assessing Pain and Other Symptoms

Careful assessment and reassessment of pain and other symptoms is central to pain and symptom management. This assessment may include the patient's description of current pain, a "pain history" of past and ongoing experiences of pain and their effect on the patient's life, a history of analgesic (pain-relieving) medications taken by the patient and their effects, and physical examination and general evaluation of the patient. Determining the cause of pain often helps to guide effective treatment. Evaluation of concurrent physical symptoms is important as well, both because of their direct impact on the patient's quality of life and because of their effect on the patient's pain. Palliative care experts recommend that health care professionals consider the patient's emotional, social, and economic concerns. Like physical symptoms, these factors contribute to the patient's experience of pain and are often a direct cause of suffering.[3]

---

[1]W. M. O'Neill and J. S. Sherrard, "Pain in Human Immunodeficiency Virus Disease: A Review," *Pain* 54 (1993): 3-14. See also R. K. Portenoy, "Chronic Opioid Therapy in Nonmalignant Pain," *Journal of Pain and Symptom Management* 5 (1990): S46-62.

[2]J. D. Loeser et al., "Interdisciplinary, Multimodal Management of Chronic Pain," in *The Management of Pain*, ed. J. J. Bonica, 2d ed. (Philadelphia: Lea and Febiger, 1990), 2107-20; H. Flor, T. Fydrich, and D. C. Turk, "Efficacy of Multidisciplinary Pain Treatment Centers: A Meta-Analytic Review," *Pain* 49 (1992): 221-30.

[3]Acute Pain Management Guideline Panel, *Acute Pain Management: Operative or Medical Procedures and Trauma, Clinical Practice Guideline*, AHCPR pub. no. 92-0032 (Rockville, Md.: U. S. Department of Health and Human Services, Public Health Service, Agency for Health Care Policy and Research, February 1992), 7-14; World Health Organization, *Cancer Pain Relief* (Geneva: World Health Organization, 1986), 45-48; V. Ventafridda, "Continuing Care: A Major Issue in Cancer Pain Management," *Pain* 36 (1989): 138; D. E. Weissman et al., *Handbook of Cancer Pain Management*, 3d ed. (Madison: Wisconsin Pain Initiative, 1992), 2-3; Loeser et al., 2108, 2112.

For both chronic and acute conditions, palliative care experts recommend an interdisciplinary approach to pain and symptom management. Input from the patient and family members is crucial. Health care professionals should develop an individualized plan for pain and symptom management, in response to the patient's symptoms and physical and personal characteristics. For example, if a patient requires an opioid medication such as morphine, individualized decisions must be made about the route of administration, the dosage, and the schedule of administration. For patients undergoing surgery, the plan should be formulated preoperatively. Frequent reassessment of the patient's pain and symptoms is also important, in order to determine the effectiveness of the plan and to respond to changes in the patient's condition.[4]

Managing Pain

For some patients, pain can be reduced by treatments aimed at the underlying cause. Pain often indicates a disease or injury that can be treated. Even if a patient is terminally ill and no longer receiving curative therapy, interventions aimed at the patient's underlying illness may serve a palliative function. For example, a cancer patient may benefit from localized radiation intended to shrink a tumor and lessen pain.[5] For some acquired immunodeficiency syndrome (AIDS) patients, oral pain arising from infection, or headaches caused by toxoplasmosis, could be alleviated by treating the underlying infection.[6]

Medications are a basic component of pain management for most patients. According to the American Pain Society, "drug therapy is the mainstay of treatment for the management of acute pain and cancer pain in all age groups."[7] Two types of analgesic medications are most widely used: nonsteroidal anti-inflammatory drugs (NSAIDS), such as

---

[4]Acute Pain Management Guideline Panel; American Pain Society, *Principles of Analgesic Use in the Treatment of Acute Pain and Cancer Pain*, 3d ed. (Skokie, Ill.: American Pain Society, 1992). Palliative care experts also note that it is easier to prevent pain than to bring pain under control. Accordingly, they recommend that patients generally receive analgesics on a regular basis, around the clock, rather than in response to pain or "as needed" (PRN).

[5]Weissman et al., 3-4; Ventafridda, 140; World Health Organization, *Cancer Pain Relief and Palliative Care: Report of a WHO Expert Committee*, WHO Technical Report Series 804 (Geneva: World Health Organization, 1990), 11.

[6]O'Neill and Sherrard.

[7]American Pain Society, 3.

aspirin and acetaminophen; and opioids, such as codeine and morphine. In some cases, other "adjuvant" analgesics would be effective. For example, antidepressant or anticonvulsant drugs could serve to reduce neuropathic pain.[8]

Nonsteroidal anti-inflammatory drugs are generally used to treat mild to moderate pain. These drugs often provide adequate palliation for patients after a relatively noninvasive surgical procedure, or for cancer patients with mild pain. If pain persists or increases, patients may be given opioid medications.[9] Opioids are frequently used to treat patients with moderate to severe pain after surgery or patients with a potentially terminal illness. While ongoing opioid therapy raises special concerns for patients with chronic pain who are not terminally ill because of the risk of tolerance and long-term physical dependence, such treatment can be appropriate in some cases.[10]

An approach of an "analgesic ladder," proposed by the World Health Organization (WHO), has been widely accepted in treating patients with cancer and other diseases. The next "step" after NSAIDS would be a weak opioid drug combined with a non-opioid; for example, codeine combined with acetaminophen. Patients with continuing severe pain would receive a strong opioid, such as morphine.[11]

With all drugs, health care professionals must be alert to possible side effects and treat them appropriately. Dosages must be adjusted carefully to provide adequate palliation while minimizing side effects. The analgesic needs of patients often change. For example, a cancer patient may require increasing doses of morphine as the disease worsens.

Patients may develop tolerance to pain medication such as opioids. When this occurs, larger or more frequent doses are needed to produce the same analgesic effect. If a patient becomes physically dependent on opioids or other drugs, any reduction of dosage must be gradual to

---

[8]World Health Organization, *Cancer Pain Relief*; American Pain Society; Weissman et al.

[9]Acute Pain Management Guideline Panel, 16-17. Especially when patients have multiple sources and types of pain, more than one type of analgesic may be administered simultaneously.

[10]R. K. Portenoy, "Opioid Therapy for Chronic Nonmalignant Pain: Current Status," in *Progress in Pain Research and Management*, ed. H. L. Fields and J. C. Liebeskind (Seattle: IASP Press, 1993), 247-87.

[11]World Health Organization, *Cancer Pain Relief*; American Pain Society; Weissman et al. People frequently have more than one site and type of pain, requiring a combination of drug therapies.

avoid symptoms of abstinence syndrome, or withdrawal. Physical dependendence should not be confused with psychological dependence, or addiction. Addiction has been defined as a "behavioral pattern of drug use, characterized by overwhelming involvement with a drug (compulsive use), the securing of its supply, and the tendency to relapse after withdrawal."[12] Psychological dependence is extremely rare in patients receiving opioids or other medications for pain control. These patients do not exhibit the compulsive behavior, or the uncontrolled escalation of dosage in the absence of symptoms, that characterize addiction.[13]

The appropriate dosage of pain medication can vary tremendously among patients or for the same patient over time. For example, a study of 90 advanced cancer patients found that more than half changed their dosage of opioids by 25 percent or more during the last four weeks of life. While half the patients received less than 100 IM morphine equivalent milligrams per day of opioid analgesics, some patients with neuropathic pain required more than nine times that dosage. When opioid dose is carefully adjusted to control side effects, large doses of opioids can be administered safely, either in the hospital or the patient's home.[14]

Nonpharmacologic treatments can also be effective, independently or in conjunction with medications. Cognitive and behavioral approaches can lessen pain and give patients a sense of control, whether the patient is experiencing acute pain following surgery or chronic pain associated with cancer. These approaches include relaxation exercises, imagery, and distraction. Physical agents, such as applications of heat or cold, may also help to alleviate pain. Anesthetic interventions can block nerve transmission on a temporary or ongoing basis. In some extreme cases, neurosurgery to cut nerves may be appropriate.[15] In

---

[12]J. H. Jaffe, "Drug Addiction and Drug Abuse," in *The Pharmacological Basis of Therapeutics*, ed. A. G. Gilman et al., 7th ed. (New York: Macmillan, 1985), 532-81, cited by Portenoy, S53.

[13]Portenoy, S53-54; Weissman et al., 12-13; A. Jacox et al., *Management of Cancer Pain, Clinical Practice Guideline* no. 9, AHCPR pub. no. 94-0592 (Rockville, Md.: U. S. Department of Health and Human Services, Public Health Service, Agency for Health Care Policy and Research, March 1994), 50-51. See chapter 8, n. 20.

[14]N. Coyle et al., "Character of Terminal Illness in the Advanced Cancer Patient: Pain and Other Symptoms During the Last Four Weeks of Life," *Journal of Pain and Symptom Management* 5 (1990): 83-93.

[15]Weissman et al.; G. W. Hanks and D. M. Justin, "Cancer Pain: Management," *Lancet* 339 (1992): 1035; Acute Pain Management Guideline Panel, 21-26.

other cases, when pain is otherwise intractable, the combination of intraspinal administration of opioids and local anesthetic can provide effective palliation.[16]

Taken together, modern pain relief techniques can alleviate pain in all but extremely rare cases. Effective techniques have been developed to treat pain for patients in diverse conditions.[17] On the basis of studies, for example, it has been estimated that for 90 percent of cancer patients, pharmacological treatments alone can alleviate pain and symptoms to an extent that patients find adequate.[18] Other patients can benefit from different approaches. Some patients whose symptom palliation is "inadequate" may nonetheless gain significant relief from pain. For example, a patient's pain may be alleviated when he or she is stationary, but pain arising from movement might confine the patient to bed most of the time.[19]

Palliative care experts believe that the number of patients with unavoidable and intolerable pain is very small. For these patients, sedation to a sleeplike state, while far from an ideal option, would prevent the patient from experiencing severe pain and suffering.[20] This option is considered in rare cases for terminally ill patients during the last days or weeks of their lives.[21]

Treating Other Symptoms of Illness

Seriously ill patients generally require treatment for distressing symptoms other than pain, which may arise from the disease or as a side effect of treatment. Symptoms such as nausea, inability to sleep,

---

[16]E. S. Krames, "The Chronic Intraspinal Use of Opioid and Local Anesthetic Mixtures for the Relief of Intractable Pain: When All Else Fails!" *Pain* 55 (1993): 1-4.

[17]See, e.g., Acute Pain Management Guideline Panel, 4.

[18]Jacox et al., 8. An estimate of 90-95% adequacy is given by Elliot S. Krames (2), citing World Health Organization, *Cancer Pain Relief*, 2d ed. (Geneva: World Health Organization, 1989).

[19]Personal communication, Russel K. Portenoy, M.D., Director of Analgesic Studies, Pain Service, Department of Neurology, Memorial Sloan-Kettering Cancer Center.

[20]See chapter 5, n. 59.

[21]In one case reported in the medical literature, a 28-year-old woman with metastatic cancer suffered from increasing pain that was only partially relieved by opioids. Radiation therapy and anesthetic interventions also failed to provide adequate pain relief. Following the wishes of the patient and her surrogate decision maker, the patient was kept in a state of light sedation until her death two days later. R. D. Truog et al., "Barbiturates in the Care of the Terminally Ill," *New England Journal of Medicine* 327 (1992): 1678.

and loss of appetite can be addressed by pharmacological and other means. For example, a patient experiencing dyspnea (difficulty in breathing) might be helped by the administration of oxygen or by opioids to reduce the sensation of breathlessness.[22] In some instances, relatively simple measures, such as dietary changes, can ameliorate a particular symptom.

While evaluating the patient's physical pain or symptoms, health care professionals may identify symptoms of depression or other psychiatric disorders. Psychiatric consultation should be considered in these cases. As discussed above, major depression is relatively common among severely ill patients. While often difficult to diagnose, depression is distinct from normal feelings of sadness that generally accompany terminal illness. Depression in terminally ill patients generally can be treated successfully using antidepressant medications and psychotherapeutic interventions.[23]

In general, symptom management requires a comprehensive approach. Health care professionals should encourage patients to talk about their symptoms, formulate and implement means to relieve each of the multiple symptoms that may be distressing a patient, and continue to reassess and respond to the patient's needs.[24] As the World Health Organization notes, "Treatment of multiple symptoms is demanding. Therapeutic efforts must consider the interaction of symptoms, the causal factors involved, and maintenance of the delicate balance between relief, adverse drug effects, and patients' expectations."[25] WHO and others suggest that these efforts can best be carried out by an interdisciplinary palliative care team working together with the patient, family members, and other health care professionals involved in the patient's care.[26]

---

[22]F. DeConno, A. Caraceni, and E. Spoldi, "Pharmacological Treatment of Dyspnoea in Terminal Cancer Patients," in *Why Do We Care?*, Syllabus of the Postgraduate Course, Memorial Sloan-Kettering Cancer Center, New York City, April 2-4, 1992, 329-40.

[23]See A. J. Roth and J. C. Holland, "Treatment of Depression in Cancer Patients," *Primary Care in Cancer* 14 (1994): 24-29; and the discussion in chapter 1.

[24]Ventafridda 140; Coyle et al. 90; J. Schiro, "Symptom Management and the Hospice Patient," in Washington State Medical Association, Washington State Physicians Insurance, and Washington State Cancer Pain Initiative, *Pain Management and Care of the Terminal Patient* (Seattle: Washington State Medical Association, 1992), 165-83.

[25]World Health Organization, *Cancer Pain Relief and Palliative Care*, 41-42.

[26]World Health Organization, *Cancer Pain Relief and Palliative Care*, 42; Ventafridda.

Palliative care experts underscore the importance of a comprehensive approach that addresses the broad range of needs of severely ill patients. This approach is often referred to as continuing care or supportive care.[27] The goals of continuing care include relief from pain and other distressing symptoms, psychological and personal support for the patient and family, and assistance to help the patient maintain his or her daily activities, independence, and dignity.[28] Initially developed by hospices caring for the terminally ill, this approach has since expanded to other health care contexts. Continuing care may be provided to patients in a variety of health care settings, including hospitals and home care. Such care may be crucial for patients at any stage of disease, including those who have just been diagnosed and those nearing the end of a long illness.[29]

Patients with severe ongoing pain often benefit from a multidisciplinary approach that helps them to modify behavioral patterns and increase their ability to function.[30] Chronically ill patients and others can benefit from rehabilitative therapy, modification of their home and working environment, and technological aids such as adapted telephones.[31] For all severely ill patients, communication and personal

---

[27]Ventafridda; N. M. Coyle, "Continuing Care for the Cancer Patient with Chronic Pain," in *Why Do We Care?*, Syllabus of the Postgraduate Course, Memorial Sloan-Kettering Cancer Center, New York City, April 2-4, 1992, 371-77.

[28]World Health Organization, *Cancer Pain Relief*, 22-23; Ventafridda; Coyle, "Continuing Care."

[29]World Health Organization, *Cancer Pain Relief*, 22-23; Ventafridda; Coyle, "Continuing Care."

[30]Loeser et al.

[31]S. S. Dittmar, *Rehabilitation Nursing: Process and Application* (St. Louis: C. V. Mosby, 1989). For example, journalist Terry Mayo Sullivan found the loss of the ability to speak one of the most devastating effects of her ALS. "It was another cruel irony: I had devoted my professional life to the business of communication, yet I couldn't make my simplest desire known." She became angry and frustrated, and wanted to end her life. Her quality of life improved dramatically when her husband devised a means for her to communicate via a personal computer using her neck muscles. "Rather than being bound by despair, I look forward to living each day, sharing laughter and joy with my husband, family, friends, and wonderful caretakers. That's not to say my life is easy: Fighting ALS is frustrating, heart-breaking, and time-consuming. ... [But] my life has meaning again, and I plan to live it fully in the time I have remaining." T. M. Sullivan, "The Language of Love," *Ladies' Home Journal*, March 1994, 24-28.

support can be crucial. In the words of one physician suffering from amyotrophic lateral sclerosis (ALS):

> The absence of a magic potion against the disease does not render the physician impotent. There are many avenues that can be helpful for the victim and his family. I am often surprised and moved by the acts of kindness and affection that people perform. Fundamentally, what the family needs is a sense that people care. No one else can assume the burden, but knowing that you are not forgotten does ease the pain.[32]

Current Clinical Practice

Despite dramatic advances in pain management, the delivery of pain relief is grossly inadequate in clinical practice. The assessment of one physician a decade ago, that the treatment of severe pain in hospitalized patients is "regularly and systematically inadequate," remains true today.[33] Studies have shown that only 25 to 70 percent of post-operative pain, and 20 to 60 percent of cancer pain, is treated adequately.[34] In one study of 897 physicians caring for cancer patients, 86 percent reported that most patients with cancer are undermedicated. Only 12 percent characterized their pain management training in medical school as excellent or good.[35] In another study of 687 physicians and 759 nurses, 81 percent of respondents agreed with the statement, "The most common form of narcotic abuse in the care of the dying is undertreatment of pain."[36] A recent study reported that patients with pain that is not attributed to cancer receive even poorer analgesic

---

[32]D. Rabin, P. L. Rabin, and R. Rabin, "Compounding the Ordeal of ALS: Isolation from My Fellow Physicians," *New England Journal of Medicine* 307 (1982): 506-9.

[33]M. Angell, "The Quality of Mercy," *New England Journal of Medicine* 306 (1982): 98-99.

[34]Russell K. Portenoy, presentation to the Task Force, May 13, 1992.

[35]J. H. Von Roenn et al.,, "Physician Attitudes and Practice in Cancer Pain Management: A Survey from the Eastern Cooperative Oncology Group," *Annals of Internal Medicine* 119 (1993): 121-26.

[36]M. Z. Solomon et al., "Decisions Near the End of Life: Professional Views on Life-Sustaining Treatments," *American Journal of Public Health* 83 (1993): 18-19. The majority of respondents expressed dissatisfaction with the current lack of patient involvement in treatment decisions; most were not satisfied with the extent to which patients are informed of care alternatives, staff finds out what critically and terminally ill patients want, or patients' wishes are recorded in the medical record.

treatment than patients with cancer-related pain. It also found that individuals treated at centers that served predominantly minority patients were three times more likely than those treated elsewhere to receive inadequate pain treatment. Elderly individuals and women were also more likely than others to receive poor treatment.[37]

Diverse factors hamper pain and symptom management and pain relief in particular. The knowledge and attitudes of health care professionals are a principal barrier. Some studies reveal significant gaps in health care professionals' knowledge and training about pain relief.[38] In general, researchers report that many doctors and nurses are poorly informed about, and have limited experience with, pain and symptom management. Health care professionals appear to have a limited understanding of the physiology of pain and the pharmacology of narcotic analgesics. Accordingly, many lack the understanding, skills, and confidence necessary for effective pain and symptom management.[39]

Studies also indicate that physicians and other health care professionals are excessively and unjustifiably concerned about the risk of addiction and respiratory depression, even though these responses to pain medication are extremely rare and can be prevented when treatment is appropriately monitored.[40] In one study of 2,459 nurses, only 24.8 percent knew that the rate of psychological dependence in patients treated with narcotic drugs for pain is less than one percent; 21.6 percent thought that addiction occurs in 25 percent or more of these

---

[37] C. S. Cleeland et al., "Pain and Its Treatment in Outpatients with Metastatic Cancer," *New England Journal of Medicine* 330 (1994): 592-96. See also Jacox et al., 138-39.

[38] For example, in one study of 2,459 nurses participating in workshops on pain, only 25% correctly identified propoxyphene (Darvon) as a narcotic. M. McCaffery et al., "Nurses' Knowledge of Opioid Analgesic Drugs and Psychological Dependence," *Cancer Nursing* 13 (1990): 21-27. See also J. Hamilton and L. Edgar, "A Survey Examining Nurses' Knowledge of Pain Control," *Journal of Pain and Symptom Management* 7 (1992): 18-26; T. E. Elliot and B. A. Elliot, "Physician Attitudes and Beliefs about Use of Morphine for Cancer Pain," *Journal of Pain and Symptom Management* 7 (1992): 141-48.

[39] J. L. Dahl et al., "The Cancer Pain Problem: Wisconsin's Response," *Journal of Pain and Symptom Management* 3 (1988): S3; K. M. Foley, "The Relationship of Pain and Symptom Management to Patient Requests for Physician-Assisted Suicide," *Journal of Pain and Symptom Management* 6 (1991): 290; personal communication, Kathleen M. Foley, Chief, Pain Service, Department of Neurology, Memorial Sloan-Kettering Cancer Center, March 4, 1993.

[40] Foley, 291-92; Solomon et al., 18-20.

patients.[41] In a more recent study of practicing physicians, 20 percent incorrectly reported that addiction is a serious concern in prescribing opioids in cancer pain management.[42]

Other factors are also significant obstacles for the delivery of good palliative care. Professional training and patterns of practice may lead health care professionals to focus on diagnosable or measurable clinical indicia, such as structural lesions, laboratory tests, and measurements of vital signs, to the exclusion of pain. Pain and distressing symptoms may not be entered in the medical record or clearly displayed. The care of a hospitalized patient is often fragmented among many health care professionals, none of whom regards pain management as his or her responsibility. In addition, accountability for pain and symptom management does not clearly rest with any one member of the care team, nor are these areas of clinical practice usually addressed by quality assurance procedures.[43]

Patients at home can face special difficulties in receiving pain medication. In some cases, regulations intended to prevent diversion and illegal use of opioids may make it more difficult for patients to receive medications. For example, some states limit the dosage of certain pain medications that a patient can obtain with a prescription, effectively restricting a patient to one week's supply. Other regulations designed to prevent abuse may stigmatize patients by requiring that physicians report patients using such drugs as "habitual users." Some physicians may fail to prescribe opioids because of fears about regulatory scrutiny, although it appears that these concerns may often reflect misunderstanding about regulatory requirements.[44]

Pharmacy practices may also be a stumbling block for patients seeking to obtain adequate pain relief. Some pharmacies do not stock

---

[41]McCaffery et al., 21-27. In another study of 318 nursing staff members, 21% of respondents believed that the risk of addiction was 50% or greater. Hamilton and Edgar.

[42]Elliot and Elliot, 144.

[43]Dahl et al.; M. B. Max, "Improving Outcomes of Analgesic Treatment: Is Education Enough?" *Annals of Internal Medicine* 113 (1990): 885-89.

[44]Dahl et al.; D. E. Joranson, "Federal and State Regulation of Opioids," *Journal of Pain and Symptom Management* 5 (1990): S12-23; K. M. Foley, personal communication. Some physicians in New York State point to the requirement for triplicate prescription forms as a significant barrier to adequate pain relief practices. Data collected by the Department of Health about prescribing practices for opioids as well as other drugs do not support this contention. For further discussion see the Task Force's recommendations for regulatory change, chapter 8, pp. 171-75.

certain pain relief medications for a variety of reasons, including low profit margins and the fear of theft. Pharmacists also may desire to avoid both paperwork and potential regulatory scrutiny. According to one estimate, only 10 to 20 percent of pharmacies in New York City carry regulated drugs such as morphine. In some cases, inaccurate knowledge or negative attitudes may lead pharmacists to convey to patients an exaggerated sense of the risks of opioid treatment and to discourage them from using adequate amounts of a prescribed drug.[45]

The attitudes and knowledge of patients and their families are also crucial for pain management. Patients may not be aware of the possibilities for managing pain, and so may "suffer in silence." They also may not know how to obtain desired therapy. Many patients are misinformed and deeply concerned about the risks of addiction and side effects. Others may believe that using strong analgesics will preclude adequate palliation in later stages of the disease. Patients may also underreport pain to avoid confirming the progress of disease, because they are fearful of distracting their doctor from curative therapy, or because they do not want to seem difficult or demanding to health care professionals. In one study, 45 percent of patients agreed with the statement, "Good patients avoid talking about pain." This belief was especially common among older patients and those with lower levels of education and income.[46]

Finally, patients often face financial barriers in receiving adequate palliative care. In some cases, insurance coverage will not pay for hospitalization when needed to control pain or for the home use of equipment such as infusion pumps. In other cases, policies may pay for the use of technological interventions but not for simpler and less expensive medications.[47]

In recent years, various programs have been developed and implemented to address these barriers. Some focus on education for health care professionals, including continuing education as well as training in nursing schools, medical schools, and residencies. Others attempt to change practice by formulating practice guidelines, developing clinical models, and establishing quality assurance procedures. Infor-

---

[45]Dahl et al.; Foley, 292; K. M. Foley, personal communication.

[46]S. E. Ward et al., "Patient-Related Barriers to Management of Cancer Pain," *Pain* 52 (1993): 319-24; Dahl et al. See also Mellman Lazarus Lake, "Presentation of Findings: Mayday Fund," September 1993, and the discussion in chapter 8.

[47]Foley, 292; B. R. Ferrell and M. Rhiner, "High-Tech Comfort: Ethical Issues in Cancer Pain Management for the 1990s," *Journal of Clinical Ethics* 2 (1991): 108-112.

mational materials and programs have been developed to educate patients. Some states have undertaken regulatory changes to increase the availability of opioids to patients while continuing to guard against drug diversion and misuse.[48]

---

[48]See, e.g., J. L. Dahl and D. E. Joranson, "The Wisconsin Cancer Pain Initiative," in *Advances in Pain Research and Therapy*, ed. K. M. Foley et al., vol. 16 (New York: Raven Press, 1990), 499-503; J. A. Spross, "Cancer Pain Relief: An International Perspective," *Oncology Nursing Forum* 19 (suppl.): 5-11; and the discussion in chapter 8.

4

Decisions at Life's End: Existing Law

New York law distinguishes between four types of practices that can arise at the end of a person's life: the withdrawal and withholding of life-sustaining treatment, whether based on the consent of patients or others close to them; suicide; assistance to commit suicide; and active euthanasia. The laws governing each of these practices reflect a judgment about the appropriate balance between individual autonomy and society's interest in preventing harm. At one end of the spectrum, the law covering treatment decisions embraces individual autonomy as its central concern, granting competent individuals a broad right to refuse medical treatment necessary to sustain their lives. Decisions about suicide and euthanasia fall at the other end of the continuum, where the law constrains individuals' actions for their own benefit and for the sake of the common good. Societal limits on suicide are reflected in laws that prohibit assisted suicide and euthanasia, regardless of the individual's consent. Likewise, while it is no longer illegal in New York State to commit suicide, there is no "right" to commit suicide as a matter of constitutional or common law.

The Right to Decide About Treatment

Under New York law, competent adults have a firmly established right to accept or reject medical treatment. This right includes the right to refuse medical interventions necessary to prolong the patient's life. The New York Court of Appeals, the state's highest court, first enunciated this principle in a 1981 decision, *In re Eichner.*[1] While the Court of Appeals in *Eichner* based its decision on the common-law right to refuse treatment,[2] it later recognized that "[t]his fundamental com-

---

[1] 52 N.Y.2d 363, 438 N.Y.S.2d 266 (authorizing the withdrawal of a respirator from an 83-year-old permanently unconscious man who had clearly expressed his opposition to the artificial prolongation of his life), *cert. denied*, 454 U.S. 858 (1981).

[2] For an early articulation of this common law principle, see *Schloendorff v. Society of N.Y. Hosp.*, 211 N.Y. 125, 129-30, 105 N.E. 92 (1914) (Cardozo, J.) ("[E]very individual of sound mind and adult years has a right to determine what should be done with his own body.").

mon-law right is coextensive with the patient's liberty interest protected by the due process clause of [the New York State] Constitution."[3] In *Cruzan v. Director, Missouri Department of Health*,[4] the United States Supreme Court similarly concluded that the right to refuse treatment is a protected "liberty interest" under the due process clause of the United States Constitution.

Courts have identified several state interests that, in theory, could overcome a patient's right to refuse life-sustaining treatment in a particular case. Most often, courts have mentioned the state's interest in preserving life, preventing suicide, protecting third persons, and maintaining the ethical integrity of the medical profession.[5] In cases decided to date, however, the competent patient's right to refuse life-sustaining treatment has generally prevailed over these interests.[6] Moreover, the New York Court of Appeals has expressly held that the right to refuse life-sustaining interventions should prevail even when the patient is not terminally or hopelessly ill.[7]

In New York, as in all other states, competent adults have the right to create advance directives regarding treatment decisions, including life-sustaining measures, to be used in the event they lose the capacity to make medical decisions for themselves. The most comprehensive type of advance directive is the "health care proxy," also known as the "health care durable power of attorney."[8] By executing a health care

---

[3]*Rivers v. Katz*, 67 N.Y.2d 485, 504 N.Y.S.2d 74, 78 (1986).

[4]497 U.S. 261, 110 S. Ct. 2841 (1990).

[5]See, e.g., *In re Farrell*, 108 N.J. 335, 529 A.2d 404 (1987). In *Farrell*, the court concluded that these state interests did not outweigh the right of a competent, paralyzed patient to be disconnected from the respirator that sustained her breathing.

[6]See, e.g., *Fosmire v. Nicoleau*, 75 N.Y.2d 218, 551 N.Y.S.2d 876 (1990) (upholding the right of a 36-year-old pregnant patient to refuse blood transfusions following a Cesarean section delivery despite the fact that the patient was responsible for the care of her infant).

[7]Ibid. The New Jersey Supreme Court, when first confronted with this issue, suggested that the patient's right to refuse treatment is weaker when the chance of recovery is great and the invasiveness of the treatment is minimal. See *In re Quinlan*, 70 N.J. 10, 355 A.2d 647, 664, *cert. denied sub nom. Garger v. New Jersey*, 429 U.S. 922 (1976). In *In re Conroy*, 98 N.J. 321, 486 A.2d 1209 (1985), however, the New Jersey Supreme Court rejected this formulation.

[8]N.Y. Public Health Law, Article 29-C (McKinney 1993). See generally New York State Task Force on Life and the Law, *Life-Sustaining Treatment: Making Decisions and Appointing a Health Care Agent* (New York: New York State Task Force on Life and the Law, 1987) (providing social, ethical, and legal background to New York's health care proxy law); see also New York State Department of Health, *The Health*

proxy, adults can delegate to a trusted individual (referred to as an "agent") the authority to make health care decisions in the event of a future loss of capacity.

New York's health care proxy law permits adults to grant an agent the authority to make some or all treatment decisions, including decisions about life-sustaining measures. Under the law, the agent must decide in accord with the patient's wishes, if they are reasonably known, or, if they are not reasonably known, in accord with a judgment about the patient's best interests. The only exception applies to decisions about artificial nutrition and hydration. If the agent does not have reasonable knowledge of the patient's wishes about these measures, the agent cannot decide about them. Health care professionals must honor decisions by the agent to the same extent as if they had been made by the patient, and they are protected from liability for doing so.[9]

In addition to appointing a health care agent, adults can also provide specific advance instructions about treatment, commonly known as a "living will." A living will contains treatment instructions to be followed in the event the individual becomes incapable of making decisions directly. Unlike health care proxies, living wills usually apply only to life-sustaining treatment. While New York does not have a statute governing living wills,[10] the New York Court of Appeals has indicated that living wills can provide the basis for withdrawing or withholding life-sustaining measures if the instructions qualify as "clear and convincing evidence" of the patient's wishes.[11] Advance oral instructions can also satisfy the clear and convincing evidence standard, provided

---

Care Proxy Law: A Guidebook for Health Care Professionals (New York: New York State Department of Health, 1991)(explaining key provisions of the health care proxy law).

[9]Under the health care proxy law, hospitals and other health care facilities must provide patients with a health care proxy form and information about creating a proxy. See N.Y. Public Health Law § 2991 (McKinney 1993). In addition, the federal Patient Self-Determination Act requires health care facilities to notify patients of their rights under state law to create advance directives. See 42 U.S.C. § 1395cc(f) (1992).

[10]Forty-seven states and the District of Columbia have enacted living will statutes that delineate the circumstances under which living wills are valid and set forth the rights and obligations of patients and health care providers under the documents. See Choice in Dying, *Refusal of Treatment Legislation* (1991 & Supp.). The states without living will legislation are Massachusetts, Michigan, and New York. Ibid.

[11]See *In re Westchester County Medical Center (O'Connor)*, 72 N.Y.2d 517, 531, 534 N.Y.S.2d 886, 892 (1988).

they are sufficiently specific and reflect "a firm and settled commitment to the termination of life supports under the circumstances like those presented."[12] Individuals can use both written and oral advance instructions in conjunction with a health care proxy, to guide the agent in making treatment decisions.

At present, New York law does not permit the withdrawal or withholding of life-sustaining treatment from an incapacitated adult patient who has neither created a health care proxy nor left written or oral treatment instructions that satisfy the clear and convincing standard. The New York Court of Appeals first reached this conclusion in its 1981 decision, *In re Storar*, the companion case to *In re Eichner*.[13] In *Storar*, the court rejected a mother's request to terminate blood transfusions for her 52-year-old developmentally disabled son, because he never had the capacity to make treatment decisions for himself. In its ruling, the court explicitly held that no one, not even a concerned family member, can refuse life-sustaining treatment for another person without clear and convincing evidence of the patient's own wishes.[14] The health care proxy law now provides an important exception to this

---

[12]Ibid. In *O'Connor*, the court denied permission to withdraw artificial nutrition and hydration from a 77-year-old severely incapacitated woman, despite the woman's previous statements to her daughters suggesting that she would not wish to continue her life by artificial means. The court reasoned that the woman's prior statements were not clear and convincing evidence of a desire to withdraw treatment, because her medical condition and treatment differed from those she had confronted and discussed with her daughters over the years. The decision in *O'Connor* demonstrates the difficulty of meeting the stringent clear and convincing standard. But cf. *In re Halperin*, N.Y.L.J., August 20, 1993, p. 25, col. 5 (Sup. Ct. Nassau Cty.) (concluding that the patient's "strong and unwavering conviction to refuse those life-prolonging measures to which he had been exposed through multiple contacts with peers and family in similar, if not identical, medical circumstances" satisfied the clear and convincing standard).

In 1991, the New York State Department of Health established regulations requiring facilities to assess whether proof of a patient's wishes is sufficiently specific to satisfy the clear and convincing standard, and to document advance oral and written instructions about treatment. N.Y. Comp. Codes R. & Regs. tit. 10, §§ 400.21 & 700.5 (1991). As stated in the regulations, health care providers need not obtain court approval before honoring living wills or other clear advance expressions of treatment choices. But see *Grace Plaza v. Elbaum*, 82 N.Y.2d 10, 603 N.Y.S.2d 386 (1993) (holding that nursing home could refuse to follow advance directive until ordered to do so by a court, and awarding nursing home costs of providing unwanted treatment while court proceeding was pending).

[13]52 N.Y.2d 363, 438 N.Y.S.2d 266, *cert. denied*, 454 U.S. 858 (1981).

[14]438 N.Y.S.2d at 275. In *Cruzan v. Director, Missouri Department of Health*, 497 U.S. 261, 110 S. Ct. 2841 (1990), the United States Supreme Court held that requiring clear and convincing evidence of an incapacitated patient's wish to forgo life-sustaining treatment does not violate the patient's constitutional rights.

rule, as does New York's statute permitting family members and others close to the patient to refuse cardiopulmonary resuscitation in the event of cardiac or respiratory arrest.[15] Other than these two situations, however, the patient's clearly expressed wishes are the sole basis for decisions to forgo life-sustaining treatment.[16]

New York and Missouri are the only two states that condition the withdrawal or withholding of life-sustaining treatment on clear and convincing evidence of the patient's wishes.[17] The District of Columbia and 23 other states have statutes that explicitly grant surrogate decision makers the right to make medical decisions for an incapacitated patient.[18] Courts in many other states have granted family members similar authority.[19] The Task Force has proposed a statute that would allow family members and others close to the patient to decide about treatment, including life-sustaining measures, for patients who lack decision-making capacity.[20] If enacted, the legislation would bring New York law into line with existing laws in the vast majority of other states. The Task Force's proposed statute is currently under consideration by the New York State Legislature.[21]

---

[15]N.Y. Public Health Law § 2965 (McKinney 1993) (setting forth circumstances under which surrogates can consent to "do not resuscitate" (DNR) orders). Recent amendments to this statute facilitate the ability of surrogates to consent to DNR orders for patients in hospice and home care settings.

[16]The law is less clear with respect to the withdrawal or withholding of life-sustaining treatment from minors. On the one hand, judicial decisions underscore that parents have broad authority to make health care decisions for their minor children, as long as those decisions do not violate legal prohibitions on abuse and neglect. See *Weber v. Stony Brook Hospital*, 60 N.Y.2d 208, 469 N.Y.S.2d 63 (1983); *In re Hofbauer*, 47 N.Y.2d 648, 419 N.Y.S.2d 936 (1979). On the other hand, cases like *Storar* cast doubt on whether this broad parental authority extends to decisions to refuse life-sustaining measures on a child's behalf.

[17]In *Mack v. Mack*, 329 Md. 188, 618 A.2d 744 (1993), the Maryland Court of Appeals held that life-sustaining treatment could not be withdrawn or withheld from an incapacitated patient absent clear and convincing evidence of the patient's wishes. Almost immediately after the decision was announced, the state legislature enacted the Health Care Decisions Act, which authorizes family members and other interested individuals, in a listed order of priority, to act as surrogate decision makers for incapacitated patients who have not executed advance directives. Md. Health-Gen. Code Ann. §§ 5-601 to 5-618 (1993 Supp.).

[18]See Choice in Dying, *Right-to-Die Law Digest* (December 1993 Supp.).

[19]Ibid.

[20]New York State Assembly Bill No. 7166 (1994).

[21]Public hearings held on the Task Force's proposal indicated that the surrogate decision making law commands broad public support. See New York State, Assembly

Suicide and the Law

The legal treatment of suicide has ancient roots, reflecting cultural, religious, and pragmatic beliefs about human life, individual responsibility, and the relationship between the individual and the state. While suicide has been illegal throughout most of history, it is no longer considered a crime anywhere in the United States. However, as discussed below, many states prohibit assisting a suicide, and no state permits euthanasia, regardless of the individual's consent.

In England, under the common law, suicide was considered "self-murder" and was ranked "among the highest crimes."[22] Writing in the 18th century, William Blackstone asserted that "the suicide is guilty of a double offence; one spiritual, in invading the perogative of the Almighty, and rushing into his immediate presence uncalled for; the other temporal, against the king, who hath an interest in the preservation of all his subjects."[23] The usual punishment for committing suicide was burial in the public highway with a stake driven through the body and forfeiture of the suicide's property to the crown.[24] The extent of the property forfeited depended on the motivations behind the suicidal act. If the suicide was committed "without any cause, through anger or ill will," the suicide lost both his lands and his chattels to the king. If, however, the suicide was committed "from weariness of life or impatience of pain," only the chattels were forfeited, and the land descended to the suicide's heirs. Finally, if the individual who committed suicide was insane at the time of his or her act, neither land nor chattels were forfeited to the king.[25] Implicit in this gradation of punishment was the notion that suicide, while always wrong, was less blameworthy under certain circumstances.

Standing Committee on Health, Public Hearings on Legislation Regarding Health Care Surrogate Decision Making, Buffalo, New York, December 14, 1992; Albany, New York, January 13, 1993; and New York, New York, January 15, 1993.

[22] W. Blackstone, *Commentaries*, vol. 4, *189.

[23] Ibid.

[24] Similar penalties were imposed throughout Europe. In France, for example, the corpse was dragged through the streets and thrown on the public garbage heap, while at Metz, "each suicide was put in a barrel and floated down the Moselle away from the places he might wish to haunt." A. Alvarez, *The Savage God: A Study of Suicide* (New York: Random House, 1970): 46-47.

[25] See S. W. Brenner, "Undue Influence in the Criminal Law: A Proposed Analysis of the Criminal Offense of 'Causing Suicide,'" *Albany Law Review* 47 (1982): 64.

In America, the colonies soon abolished the traditional penalties of forfeiture, on the theory that the penalty simply punished the suicidal individual's innocent family.[26] However, many states, including New York, imposed punishment on persons who unsuccessfully attempted to commit suicide, and continued to describe suicide as a "grave public wrong." In 1919, New York State decriminalized attempted suicide, although the description of suicide as a "grave public wrong" remained in the statutes until 1965.[27]

At present, neither suicide nor attempted suicide is a criminal offense in any state. The decriminalization of suicide did not stem from an acceptance of the practice, but rather from a more pragmatic judgment that "there is no form of criminal punishment that is acceptable for a completed suicide and that criminal punishment is singularly inefficacious to deter attempts to commit suicide."[28] Moreover, although suicide is not illegal, there is no "right" to commit suicide under the common law or the Constitution.[29]

Assisted Suicide

New York is among 32 states that make assisting a suicide a specific statutory offense.[30] In states without statutes prohibiting suicide assistance, persons who aid in suicides may be subject to prosecution for murder or manslaughter.[31] Dr. Jack Kevorkian's widely publicized acts of suicide assistance have led several states to adopt new prohibitions

---

[26]See T. J. Marzen et al., "Suicide: A Constitutional Right?" *Duquesne Law Review* 24 (1985): 69.

[27]Ibid., 208-09.

[28]American Law Institute, *Model Penal Code and Commentaries*, vol. 2 (Philadelphia: The American Law Institute, 1980): § 210.5, Comment at 94 (also noting "a certain moral extravagance in imposing punishment on a person who has sought his own self-destruction, who has not attempted direct injury to anyone else and who more properly requires medical or psychiatric attention"). Some commentators, however, have argued that the decriminalization of suicide reflects a societal acceptance of that practice. See, e.g., D. W. Brock, "Voluntary Active Euthanasia," *Hastings Center Report* 22, no. 2 (1992): 19 ("That suicide or attempted suicide is no longer a criminal offense in virtually all states indicates an acceptance of individual self-determination in the taking of one's own life ....").

[29]See p. 67 *et seq.*

[30]For a list of the relevant state statutes, see Choice in Dying, *Right-to-Die Law Digest.*

[31]See C. K. Smith, "What About Legalized Assisted Suicide?" *Issues in Law and Medicine* 8 (1993): 505.

on assisted suicide, including Illinois, Indiana and Tennessee.[32] In Michigan, where Kevorkian resides, the legislature has enacted a temporary ban on suicide assistance pending a commission study on the issue.[33] Legislation prohibiting assisted suicide is also pending in other states.[34]

Specific laws prohibiting assisted suicide are a relatively recent phenomenon. When suicide itself was considered murder, persons who assisted in suicides were guilty of murder as well.[35] Early court decisions generally grounded liability on the defendant's presence during the suicide,[36] or on the defendant's agreement to participate with the victim in a suicide pact.[37] According to one commentator, courts considered these factors evidence of the defendant's causal role in the victim's decision to take his or her own life.[38]

Current New York law classifies assisting a suicide as an independent criminal offense. A person who assists a suicide will be guilty of manslaughter in the second degree, unless the suicide is caused by duress or deception, in which case a defendant could be found guilty of second-degree murder.[39] Liability for assisting a suicide can arise if a person acts intentionally to cause or to aid a suicide, or engages in reckless conduct that causes a suicide. While manslaughter liability

---

[32] See Choice in Dying, *Right-to-Die Law Digest*.

[33] Mich. Comp. Laws § 752.1027 (1993). The statute has been challenged on both procedural and substantive constitutional grounds. See p. 67 n.86.

[34] See generally Choice in Dying, *Right-to-Die Law Digest*.

[35] At common law, if the defendant was present during a suicide, he was guilty as a principal to murder; if he counseled the suicide beforehand, he was guilty as an accessory. Under this formulation, defendants who counseled successful suicides without being present for the suicide itself escaped prosecution, as an accessory could not be prosecuted until the principal was convicted first. See Brenner, 66-67.

[36] See, e.g., *Blackburn v. State*, 23 Ohio St. 146 (1872).

[37] See, e.g., *Burnett v. People*, 204 Ill. 208, 68 N.E. 505 (1903).

[38] See Brenner, 86.

[39] Under the 1881 Penal Law, it was unclear whether the specific provisions on assisted suicide were the exclusive penalties for such conduct, or whether persons who assisted in suicides could also be prosecuted for murder, as they could at common law. The confusion stemmed from the definition of murder itself, which based liability on the defendant's role in "causing" the victim's death. Because persons who assisted in suicides could be said to have "caused" the death of the victim, the act of assisting a suicide "would certainly have been prosecutable as [murder] under the former law in the absence of any specific [assisted] suicide provision." N.Y. Penal Law § 125.15, Denzer and McQuillan Practice Commentary, 226 (McKinney 1967).

would not apply to the person who causes or aids an unsuccessful suicide *attempt*, such persons could face liability for "promoting a suicide attempt," an independent statutory offense.[40]

The scope of liability under New York's laws on assisted suicide is comparable to that in most other states that make assisted suicide a specific statutory offense. A few states, however, impose liability in a wider range of situations than New York. California, for example, criminalizes the act of "encourag[ing]" a suicide,[41] and Oklahoma, in addition to its general prohibition on assisted suicide, separately prohibits the act of providing "any deadly weapon or poisonous drug" with the knowledge that the recipient intends to take his or her own life.[42]

No person has been convicted in New York State of manslaughter for intentionally aiding or causing a suicide. Nor has anyone been convicted of murder for causing a suicide by duress or deception. In one prominent case, however, a man was found guilty of reckless manslaughter when he provided a loaded gun to a drunk and despondent individual and actively challenged the individual to commit suicide.[43]

The paucity of cases dealing with assisted suicide probably stems from a variety of factors: the private, consensual nature of assisted suicide, the difficulties of proving intention in such cases, and the reluctance of prosecutors to pursue the types of cases that are likely to be most common — assistance provided by physicians or family members to terminally or severely ill individuals.[44] The reluctance to bring such cases no doubt rests in part on the degree of public sympathy they often arouse, and the resulting difficulty of securing an indictment and conviction.

---

[40]N.Y. Penal Law § 120.30 (McKinney 1987).

[41]Cal. Penal Code § 401 (1988).

[42]Okla. Sta. Ann. tit. 21, § 814 (1985).

[43]See *People v. Duffy*, 79 N.Y.2d 611, 595 N.Y.S.2d 814 (1992); see also the discussion on pp. 61-62.

[44]Indeed, according to one commentator's search of reported decisions nationwide, no health care professional has ever been convicted of "causing, inducing, or assisting" in the death of his or her patient. L. O. Gostin, "Drawing a Line Between Killing and Letting Die: The Law, and Law Reform, on Medically Assisted Dying," *Journal of Law, Medicine and Ethics* 21 (1993): 97.

Assisted Suicide as Murder: Requirement of Duress or Deception

Section 125.25 of the Penal Law establishes that causing a suicide through the use of duress or deception constitutes second-degree murder. It does this by providing that causing a suicide does *not* fall within the definition of intentional murder *unless* the suicide is caused by the defendant's use of duress or deception.[45] Causing a suicide through duress or deception is different from other assisted suicide cases because the defendant does not seek to effectuate the victim's own wish to commit suicide, but instead exerts pressure to cause a suicide that would otherwise not have taken place.[46]

As in all murder cases, proof that the defendant's acts played a causal role in the victim's death is essential to establish the defendant's guilt.[47] Causation in this context refers to both causation-in-fact (i.e., proof that the defendant's actions "forged a link in the chain of causes which actually brought about the death") and proximate cause (i.e., proof that the defendant's actions were a "sufficiently direct cause of the ensuing death").[48] Under this formulation, a defendant will not be held to have caused the victim's death based on an "obscure or merely probable connection between an assault and death."[49] At the same time, it is not necessary to establish that the defendant's acts were the sole cause of death, as long as "the ultimate harm is something which should have been foreseen as being reasonably related to the acts of the accused."[50]

---

[45]"This rule is designed to restrict the more sympathetic cases to manslaughter and, at the same time, to permit the more heinous ones to be prosecuted as murder." N.Y. Penal Law § 125.15, Denzer and McQuillan Practice Commentary, 226 (McKinney 1967); cf. American Law Institute, § 210.5(1) (classifying as criminal homicide the act of causing suicide through force, duress or deception). If the result of the defendant's duress or deception is an unsuccessful suicide attempt, the defendant can be prosecuted for attempted murder. See N.Y. Penal Law § 120.35 (McKinney 1987).

[46]See Brenner, 87-93 (arguing that "causing" a suicide under Section 210.5(1) of the Model Penal Code should depend on the defendant's exertion of "undue influence" that overcomes the victim's independent free will).

[47]See N.Y. Penal Law § 125.00 (McKinney 1987) ("Homicide means conduct which causes the death of a person ....").

[48]*People v. Stewart*, 40 N.Y.2d 692, 697, 389 N.Y.S.2d 804, 807-08 (1976).

[49]Ibid.

[50]*People v. Kibbe*, 35 N.Y.2d 407, 412, 362 N.Y.S.2d 848, 851-52 (1974). Based on this rationale, the *Kibbe* court affirmed the murder convictions of defendants who had beaten the victim and left him lying in the middle of the street, where he was subsequently hit and killed by an oncoming truck. The court found that the victim's death was a sufficiently foreseeable consequence of the defendants' acts. By contrast,

There are no reported cases in New York charging a defendant with murder for causing or assisting a suicide by duress or deception. The New Jersey case of *State v. Lassiter*,[51] however, suggests the extreme nature of the acts that might constitute this offense. In *Lassiter*, the defendant, who employed the victim as a prostitute, beat the victim severely with a shovel. The next day, when the victim was already badly injured, the defendant returned and beat her again. Eventually, the victim pleaded that she could not tolerate the beatings and that she was going to jump out the window. When the defendant replied "go ahead and jump," the victim leaped to her death. In affirming the defendant's murder conviction, the appellate court held that the victim's suicide "was provoked entirely by abuse and coercion on the part of defendant and was unrelated to any suicidal purpose."[52] Cases like *Lassiter* underscore that suicide caused by duress or deception is a different, and more serious, crime than suicide assistance provided at a person's request.

Assisted Suicide as Manslaughter:
"Intentionally" Causing or Aiding Death

Section 125.15(3) of the Penal Law provides that a person who "intentionally causes or aids another person to commit suicide," without the use of duress or deception, is guilty of second-degree manslaughter.[53] There are no reported convictions in New York State for this offense, and the scope of liability under this provision is therefore not entirely clear. The reach of the statute will depend largely on how courts and juries interpret the requirement that the defendant act with an "intentional" state of mind.

---

in *People v. Stewart*, 40 N.Y.2d 692, 389 N.Y.S.2d 804 (1976), where the victim of knife wounds died in the course of a hernia operation, the court reversed the defendant's conviction for manslaughter, even though the operation was performed only because a hernia was discovered while operating on the victim for wounds caused by the defendant's assault.

[51] 197 N.J. Super. 2, 484 A.2d 13 (1984).

[52] Ibid. at 13, 484 A.2d at 19. For a discussion of similar cases, see C. D. Shaffer, Note, "Criminal Liability for Assisting Suicide," *Columbia Law Review* 86 (1986): 364-66 (noting that these cases manifest "a classic murder motive — anger, jealousy, hatred, greed, or desire to end marriage," and involve defendants who "seem truly evil, or heartlessly callous").

[53] Intentionally causing or aiding another person to *attempt* suicide constitutes the separate offense of "promoting a suicide attempt." See N.Y. Penal Law § 120.30 (McKinney 1987).

Under the Penal Law, a person is considered to act intentionally with respect to a result or to conduct "when his conscious objective is to cause such result or to engage in such conduct."[54] The word "intentionally," when used in a criminal statute, "is presumed to apply to every element of the offense unless an intent to limit its application clearly appears."[55] Accordingly, liability under Section 125.15(3) would require proof that the defendant's "conscious objective" extended to each of the elements set forth in the statute — engaging in the *conduct* of causing or aiding another person's suicide, and bringing about the *result* of achieving the other person's death.[56]

It is often hard to prove intention in criminal cases. Such proof is particularly difficult in cases of assisted suicide, where the assistance is usually rendered in the context of a private relationship. Proving that a physician intentionally aided a suicide is especially complicated because many medications used to commit suicide also have legitimate medical purposes, particularly for patients in severe pain. For example, if a physician prescribes morphine with the conscious objective of relieving pain, not of bringing about the patient's death, and the patient uses the morphine to commit suicide, the physician would not be guilty of aiding or causing a suicide under Section 125.15(3).[57] In this case, the physician would lack both the intent to aid the patient's suicidal plan and the intent to bring about the patient's death.[58]

---

[54] N.Y. Penal Law § 15.05(1) (McKinney 1987).

[55] N.Y. Penal Law § 15.15 (McKinney 1987); see also *People v. Ryan*, 82 N.Y.2d 497, 605 N.Y.S.2d 235 (1993) ("[I]f a single mens rea element is set forth, ... it presumptively applies to all elements of the offense unless a contrary legislative intent is plain.").

[56] Achieving the result of the principal's death is an essential element of Section 125.15(3). If the result of the defendant's assistance is a suicide attempt, rather than a completed suicide, Section 125.15(3) would not apply; rather, the defendant would be subject to prosecution for "promoting a suicide attempt" under Section 120.30 of the Penal Law.

[57] According to one commentator, however, if the physician, at the time of prescribing the morphine, is "substantially certain" that the patient will use the medication to commit suicide, a finding of intent would be appropriate. See J. A. Alesandro, Comment, "Physician-Assisted Suicide and New York Law," *Albany Law Review* 57 (1994): 847.

[58] Cf. W. R. LaFave and A. W. Scott, Jr., *Substantive Criminal Law*, vol. 2 (St. Paul: West Publishing Co., 1986), § 6.7, p. 143 ("[I]t is not sufficient that [an accomplice] intentionally engaged in acts which, as it turned out, did give assistance or encouragement to the principal. Rather, the accomplice must intend that his acts have the effect of assisting or encouraging another."). In New York, knowingly providing assistance to a crime, without the specific intent of assisting the principal, constitutes

Nonetheless, proof of intent need not be based on direct evidence of the physician's state of mind. Rather, in some cases, juries might *infer* the physician's intent to assist a patient's suicide from the circumstances surrounding the particular case. For example, juries might make such an inference if the physician provides an amount or type of medication that has no legitimate medical purpose for the particular patient in light of identified treatment goals. In the most obvious case, this would be true of the various machines devised by Dr. Kevorkian to provide lethal medication, none of which has any legitimate medical use. Proof of intent could also be inferred from other surrounding circumstances, including the physician's knowledge of the patient's suicidal tendencies.[59] In this regard, it is significant that intent does not mean motive, and does not imply an evil state of mind. The fact that the physician acts benevolently, out of compassion for the patient, would not be a defense to liability under Section 125.15(3).

Assisted Suicide as Manslaughter: Recklessly Causing The Victim's Death

Under New York law, reckless conduct leading to suicide can also be the basis for a charge of manslaughter, even if the defendant did not intentionally cause or aid the suicide within the meaning of Section 125.15(3). The New York Court of Appeals reached this conclusion in a 1992 decision, *People v. Duffy*.[60] *Duffy* involved a 17-year-old, Jason Schuhle, who was extremely distraught over a recent breakup with his girlfriend. The defendant talked with Schuhle at length about Schuhle's suicidal thoughts and Schuhle asked the defendant to shoot him. When the defendant became "tired" of hearing Schuhle complain about wanting to die, he handed Schuhle a gun and urged him to "blow his

the independent offense of "criminal facilitation." See N.Y. Penal Law § 115. Persons who knowingly assist in suicides could not, however, be charged with criminal facilitation, as suicide itself is not a crime. However, if the physician violates accepted medical standards in providing the medication or prescription, he or she could face civil or criminal liability for reckless or negligent conduct.

[59] Cf. American Law Institute, § 2.06, Comment at 316 ("[O]ften, if not usually, aid rendered with guilty knowledge implies purpose since it has no other motivation."). While juries would not be required to make such an inference in any particular case, see *Sandstrom v. Montana*, 442 U.S. 510, 99 S. Ct. 2450 (1979) (finding it error to instruct the jury to presume conclusively that a defendant intends the natural consequences of his voluntary acts), they would be permitted to rely on evidence of the patient's known suicidal tendencies to support such a finding if they so chose. See, e.g., *People v. Johnson*, 101 A.D.2d 684, 475 N.Y.S.2d 942 (3d Dep't 1984) (circumstantial evidence is admissible to prove intent).

[60] 79 N.Y.2d 611, 595 N.Y.S.2d 814 (1992).

head off." Shortly thereafter, Schuhle shot himself. At trial, the defendant was acquitted of intentionally causing or aiding Schuhle's suicide, but convicted of recklessly causing Schuhle's death. On appeal, the Court of Appeals held that the defendant's liability for causing a suicide was properly based on grounds of recklessness, under the general reckless manslaughter statute. The Court of Appeals' decision in *Duffy* established that intentionally assisting a suicide, as defined in Section 125.15(3), is not the exclusive basis for manslaughter liability for conduct that causes another person to take his or her life.[61]

New York law defines recklessness as the conscious disregard of "a substantial and *unjustifiable* risk."[62] This definition necessarily excludes situations where the benefit of taking action outweighs the likelihood that the action will cause harm.[63] Accordingly, in the medical context, if a physician's actions are useful in achieving a beneficial result (e.g., providing medication to relieve pain) and are an acceptable medical means of realizing that goal, the fact that they create a risk of causing a suicide would not, in itself, make the physician's actions reckless within the meaning of Section 125.15(1).[64] Indeed, where a

---

[61]While no New York case has considered whether a person can be charged with *negligently* causing a suicide under the general negligent homicide statute, the logic of *Duffy* would suggest that such a charge would be possible. Cf. *State v. Bier*, 181 Mont. 27, 591 P.2d 1115 (1979) (affirming negligent homicide conviction of defendant who provided his intoxicated wife with a loaded gun, which the wife immediately used to kill herself). However, the standard of criminal negligence is "'appreciably greater than that required for ordinary civil negligence by virtue of the "substantial and unjustifiable" character of the risk involved and the factor of "gross deviation" from the ordinary standard of care.'" *People v. Haney*, 30 N.Y.2d 328, 333, 333 N.Y.S.2d 403, 407 (1972) (citations omitted). In the medical context, criminal charges of negligent homicide are extremely rare, and generally involve conduct that falls well outside the bounds of accepted medical practice. See, e.g., *People v. Ketchum*, 35 N.Y.2d 740, 361 N.Y.S.2d 911 (1974) (affirming doctor's conviction for negligent homicide based on use of dangerous procedure for performing abortion, combined with failure to provide medical care after abortion was performed), *cert. denied*, 420 U.S. 928 (1975). Such a degree of negligence would also subject physicians to charges of professional misconduct by the New York State Department of Health. See pp. 64-67.

[62]N.Y. Penal Law § 15.05(3) (McKinney 1987) (emphasis added).

[63]See LaFave and Scott, vol. 1, § 3.7, p. 327 ("The test for reasonableness in creating risk is ... said to be determined by weighing the magnitude of the risk of harm against the utility of the actor's conduct.").

[64]Cf. President's Commission for the Study of Ethical Problems in Medicine and Biomedical and Behavioral Research, *Deciding to Forgo Life-Sustaining Treatment* (Washington, D.C.: U.S. Government Printing Office, 1983), 82 ("[T]he moral issue is whether or not the decisionmakers have considered the full range of foreseeable effects, have knowingly accepted whatever risk of death is entailed, and have found the risk to be justified in light of the paucity and undesirability of other options.").

patient is experiencing pain, physicians are not only permitted but are ethically obligated to prescribe appropriate pain relief, even though the pain medication may itself create some risk of death.[65]

Euthanasia

Although it is frequently argued that suicide assistance and active euthanasia are morally equivalent,[66] the law in all states draws a clear distinction between these two types of acts. In New York, assisting a suicide, except in certain limited circumstances, is a form of second-degree manslaughter. Euthanasia, however, falls under the definition of second-degree murder, as the defendant intentionally causes the death of the victim through his or her direct acts.[67] Because the consent of the victim is not a defense to murder,[68] euthanasia is therefore prosecutable as murder in the second degree.

While there are no reported cases in New York dealing with murder-by-consent, courts in other states have routinely rejected defendants' requests to instruct the jury on the lesser crime of assisted suicide, rather than murder, where the victim has consented to the defendant's acts.[69] However, in determining the punishment that will be imposed, judges and juries are likely to give substantial weight to both the consent of the victim and the defendant's motive.[70] In addition, although the victim's consent is irrelevant to the defendant's underlying guilt, if the defendant acted in a state of extreme emotional

---

[65]See chapter 7. However, physicians who violate accepted medical standards in determining the appropriate dose or type of drug might be considered to have acted recklessly, particularly if their conduct leads to the patient's death.

[66]See chapter 5, pp. 82-85.

[67]See N.Y. Penal Law § 125.25(1) (McKinney 1987).

[68]See Shaffer, 351 ("No jurisdiction in the United States recognizes consent to homicide."); *State v. Fuller*, 203 Neb. 233, 241, 278 N.W.2d 756, 761 (1979) ("'Murder is no less murder because the homicide is committed at the desire of the victim.'") (quoting *Turner v. State*, 119 Tenn. 663, 671, 108 S.W. 1139, 1141 (1908)).

[69]See, e.g., *State v. Cobb*, 229 Kan. 522, 525-26, 625 P.2d 1133, 1136 (1981) (rejecting defendant's claim that the court should have instructed the jury on suicide assistance, rather than murder, where the defendant "was a direct participant in the overt act of shooting [the victim], which caused his death"). But cf. Shaffer, 374 ("There is too little difference between handing a lethal dosage to another person and placing it in that person's mouth to justify completely different criminal charges – especially when those persons who actively participate in suicide, like those who provide the means, generally do not have a murder motive.").

[70]See American Law Institute, § 210.5, Commentary at 106.

distress — as occurs in some cases of "mercy killing" — the charge may be reduced from murder to manslaughter.[71]

As with the crime of suicide assistance, proof of the defendant's intent is essential to a prosecution for second-degree murder.[72] A physician who administers medication for pain relief would lack the intent to kill, provided that the physician does not intend to relieve pain by killing the patient. In these circumstances, even if pain medication hastens the patient's death, a physician would not be guilty of second-degree murder.

Professional Misconduct Proceedings

In addition to standards set forth in the civil and criminal law, physicians must practice medicine within the standards established by the medical profession itself. These standards are set in a variety of ways, including policies set by the legislature, statements of professional bodies such as the American Medical Association, and the actual practice of physicians, commonly referred to in legal terms as "accepted medical practice."

Through quality assurance programs, hospitals and other health care providers review patient care to determine if physicians are practicing in accord with accepted medical standards. Professional medical standards are also enforced in each state through an administrative disciplinary process. In New York, that process is governed by the State Board for Professional Medical Conduct.[73] Operating within the New York State Department of Health, the board is comprised of 230 members, three quarters of whom are physicians. The board has a duty to investigate complaints of misconduct, to bring

---

[71]See N.Y. Penal Law §§ 125.20(2); 125.25(1)(a) (McKinney 1987).

[72]New York law also provides that reckless conduct "evinc[ing] a depraved indifference to human life" can support a charge of second-degree murder. See N.Y. Penal Law § 125.25(2) (McKinney 1987). However, "depraved-mind" murder is almost never applied in the medical context. See R. Sullivan, "Doctor Faces Murder Count in Abortion," *New York Times*, August 13, 1993, p. B1, col. 5 (noting that no physician has ever been convicted of depraved-mind murder in New York). It is highly unlikely that this kind of charge would arise in the context of physician-assisted suicide.

[73]See generally N.Y. Public Health Law § 230 *et seq.* (McKinney Supp. 1994) (setting forth procedures governing the Board for Professional Medical Conduct); P. J. Millock, "Legal Aspects of Physician-Assisted Suicide, New York Law and Professional Standards," paper delivered to the New York State Task Force on Life and the Law, Arden House, New York, October 26, 1992.

appropriate charges, and to sanction physicians found to violate accepted medical standards.

Disciplinary proceedings before the board can arise from complaints by patients, other physicians, hospitals, or the Department of Health itself. The board investigates complaints referred to it and decides whether or not to recommend that formal charges be brought. In many cases, the board chooses not to proceed; of more than 4,000 complaints filed annually, only 5 percent result in formal charges.

If the board does proceed, the Department of Health formally serves charges against the physician, which trigger an administrative adjudicatory hearing before a three-person committee. The decision of that committee may be appealed to a five-person administrative review board, and that decision may be challenged in court. If disciplinary charges are ultimately sustained, penalties can include censure and reprimand, license suspension or revocation, retraining, fines, and public service.

Disciplinary proceedings differ from criminal prosecutions in several important respects. First, unlike criminal prosecutions, which are investigated by the police and decided by juries drawn from the community at large, disciplinary complaints are investigated and decided by panels of the State Board for Professional Medical Conduct. Each panel has three members, two of whom must be physicians. As such, while criminal liability for assisted suicide and euthanasia depends on moral and legal judgments by members of the general public, disciplinary proceedings reflect the views and standards of the medical community itself.[74]

In addition, unlike criminal prosecutions for assisted suicide or euthanasia, which focus on the defendant's state of mind and the degree to which the defendant caused or assisted the suicidal act, disciplinary proceedings are concerned with the physician's conduct in an objective sense. Thus, rather than examining the physician's "conscious objective" or whether the physician was the proximate cause of the patient's death, the board applies a general negligence standard, with the accepted standards of the medical profession as its overall guide.[75]

---

[74]Opinion within the medical community about the acceptability of assisted suicide and euthanasia is discussed in chapter 5, pp. 108-09.

[75]No New York statute or court decision has explicitly addressed the definition of negligence in the context of disciplinary proceedings. As a result, the definitions of negligence in civil case law are usually employed in the disciplinary setting.

Ordinary negligence on one occasion is not sufficient to subject a physician to professional discipline. Rather, the physician must act with "gross negligence" (i.e., negligence of egregious proportions or conspicuously bad behavior) or with ordinary negligence on more than one occasion.[76] The New York Court of Appeals has held that "occasion" in this context refers to an "event of some duration, occurring at a particular time and place, and not simply to a discrete act of negligence which can occur in an instant."[77] Charges will be sustained only if the board concludes that the physician owed a duty to the patient and that he or she deviated from the generally accepted professional standard of care in performing that duty in the overall circumstances of the particular case.

Few precedents relevant to assisted suicide and euthanasia exist, as the overwhelming majority of cases before the board involve issues of incompetence, as opposed to professional ethics. One notable exception was the case of Dr. Timothy Quill, who published an article in the *New England Journal of Medicine* about a patient who committed suicide with medication that Quill had prescribed for insomnia. In his article, Quill wrote that he discussed the possibility of suicide with his patient on several occasions, and "made sure that she knew ... the amount [of medication] needed to commit suicide."[78] After reviewing the case, the board decided not to bring charges for professional misconduct. The board's decision emphasized that Quill could not "know with certainty" that his patient would use the drugs he prescribed to take her own life.[79]

The final difference between disciplinary proceedings and criminal prosecutions is the burden of proof the state must meet. While a conviction in a criminal prosecution requires proof of guilt "beyond a reasonable doubt," disciplinary proceedings are governed by the less stringent "preponderance of the evidence" standard, which requires

[76] See N.Y. Education Law § 6530(3) (McKinney Supp. 1994).

[77] *Yong-Myu Rho v. Commissioner of Education*, 74 N.Y.2d 318, 546 N.Y.S.2d 1005 (1989).

[78] T. E. Quill, "A Case of Individualized Decision Making," *New England Journal of Medicine* 324 (1991): 693.

[79] "Dr. Timothy Quill," Determination of the New York State Board for Professional Medical Conduct, August 16, 1991, p. 2. In a subsequent article published in the *New England Journal of Medicine* after the investigation into his activities had been concluded, Quill examined his motivations in more detail, asking at one point, "if I did not ... intend to ensure that Diane had the option of death should she find her suffering unbearable, why the prescription for barbiturates?" T. E. Quill, "The Ambiguity of Clinical Intentions," *New England Journal of Medicine* 329 (1993): 1039.

the state to prove only that it is more likely than not that the prohibited conduct occurred.[80] As a result of this distinction, physicians who are acquitted under the criminal law may still face disciplinary charges. If a physician is convicted of a crime, the conviction itself is an act of professional misconduct and can provide the basis for disciplinary sanctions without a full administrative hearing.[81]

The Constitutional Issues

The common law has long protected the individual's right to decide about medical treatment, including the right to refuse treatment necessary to sustain an individual's life.[82] In *Cruzan v. Director, Missouri Department of Health*,[83] the United States Supreme Court held that the right to refuse treatment is also a protected "liberty interest" under the due process clause of the federal Constitution.[84] Likewise, in *Rivers v. Katz*,[85] the New York Court of Appeals concluded that the right to refuse medical treatment is protected under the due process clause of the New York State Constitution.

In contrast, many states, including New York, prohibit assisted suicide and euthanasia. Recently, Michigan passed a law against assisted suicide designed to halt Kevorkian's activities while a state commission develops recommendations for policies on assisted suicide and euthanasia. Both Kevorkian and the Michigan chapter of the American Civil Liberties Union have challenged the law as unconstitutional, on the ground that it violates the rights of terminally ill individuals who wish to die.[86] Some commentators have also argued that

---

[80]See N.Y. Public Health Law § 230(10)(f).

[81]See N.Y. Education Law § 6530(9)(a) (McKinney Supp. 1994); N.Y. Public Health Law § 230(10)(p) (McKinney Supp. 1994).

[82]See pp. 49-50.

[83]497 U.S. 261, 110 S. Ct. 2841 (1990).

[84]Prior to *Cruzan*, many courts had held that the right to refuse treatment is part of the general constitutional right of privacy. In *Cruzan*, however, the Supreme Court found that "this issue is more properly analyzed in terms of a Fourteenth Amendment liberty interest." 110 S. Ct. at 2851 n.7.

[85]67 N.Y.2d 485, 504 N.Y.S.2d 74 (1986).

[86]See *People v. Jack Kevorkian*, No. 93-11482 (Mich. Cir. Ct. Wayne County); *Hobbins v. Attorney General*, No. 93-306-178 CZ (Mich. Cir. Ct. Wayne County). See generally R. A. Sedler, "The Constitution and Hastening Inevitable Death," *Hastings Center Report* 23, no. 5 (1993): 20 (outlining and defending the ACLU's position in *Hobbins*). A similar challenge is pending in federal district court in Washington State. See *Compassion in Dying et al. v. State of Washington*, No. C94-119 (W.D. Wash.).

the constitutional right to refuse unwanted medical treatment necessarily includes the right to suicide assistance or euthanasia.[87]

After examining state and federal law, the Task Force concluded
that neither the United States nor the New York State Constitution
grants individuals a "right" to commit suicide. In cases affirming the
right to forgo life-sustaining treatment, courts have consistently distinguished the right to refuse treatment from a right to commit suicide,
and have acknowledged the state's interest in preventing individuals
from taking their own lives. Rather than establishing a broad constitutional right to determine the timing and manner of death, these cases
stand for the more limited proposition that individuals have a right to
resist bodily intrusions, and to preserve the possibility of dying a natural
death. However, even if suicide implicated a constitutionally-protected
right or liberty interest, prohibitions on assisted suicide or euthanasia
would still be justified by the state's interest in preventing the error and
abuse that would inevitably occur if physicians or others were
authorized to cause or aid another person's death.

The "Right" To Commit Suicide

The Supreme Court has classified certain individual rights as "fundamental," and subjects laws infringing those rights to "strict scrutiny."
A law will survive strict scrutiny only if it is justified by "compelling
governmental interest[s]" and if it is "narrowly tailored" to achieve
those interests.[88] The Supreme Court has also recognized that certain
other rights, while not rising to the status of fundamental rights,
implicate constitutionally protected "liberty interests." Laws that infringe on these liberty interests are subjected to a balancing test, under
which the court must weigh the "individual's interest in liberty against
the State's asserted reason for restraining individual liberty."[89] Laws
that do not infringe on either fundamental rights or constitutionally

---

[87]Compare, e.g., Note, "Physician-Assisted Suicide and the Right to Die with
Assistance," *Harvard Law Review* 105 (1992): 2021 (arguing for recognition of
constitutional right to suicide); S. J. Wolhandler, Note, "Voluntary Active Euthanasia
for the Terminally Ill and the Constitutional Right to Privacy," *Cornell Law Review* 69
(1984): 363 (same); A. Sullivan, "A Constitutional Right to Suicide," in *Suicide: The
Philosophical Issues*, ed. M. P. Battin and D. J. Mayo (New York: St. Martin's Press,
1980): 229 (same) with Y. Kamisar, "Are Laws Against Assisted Suicide
Unconstitutional?" *Hastings Center Report* 23, no. 3 (1993): 32 (arguing against
recognition of constitutional right to suicide); Marzen et al. (same).

[88]See, e.g., *Austin v. Michigan State Chamber of Commerce*, 494 U.S. 652, 666, 110 S.
Ct. 1391, 1401 (1990).

[89]*Youngberg v. Romeo*, 457 U.S. 307, 320, 102 S. Ct. 2452, 2460 (1982).

protected liberty interests receive only minimal judicial scrutiny, and will be upheld as long as they are "rationally related" to a legitimate governmental goal.[90]

Advocates of a constitutional right to assisted suicide contend that the individual's right to self-determination encompasses all decisions concerning the timing and manner of death. In their view, a right to assisted suicide is implicit in the right to refuse life-sustaining treatment, as both practices seek to give individuals "control over when they die, where they die, and their physical and mental state at the time of their death."[91] According to this position, distinctions between the refusal of treatment and suicide are artificial, because both practices stem from the individual's intent to end his or her life,[92] and require acts or omissions that directly cause the individual's death.[93] Rejecting the distinction between "actively" causing death through assisted suicide or euthanasia and "passively" allowing a patient to die by terminating treatment, advocates of a right to suicide emphasize that the law often equates omissions with deliberate acts.[94]

An examination of existing law, however, strongly undermines the contention that the Constitution guarantees individuals the right to take their own lives.[95] In *Cruzan v. Director, Missouri Department of*

---

[90]See, e.g., *Concrete Pipe & Products of California, Inc. v. Construction Laborers Pension Trust*, 113 S. Ct. 2264 (1993).

[91]Note, "Physician-Assisted Suicide," 2026.

[92]Ibid., 2030.

[93]Ibid., 2029 ("[T]he physician's act — turning off the respirator — *is* a cause-in-fact of the death: but for turning off the machine, the patient would be alive today."); see also J. Fletcher, "The Courts and Euthanasia," *Law, Medicine and Health Care* 15 (1987/88): 225 ("[T]he primary causative act is the moral one of removing the supports.").

[94]See Note, "Physician-Assisted Suicide," 2028-29; cf. Brock, 12 (agreeing that terminating treatment and assisting a suicide are both "killing," but arguing that the label of killing does not determine a practice's moral acceptability). In his concurring opinion in *Cruzan*, Justice Scalia also argued that suicide and the refusal of treatment could not be distinguished, but concluded that neither practice was constitutionally protected, not that both must be allowed. See *Cruzan*, 110 S. Ct. at 2860-63 (Scalia, J., concurring). No other justice in *Cruzan* agreed with Justice Scalia's analysis.

[95]Although two lower courts in Michigan have held that the right to commit suicide is constitutionally guaranteed, see *People v. Kevorkian*, No. 93-11482 (Mich. Cir. Ct. Wayne Cty. 1993), *Hobbins v. Attorney General*, No. 93-306-178 CZ (Mich. Cir. Ct. Wayne Cty. 1993), these decisions contained sparse constitutional analysis and are likely to carry little weight as precedent, especially outside the state of Michigan. Appellate courts generally defer only to the factual findings made in the court of first instance, not to the lower court's legal reasoning. In cases involving sensitive issues at

Health,[96] the United States Supreme Court specifically noted the prevalence of laws against assisted suicide, and suggested that a state need not "remain neutral in the face of an informed and voluntary decision by a physically-able adult to starve to death."[97] Other courts that have recognized the right to refuse medical treatment have explicitly distinguished that right from a right to commit suicide,[98] and have consistently affirmed the state's interest in preventing individuals from taking their own lives.[99] These courts have generally held that suicide and the refusal of treatment are different, because individuals who refuse medical treatment do not intend to cause death, but only to avoid unwanted medical interventions.[100] They have also affirmed that, when treatment is refused, the ultimate cause of death is the underlying disease, not the patient's own decision or act.[101]

---

the forefront of legal change, lower court opinions often bear little resemblance to the ultimate resolution of the case at the appellate level. For example, while a New Jersey trial court judge made headlines by upholding the surrogate parenting contract in the *Baby M* case, see *Matter of Baby M*, 217 N.J. Super. 313, 525 A.2d 1128 (Ch. Div., Fam. Pt. 1987), the New Jersey Supreme Court paid little attention to the lower court's legal reasoning in the final decision in the case. See *Matter of Baby M*, 537 A.2d 1227 (N.J. 1988). The reasoning of a lower court in one state carries even less weight as precedent outside that state.

[96]497 U.S. 261, 110 S. Ct. 2841 (1990).

[97]110 S. Ct. at 2852. While the New York Court of Appeals has never directly addressed the constitutionality of laws prohibiting suicide assistance or euthanasia, the Appellate Division, New York's intermediate appellate court, considers it "self-evident that the right to privacy does not include the right to commit suicide." *Von Holden v. Chapman*, 87 A.D.2d 66, 450 N.Y.S.2d 623 (4th Dep't 1982). Moreover, the Court of Appeals' conclusion that the liberty interest protected by the due process clause of the New York State Constitution "is coextensive with" the individual's common-law right to refuse unwanted medical treatment, *Rivers v. Katz*, 67 N.Y.2d 485, 504 N.Y.S.2d 74, 78 (1986), strongly suggests that suicide — which was illegal at common law — does not rise to the level of a constitutional right.

[98]See, e.g., *Fosmire v. Nicoleau*, 75 N.Y.2d 218, 551 N.Y.S.2d 876, 881 (1990) ("[M]erely declining medical care, even essential treatment, is not considered a suicidal act or indication of incompetence.").

[99]See, e.g., *In re Eichner (In re Storar)*, 52 N.Y.2d 363, 438 N.Y.S.2d 266 (noting the legitimacy of the state's interest in "prevention of suicide"), *cert. denied*, 454 U.S. 858 (1981).

[100]See, e.g., *In re Coyler*, 99 Wash.2d 114, 660 P.2d 738, 743 (1983) ("A death which occurs after the removal of life sustaining systems is from natural causes, neither set in motion nor intended by the patient.").

[101]See, e.g. *In re Conroy*, 98 N.J. 321, 486 A.2d 1209, 1224 (1985) (arguing that, although death might result from the refusal of treatment, "it would be the result, primarily, of the underlying disease, and not the result of a self-inflicted injury").

As these courts have recognized, the fact that the refusal of treatment and suicide may both lead to death does not mean that they implicate identical constitutional concerns. The imposition of life-sustaining medical treatment against a patient's will requires a direct invasion of bodily integrity and, in some cases, the use of physical restraints, both of which are flatly inconsistent with society's basic conception of personal dignity.[102] As one commentator has argued, compelled treatment results in "a life almost totally occupied. The person's body is ... so far expropriated from his own will, supposing that he seeks to die, that the most elemental acts of existence — such as breathing, digesting, and circulating blood — are forced upon him by an external agency."[103] It is this right against intrusion — not a general right to control the timing and manner of death — that forms the basis of the constitutional right to refuse life-sustaining treatment.[104] Restrictions on suicide, by contrast, entail no such intrusions, but simply prevent individuals from intervening in the natural process of dying.

While restrictions on suicide do limit individual autonomy, the bare fact that individual options are constrained does not render such limits unconstitutional. Individuals may not irrevocably waive their right against involuntary servitude, for example, regardless of whether the waiver is knowingly and intelligently made.[105] Indeed, in recent years

---

[102]Cf. *Rochin v. California*, 342 U.S. 165, 72 S. Ct. 205 (1952) (concluding that the forcible extraction of evidence from an individual's stomach "shocks the conscience").

[103]J. Rubenfeld, "The Right of Privacy," *Harvard Law Review* 102 (1989): 795; see also D. Orentlicher, "Physician Participation in Assisted Suicide," *Journal of the American Medical Association* 262 (1989): 1845 ("Would a patient dying of cancer have to accept a regimen of chemotherapy that might prolong life for several months but would be painful, nauseating, and debilitating?").

[104]See *Cruzan*, 110 S. Ct. at 2851 (basing right to refuse treatment on cases dealing with intrusions on the person); see also ibid., 110 S. Ct. at 2856 (O'Connor, J., concurring) ("A seriously ill or dying patient whose wishes are not honored may feel a captive of the machinery required for life-sustaining measures or other medical interventions. Such forced treatment may burden that individual's liberty interests as much as any state coercion.").

[105]See *Pollack v. Williams*, 322 U.S. 4, 64 S. Ct. 792 (1944). According to one commentator, while autonomy "has long been the dominant rhetorical value in American medical law and medical ethics," legal protection of autonomy "does not seem to be as dominant a value as rhetoric would suggest." For example, "[l]icensure and the control of allegedly beneficial medicines and devices are designed to ... paternalistically prevent individuals from autonomously making bad choices," while laws that prohibit abortions to protect the health of the mother "can only be understood as reflecting a paternalistic concern for maternal well-being." R. B. Dworkin, "Medical Law and Ethics in a Post-Autonomy Age," *Indiana Law Journal* 68 (1993): 727-30.

the Supreme Court has afforded constitutional protection only to those individual practices "deeply rooted in this Nation's history and tradition."[106] While the merits of this constitutional doctrine are subject to debate, its effect on the constitutional distinction between the refusal of treatment and suicide is clear. On the one hand, the right to refuse treatment has a well-established history in the laws of informed consent and battery.[107] On the other hand, individuals have never been granted a right to control the timing and manner of their death; indeed, suicide was illegal in many states for most of this nation's history, and, even after decriminalization, society continues to discourage suicide and seek to prevent individuals from taking their own lives. The historical opposition to suicide, while neither necessary nor sufficient to the Task Force's own constitutional analysis, makes it virtually inconceivable that the United States Supreme Court would recognize a constitutional right to commit suicide.

The State's Interest in Preventing Error and Abuse

In light of the distinctions set forth above, laws prohibiting assisted suicide and euthanasia would be subjected to only minimal judicial scrutiny, which considers whether a law is "rationally related" to a legitimate governmental goal.[108] Even if individuals had a right to commit suicide, however, that right would not translate into a right to obtain the assistance of others in bringing about one's own death. Rather, any burden on individual liberties that prohibitions on assisted suicide or euthanasia might entail would be outweighed by the state's interest in preventing error and abuse.

First, to the extent that laws prohibiting assisted suicide and euthanasia impose a burden, they do so only for individuals who make an informed, competent choice to have their lives artificially shortened, and who cannot do so without another person's aid. As studies have confirmed, very few individuals fall into this group, particularly if appropriate pain relief and supportive care are provided.[109] At the

---

[106] See *Michael H. v. Gerald D.*, 491 U.S. 110, 123, 109 S. Ct. 2333, 2343 (1989) (plurality opinion).

[107] As the Supreme Court recognized in *Cruzan*, "[a]t common law, even the touching of one person by another without consent and without legal justification was a battery." *Cruzan v. Director, Missouri Department of Health*, 110 S. Ct. 2841, 2846 (1990); see also *Eichner*, 52 N.Y.2d at 377, 438 N.Y.S.2d at 273 (noting the prevalence of statutes that impose civil liability on persons who perform medical treatment without consent).

[108] See pp. 68-69.

[109] See chapter 1.

same time, laws barring suicide assistance and euthanasia serve valuable societal goals: they protect vulnerable individuals who might otherwise seek suicide assistance or euthanasia in response to treatable depression, coercion, or pain; they encourage the active care and treatment of the terminally ill; and they guard against the killing of patients who are incapable of providing knowing consent. In this regard, prohibitions on assisted suicide and euthanasia are distinct from earlier statutes that barred suicide committed without another person's aid. While unassisted suicide is essentially a private, independent act, assisted suicide and euthanasia possess a uniquely *social* dimension, as they involve one individual participating directly in another person's decision to die. Such participation carries far-reaching risks of mistake and abuse.[110] While proponents of legalized assisted suicide and euthanasia suggest that safeguards could be established to minimize these dangers, the essential prerequisites for such safeguards — an attentive and caring physician-patient relationship, skilled pain management and comfort care, and universal access to effective psychiatric services — represent an idealized version of medical care that society has thus far failed to achieve. Given this reality, any effort to carve out exceptions to the prohibitions on assisted suicide or euthanasia would seriously undermine the state's interest in preventing suicide in the vast majority of cases in which patients seek this option because of pressure, undiagnosed or untreated depression, or improperly managed pain.[111] The state's interest in protecting these

---

[110]See chapter 6, pp. 121-34.

[111]As the Supreme Court of Canada recently observed in rejecting a constitutional challenge to that nation's ban on assisted suicide, "[t]here is no halfway measure that could be relied upon with assurance to fully achieve the legislation's purpose." *Rodriguez v. Attorney General*, [1993] 3 S.C.R. 519. In this country, the Supreme Court has clearly affirmed that statutes are not unconstitutional simply because they apply to some cases where the state's interest is not directly implicated. Rather, as long as the legislation does not interfere with a fundamental constitutional right, the fact that it is overbroad is generally not a basis for constitutional attack. See, e.g., *New York Transit Auth. v. Beazer*, 440 U.S. 568, 99 S. Ct. 1355 (1979) (upholding an absolute ban on employment of users of narcotic drugs, including methadone users, despite the fact that the reasons supporting the ban did not apply to patients in methadone treatment programs, because "any special rule short of total exclusion ... is likely to be less precise."). Moreover, even when fundamental rights are at stake, the Court has held that states need not make exceptions for individual cases if such exceptions would "unduly interfere with fulfillment of the governmental interest." *United States v. Lee*, 455 U.S. 252, 259, 102 S. Ct. 1051 (1982).

patients outweighs any burden on individual autonomy that prohibitions on assisted suicide and euthanasia might entail.[112]

This constitutional balancing of individual and state interests yields an entirely different result for decisions to forgo life-sustaining treatment. To be sure, allowing individuals to refuse life-sustaining treatment also presents some risk of abuse or error. However, that risk is minimized by the fact that the refusal of treatment causes death only for individuals whose continued existence requires extensive medical support. By contrast, if a right to suicide were recognized, it would apply to a far broader, more elastic class of "suffering" individuals, thus greatly expanding the number of people at risk.[113] Even more significantly, a ban on the refusal of life-sustaining treatment would impose a burden on individual liberty far more severe than any burden entailed by prohibiting assisted suicide or euthanasia. Unlike assisted suicide and euthanasia, the refusal of life-sustaining treatment is an integral dimension of medical practice; it is estimated that approximately 70 percent of all hospital and nursing home deaths follow the refusal of some form of medical intervention.[114] A prohibition on

---

[112]See Kamisar (arguing that the state's interest in prohibiting suicide assistance and euthanasia outweighs any burden such prohibitions might impose on individual autonomy). Advocates of legalized assisted suicide or euthanasia often fail to engage in this crucial balancing process. For example, Ronald Dworkin suggests that, because "[t]here are dangers both in legalizing and refusing to legalize" euthanasia, society has an obligation to carve out a middle ground. See R. Dworkin, *Life's Dominion* (New York: Knopf, 1993): 198 ("[O]nce we understand that legalizing *no* euthanasia is itself harmful to many people ... we realize that doing our best to draw and maintain a defensible line ... is better than abandoning those people altogether."). Dworkin's argument loses much of its force once it is recognized that the number of people genuinely harmed by laws prohibiting euthanasia or assisted suicide is extremely small, and that legalizing euthanasia or assisted suicide for the sake of these few — whatever safeguards are written into the law — would endanger the lives of a far larger group of individuals, who might avail themselves of these options as a result of depression, coercion, or untreated pain.

[113]See Marzen et al., 105 ("[A] jurisprudential scheme that acknowledged a constitutional right to suicide but carefully confined its exercise to a narrow class of persons or set of circumstances would be perverse."). Few of the advocates of a right to assisted suicide have argued that the right should be limited to the terminally ill or to other similarly narrow classes of individuals, and cases in the area of life-sustaining treatment suggest that such a distinction could not be made. See *Fosmire v. Nicoleau*, 75 N.Y.2d 218, 551 N.Y.S.2d 876 (1990) (rejecting the argument that the right to refuse life-sustaining treatment should be limited to the terminally ill). Indeed, Professor Tribe has suggested that the difficulty of limiting a right "to determine when and how to die" is the principal reason that courts have been reluctant to recognize such a right as a matter of constitutional law. L. Tribe, *American Constitutional Law*, 2d ed. (New York: The Foundation Press, 1988): § 15-11, p. 1370.

[114]See *Cruzan v. Director, Missouri Department of Health*, 497 U.S. 261, 110 S. Ct. 2841, 2864 (Brennan, J., dissenting).

the refusal of treatment would therefore require the widespread restraint of patients unwilling to submit to invasive procedures at the end of their lives. Such a policy would be an abuse of medicine, placing patients at the mercy of every technological advance. In addition, such prohibitions might deter individuals from seeking medical treatment in the first place, thereby undermining society's interest in caring for the seriously ill. New York, like other states in the nation, has already recognized that its interests are best served by permitting the refusal of treatment in accord with appropriate guidelines, and that individual decision making about treatment will ultimately promote the public good.[115]

---

[115]See *Eichner*, 52 N.Y.2d at 377, 438 N.Y.S.2d at 273 ("To the extent that existing statutory and decisional law manifests the State's interest on this subject, they consistently support the right of the competent adult to make his own decision by imposing civil liability on those who perform medical treatment without consent, although the treatment may be beneficial or even necessary to preserve the patient's life.").

5

The Ethical Debate

The ethics of assisted suicide and euthanasia are squarely before the public eye. A steady drumbeat of media attention and mounting concern about control at life's end have generated serious consideration of legalizing the practices. Public discussion has centered on the desire for control over the timing and manner of death, amidst warnings about the potential abuse or harm of overriding society's long-standing prohibitions against assisting suicide or directly causing another person's death.

Concurrent with this public debate, but in many ways separate from it, has been the discussion of assisted suicide and euthanasia in the medical and ethical literature. In this debate, some assert that both assisted suicide and euthanasia are morally wrong and should not be provided, regardless of the circumstances of the particular case. Others hold that assisted suicide or euthanasia are ethically legitimate in rare and exceptional cases, but that professional standards and the law should not be changed to authorize either practice. Finally, some advocate that assisted suicide, or both assisted suicide and euthanasia, should be recognized as legally and morally acceptable options in the care of dying or severely ill patients.[1]

An Historical Perspective

For thousands of years, philosophers and religious thinkers have addressed the ethics of suicide. These debates have rested on broad principles about duties to self and to society as well as fundamental questions of the value of human life. Many great thinkers of Western intellectual history have contributed to this debate, ranging from Plato

---

[1]Through most of this chapter, arguments are schematically presented as those of "proponents" of legalizing assisted suicide and euthanasia and "opponents" of legalizing these practices. Each category groups together diverse views in order to provide an overview of a debate marked by complex and nuanced positions.

and Aristotle in ancient Greece to Augustine and Thomas Aquinas in the Middle Ages, and Locke, Hume, and Kant in more modern times.[2]

Some views and practices surrounding suicide were rooted in particular cultures and beliefs that have little relevance for contemporary society. For example, in the warrior society of the Vikings, only those who died violently could enter paradise, or Valhalla. The greatest honor was death in battle; suicide was the second best alternative.[3] Likewise, the ancient Scythians believed that suicide was a great honor when individuals became too old for their nomadic way of life, thereby sparing the younger members of the tribe the burden of carrying or killing them. In other eras and civilizations, the debate about suicide touched on values that influenced the course of Western thought and still resonate to contemporary perspectives on suicide.

The word "euthanasia" derives from Greek, although as used in ancient Greece, the term meant simply "good death," not the practice of killing a person for benevolent motives.[4] In ancient Greece, euthanasia was not practiced, and suicide itself was generally disfavored.[5] Some Greek philosophers, however, argued that suicide would be acceptable under exceptional circumstances. Plato, for example, believed that suicide was generally cowardly and unjust but that it could be an ethically acceptable act if an individual had an immoral and incorrigible character, had committed a disgraceful action, or had lost control over his or her actions due to grief or suffering.[6] Unlike

---

[2]It is notable that the current debate about assisted suicide, even among academic commentators, has drawn so little from this rich history. For an excellent discussion of the intellectual history of suicide, see B. A. Brody, "Introduction," in *Suicide and Euthanasia: Historical and Contemporary Themes*, ed. B. A. Brody (Dordrecht: Kluwer Academic Publishers, 1989), 1. For an engaging literary history of suicide, see A. Alvarez, *The Savage God* (New York: Random House, 1971).

[3]Those who died peacefully in their beds of old age or illness were eternally excluded from Valhalla. Alvarez, 54.

[4]According to one author, no Greek philosopher "ever discusses euthanasia in our contemporary sense of the word." J. M. Cooper, "Greek Philosophers on Euthanasia and Suicide," in *Suicide and Euthanasia*, ed. Brody, 14. See also P. Carrick, *Medical Ethics in Antiquity* (Dordrecht: D. Reidel, Kluwer, 1985), 127-31.

[5]A. Alvarez suggests that although suicide was taboo, the Greeks tolerated suicide in some circumstances. Noting the Greek practice of burying the corpse of a suicide outside the city limits with its hand cut off, Alvarez argues that this practice was "linked with the more profound Greek horror of killing one's own kin. By inference, suicide was an extreme case of this, and the language barely distinguishes between self-murder and murder of kindred." Alvarez points out that many suicides in Greek literature reflect acceptance and even admiration of the act. Alvarez, 58.

[6]Plato, *Laws*, chap. 9, 854, 873; see Cooper, 17-19. Plato also argued that, in most

contemporary proponents of assisted suicide and euthanasia, who regard individual self-determination as central, Plato considered the individual's desire to live or die largely irrelevant to determining whether suicide might be an appropriate act. An objective evaluation of the individual's moral worthiness, not the individual's decision about the value of continued life, was critical.[7]

In contrast to Plato, the Stoics of the later Hellenistic and Roman eras focused more strongly on the welfare of the individual than on the community. They believed that, while life in general should be lived fully, suicide could be appropriate in certain rare circumstances when deprivation or illness no longer allowed for a "natural" life.[8] The Stoics did not, however, maintain that suicide would be justified whenever an individual loses the desire to live. Unlike contemporary proponents of a right to suicide assistance, the Stoics believed that suicide was appropriate only when the individual loses the ability to pursue the life that nature intended.[9]

Since ancient times, Jewish and Christian thinkers have opposed suicide as inconsistent with the human good and with responsibilities to God. In the thirteenth century, Thomas Aquinas espoused Catholic teaching about suicide in arguments that would shape Christian thought about suicide for centuries. Aquinas condemned suicide as wrong because it contravenes one's duty to oneself and the natural

---

cases, suicide would represent abandonment of one's duty and would violate divinely mandated responsibilities. Plato, *Phaedo*, 62. In contrast to Plato, Aristotle believed that suicide was unjust under all circumstances, because it deprived the community of a citizen. Aristotle, *Nicomachean Ethics*, chap. 5, 1138a; Cooper, 19-23.

[7]Plato's suggestion that medical treatment should not be provided to severely ill and disabled patients reflects a similar objective view. In the *Republic* (chap. 3, 406-7), Plato argues that no treatment should be provided to prolong the life of severely ill or disabled individuals, because they represent a burden to themselves and others. As with suicide, the individual's subjective feelings about the merits of continued life had no bearing on the appropriateness of continued medical treatment. Interestingly, Plato did not apply this analysis to the severely ill and disabled elderly, who, he argued, should be permitted to live regardless of their ability to contribute to the community. See Cooper, 13.

[8]Cooper, 24-29, 36n.

[9]Some Roman Stoics, such as Seneca, however, argued that the individual should have broad discretion to end his or her own life. He criticized those who "maintain that one should not offer violence to one's own life, and hold it accursed for a man to be the means of his own destruction; we should wait, say they, for the end decreed by nature. But one who says this does not see that he is shutting off the path to freedom. The best thing which eternal law ever ordained was that it allowed to us one entrance into life, but many exits." In Carrick, 145.

inclination of self-perpetuation; because it injures other people and the community of which the individual is a part; and because it violates God's authority over life, which is God's gift.[10] This position exemplified attitudes about suicide that prevailed from the Middle Ages through the Renaissance and Reformation.[11]

By the sixteenth century, philosophers began to challenge the generally accepted religious condemnation of suicide. Michel de Montaigne, a sixteenth-century philosopher, argued that suicide was not a question of Christian belief but a matter of personal choice. In an essay presenting arguments on both sides of the issue, he concluded that suicide was an acceptable moral choice in some circumstances, noting that "pain and the fear of a worse death seem to me the most excusable incitements."[12] Other writers employed more theological arguments to challenge the religious prohibition on suicide. In the early seventeenth century, for example, John Donne asserted that while suicide is morally wrong in many cases, it can be acceptable if performed with the intention of glorifying God, not serving self-interest. Donne acknowledged the merit of laws against suicide that discouraged the practice, but he argued that civil and common laws ordinarily admit of some exceptions, suggesting that suicide could be morally acceptable in certain cases.[13]

In the eighteenth century, David Hume made the first unapologetic defense of the moral permissibility of suicide on grounds of individual autonomy and social benefit. He asserted that even if a person's death would weaken the community, suicide would be morally permissible if

---

[10]Thomas Aquinas, *Summa Theologiae*, II-II, 64; D. W. Amundsen, "Suicide and Early Christian Values," in *Suicide and Euthanasia*, ed. Brody, 142-44; T. L. Beauchamp, "Suicide in the Age of Reason," in *Suicide and Euthanasia*, ed. Brody, 190-93.

[11]These principles continue to influence contemporary religious and secular views about suicide. See the discussion below in this chapter.

[12]G. B. Ferngren, "The Ethics of Suicide in the Renaissance and Reformation," in *Suicide and Euthanasia*, ed. Brody, 159-61. As Ferngren notes, suicide and euthanasia were discussed a generation earlier in satirical works by Erasmus and Thomas More, but it is unclear whether the authors intended to advocate these practices. Ferngren, 157-59.

[13]Donne articulated these views in an essay entitled *Biathanatos*, which was published only after his death. He did not want it published during his lifetime, perhaps reflecting his discomfort with views that challenged the prevailing Christian ethics of his time. In *Biathanatos*, Donne acknowledges that he battled his own urge to commit suicide. "Whenever any affliction assails me, me thinks I have the keys of my prison in mine own hand, and no remedy presents itself so soon to my heart as mine own sword." In Ferngren, 169.

the good it afforded the individual outweighed the loss to society. Moreover, suicide would be laudatory if the person's death would benefit the group and the individual. Hume did not advocate that all suicides are justified, but argued that when life is most plagued by suffering, suicide is most acceptable.[14]

Other philosophers of the Age of Reason, such as John Locke and Immanuel Kant, opposed suicide. Locke argued that life, like liberty, represents an inalienable right, which cannot be taken from, or given away by, an individual.[15] For Kant, suicide was a paradigmatic example of an action that violates moral responsibility. Kant believed that the proper end of rational beings requires self-preservation, and that suicide would therefore be inconsistent with the fundamental value of human life.[16] Like some contemporary opponents of assisted suicide and euthanasia, Kant argued that taking one's own life was inconsistent with the notion of autonomy, properly understood. Autonomy, in Kant's view, does not mean the freedom to do whatever one wants, but instead depends on the knowing subjugation of one's desires and inclinations to one's rational understanding of universally valid moral rules.[17]

Essays advocating active euthanasia in the context of modern medicine first appeared in the United States and England in the 1870s. In an 1870 work, schoolmaster and essayist Samuel D. Williams argued that "in all cases of hopeless and painful illness it should be the recognized duty of the medical attendant, whenever so desired by the patient, to administer chloroform, or such other anaesthetics as may by and by supersede chloroform, so as to destroy consciousness at once,

---

[14] D. Hume, "On Suicide," in *Ethical Issues in Death and Dying*, ed. T. L. Beauchamp and S. Perlin (Englewood Cliffs, N.J.: Prentice-Hall, 1978), 105-10; T. L. Beauchamp, "An Analysis of Hume and Aquinas on Suicide," in *Ethical Issues in Death and Dying*, ed. Beauchamp and Perlin, 111-21; Beauchamp, "Age of Reason," 199-205.

[15] Ferngren, 173-75.

[16] See I. Kant, *Grounding for the Metaphysics of Morals*, 3d ed., trans. J. W. Ellington (Indianapolis: Hackett, 1993); and the discussion in Beauchamp, "Age of Reason," 206-15.

[17] For Kant, the fundamental moral law was expressed in the "categorical imperative": "Act only according to that maxim whereby you can at the same time will that it should become a universal law," or, in another formulation, "Act in such a way that you treat humanity, whether in your own person or in the person of another, always at the same time as an end and never simply as a means." Ellington translation, pp. 30, 36; *Ak.* 421, 429.

and put the sufferer at once to a quick and painless end."[18] Support
for euthanasia at this time was animated in part by the philosophy of
social Darwinism and concerns with eugenics — improving the biological stock of the community. In 1873, essayist Lionel A. Tollemache
asserted that euthanasia could serve the patient's interests and benefit
society in appropriate cases by removing an individual who was "un-
healthy, unhappy, and useless."[19]

Over the course of the following decades, essays discussing
euthanasia continued to appear in medical and popular journals. The
British Parliament debated a bill to legalize euthanasia in 1936. In the
United States, similar proposals were introduced in state legislatures
during the first half of the twentieth century, including New York State
in 1947. The Euthanasia Society of America, an organization advocating such proposals, was founded in 1938.[20] Following World War II,
however, the term "euthanasia" became disfavored due to sensitivity
about Nazi practices.

Distinguishing Assisted Suicide and Euthanasia

Contemporary discussion has not focused primarily on the ethics of
suicide itself, but on assistance to commit suicide and the direct killing
of another person for benevolent motives. Actions that intentionally
cause death are often referred to as active euthanasia, or simply as
euthanasia. Euthanasia performed at the explicit request of a patient
is referred to as "voluntary" euthanasia. Euthanasia of a child or an
adult who lacks the capacity to consent or refuse is often termed
"nonvoluntary."[21]

In addition, the terms "euthanasia" and "passive euthanasia" are
sometimes used to describe withholding or withdrawal of life-sustaining treatment. For example, Roman Catholic authorities often use the

---

[18]"Euthanasia," in W. B. Fye, "Active Euthanasia: An Historical Survey of Its
Conceptual Origins and Introduction into Medical Thought," *Bulletin of the History of
Medicine* 52 (1978): 498. Similar arguments were advanced in the 1936 debate on a
bill to legalize euthanasia in the British House of Lords; see S. J. Reiser, A. J. Dyck,
and W. J. Curran, *Ethics in Medicine: Historical Perspectives and Contemporary
Concerns* (Cambridge: MIT Press, 1977), 498.

[19]"The New Cure for Incurables," in Fye, 499.

[20]J. Fletcher, *Morals and Medicine* (Princeton: Princeton University Press, 1954); J.
Fletcher, "The Courts and Euthanasia," *Law, Medicine and Health Care* 15 (1987/88):
223-30.

[21]Involuntary euthanasia, performed over a patient's explicit objection, has not been
endorsed by anyone in the current debate.

word "euthanasia" to refer to inappropriate decisions to withhold or to stop treatment.[22] This report uses the term "euthanasia" to refer only to active steps, such as a lethal injection, to end a patient's life.

In assisted suicide, one person contributes to the death of another, but the person who dies directly takes his or her own life. Many individuals hold similar positions on assisted suicide and euthanasia. Others find assisted suicide more acceptable, either because of the nature of the actions or because of differences they see in the societal impact and potential harm of the two practices.

For some, assisted suicide and euthanasia differ intrinsically. A physician who writes a prescription for a lethal dose of medication, for example, is less directly involved in the patient's death than a physician who actually administers medication that causes death. With assisted suicide, the patient takes his or her own life, usually when the physician is not present. Accordingly, factors such as the physician's intentions may be more complex. In some cases, a physician may intend to make it possible for a patient to commit suicide so that the patient feels a greater sense of control, but may hope that the patient does not take this final step. In addition, because the patient's own actions intervene between the physician's actions and the patient's death, the physician's causal responsibility may be less clear.[23]

Some regard physician-assisted suicide as less subject to abuse than euthanasia. When assisted suicide occurs, the final act is solely the patient's. It would therefore be more difficult to pressure or convince

---

[22]The Vatican's 1980 "Declaration on Euthanasia" describes euthanasia as "an action or an omission which of itself or by intention causes death, in order that all suffering may in this way be eliminated." In President's Commission for the Study of Ethical Problems in Medicine and Biomedical and Behavioral Research, *Deciding to Forego Life-Sustaining Treatment* (Washington: U.S. Government Printing Office, 1983), 303. Appropriate decisions to forgo extraordinary or disproportionately burdensome treatment would not be considered euthanasia, however. Ibid.

This report does not discuss the criteria that characterize appropriate decisions to forgo life-sustaining treatment. The Task Force has addressed this issue in previous reports. See New York State Task Force on Life and the Law, *When Others Must Choose: Deciding for Patients Without Capacity* (New York: New York State Task Force on Life and the Law, 1992) and *Life-Sustaining Treatment: Making Decisions and Appointing a Health Care Agent* (New York: New York State Task Force on Life and the Law, 1987).

[23]See R. F. Weir, "The Morality of Physician-Assisted Suicide," *Law, Medicine and Health Care* 20 (1992): 116-26.

a patient to commit suicide than to secure agreement to euthanasia.[24] Further, a patient who requests assistance in suicide but then becomes ambivalent could simply put off the final step. By contrast, some patients would be too embarrassed or intimidated to express uncertainty to a physician on the verge of giving a lethal injection, or would be concerned that the doctor might be hesitant to administer the injection at a later time.[25]

Some note that the potential for intimidation or influence stems not only from the doctor's actions in euthanasia, but also from his or her presence at the time of death. Some individuals therefore distinguish cases when a physician assists a suicide by providing information or a prescription, which they believe should be permitted, from instances when the physician is present at the time of the suicide and directly aids or supervises the act, posing a greater risk.[26] Others are not troubled by this risk, and believe that the physician's presence could express caring and a desire to accompany the patient in the final moments of life.[27]

For others, no decisive distinction can be drawn between assisted suicide and voluntary euthanasia. Whatever differences may exist do not justify a policy of accepting one practice while forbidding the other. This view is shared by some who support both practices and by others who oppose both.[28] Proponents of the practices believe that the risks

---

[24]D. E. Meier, "Physician-Assisted Dying: Theory and Reality," *Journal of Clinical Ethics* 3 (1992): 35.

[25]J. Glover, *Causing Death and Saving Life* (Harmondsworth, England: Penguin Books, 1977), 184. Howard Brody writes: "There are psychological reasons to prefer patient control over physician-assisted lethal injection whenever possible. The normal human response to facing the last moment before death, when one has control over the choice, ought to be ambivalence. The bottle of pills allows full recognition and expression of that ambivalence: I, the patient, can sleep on it, and the pills will still be there in the morning; I do not lose my means of escape through the delay. But if I am terminally ill of cancer in the Netherlands and summon my family physician to my house to administer the fatal dose, I am powerfully motivated to deny any ambivalence I may feel." H. Brody, "Assisted Death — A Compassionate Response to Medical Failure," *New England Journal of Medicine* 327 (1992): 1384-88.

[26]D. T. Watts and T. Howell, "Assisted Suicide Is Not Euthanasia," *Journal of the American Geriatrics Society* 40 (1992): 1043.

[27]T. E. Quill, C. K. Cassel, and D. E. Meier, "Care of the Hopelessly Ill: Proposed Clinical Criteria for Physician-Assisted Suicide," *New England Journal of Medicine* 327 (1992): 1383.

[28]Among supporters of the practices, see E. H. Loewy, "Healing and Killing, Harming and Not Harming," *Journal of Clinical Ethics* 3 (1992): 30; G. C. Graber and J. Chassman, "Assisted Suicide Is Not Voluntary Active Euthanasia, but It's Awfully

of error and abuse are similar in both practices, and can be minimized with appropriate safeguards.[29] Many who oppose both assisted suicide and euthanasia agree that the practices pose similar risks, but reject these risks as unacceptable.[30]

Most of those who emphasize the basic similarities between assisted suicide and voluntary active euthanasia nevertheless acknowledge some difference in degree between the two practices. Some claim that while both should be allowed, assisted suicide would be a preferable option in any particular case, in order to minimize the possibility of error.[31] Others oppose both practices but view active euthanasia as more problematic.[32] As discussed above, American law draws a clear distinction between the two types of action, treating euthanasia as a far more serious offense. In New York and many other states, while both practices are felonies, assisting suicide is generally classified as manslaughter, while euthanasia constitutes second-degree murder.[33]

The Appeal to Autonomy

American society has long embraced individual liberty and the freedom to make personal choices as fundamental values. These values have always been pursued within a social context, accompanied by commitments to promote the overall good of society and protect vulnerable individuals from harm. For some, the exercise of autonomy must also be balanced against other fundamental values embraced by society, including our reverence for human life. The current debate

Close," *Journal of the American Geriatrics Society* 41 (1993): 88-89. An opponent of both practices likewise argues: "If the right to control the time and manner of one's death — the right to shape one's death in the most humane and dignified manner one chooses — is well founded, how can it be denied to someone simply because she is unable to perform the final act by herself?" Y. Kamisar, "Are Laws Against Assisted Suicide Unconstitutional?" *Hastings Center Report* 23, no. 3 (1993): 35.

[29] D. Brock, "Voluntary Active Euthanasia," *Hastings Center Report* 22, no. 2 (1992): 10; Graber and Chassman, 88.

[30] Kamisar, 35.

[31] E.g., Glover, 184; H. Brody, 1384-88. As Dr. Aadri Heiner of the Netherlands describes his practice, "I will bring a small glass bottle, and I will hand it over and say, 'This is for you.' ... He has [to] drink it by [him]self. ... And that makes me very sure that it is his own wish." "Choosing Death," *Health Quarterly*, broadcast March 23, 1993.

[32] See American Medical Association, Council on Ethical and Judicial Affairs, "Decisions Near the End of Life," *Journal of the American Medical Association* 267 (1992): 2233.

[33] See chapter 4, p. 63.

about assisted suicide and euthanasia also presents questions about the way autonomy can best be realized, and the manner in which the tension between autonomy and other ethical and societal values should be resolved.

One strand of the debate about assisted suicide and euthanasia has focused on whether the value of self-determination, which undergirds the right to refuse treatment, provides the basis for a right to assisted suicide or euthanasia as well. Would the self-determination of severely ill patients actually be promoted in practice if assisted suicide and euthanasia were legalized? Does contributing to another person's death manifest respect for that person's autonomy? Questions have also been posed about the impact of legalizing assisted suicide and euthanasia on the self-determination and well-being of individuals who do not seek out these options.

Proponents

Proponents of assisted suicide and euthanasia maintain that respect for individual self-determination mandates the legalization of these practices. Individuals have a fundamental right to direct the course of their lives, a right that should encompass control over the timing and circumstances of their death. While few if any advocates argue for an absolute right to commit suicide, most believe that in appropriate cases suicide can minimize suffering or enhance human dignity, and that people in these circumstances should have the right to take their own lives.[34]

Proponents suggest that a physician's participation in assisted suicide or euthanasia can support a choice embraced by the patient, consistent with his or her own value system. Individual beliefs about the meaning of life and the significance of death vary greatly. For proponents, establishing assisted suicide and euthanasia as accepted alternatives would respect this diversity. As stated by one commentator:

> There is no single, objectively correct answer for everyone as to when, if at all, one's life becomes all things considered a burden and unwanted. If self-determination is a fundamental value, then the great

---

[34]M. Battin, "Voluntary Euthanasia and the Risks of Abuse," *Law, Medicine and Health Care* 20 (1992): 134; M. P. Battin, "Suicide: A Fundamental Human Right?" in *Suicide: The Philosophical Issues*, ed. M. P. Battin and D. J. Mayo (New York: St. Martin's Press, 1980), 267-85. See also J. Arras, "The Right to Die on the Slippery Slope," *Social Theory and Practice* 8 (1982): 285-328, noting arguments on both sides of this issue.

variability among people on this question makes it especially important that individuals control the manner, circumstances, and timing of their death and dying.[35]

Some proponents promote legalizing assisted suicide and voluntary euthanasia as an affirmative step to grant individuals further control over their dying process.[36] For others, the decisive principle is the right to be free of state interference when individuals voluntarily choose to end their lives.[37] When differences on basic issues such as life and death go deep and involve profound values, a tolerant, pluralistic society must allow each individual to decide.[38] Many believe that, even if pain can be alleviated, the individual's right to control his or her death should prevail.

> "I wouldn't want to be kept alive that way" has become a modern motto in American society. Pain management and hospice care are better than ever before. But for some people they are simply the trees. The forest is that they no longer want to live, and they believe the decision to die belongs to them alone.[39]

Opponents

Some believe that assisted suicide and euthanasia can promote autonomy, at least in some cases, but that the dangers of the practices are overriding. For others, the value of human life outweighs the claim to autonomy, and argues decisively against permitting suicide assis-

---

[35]Brock, 11. See similarly R. Dworkin, *Life's Dominion* (New York: Knopf, 1993), 208-11; C. K. Cassel and D. E. Meier, "Morals and Moralism in the Debate over Euthanasia and Assisted Suicide," *New England Journal of Medicine* 323 (1990): 751.

[36]Weir, 124. Dick Lehr reports that in every case of assisted suicide that health care professionals discussed in interviews, "patients were middle-to-upper class, accustomed to being in charge." An oncologist who had assisted suicide stated that "these are usually very intelligent people, in control of their life — white, executive, rich, always leaders of the pack, can't be dependent on people a lot." D. Lehr, "Death and the Doctor's Hand," *Boston Globe*, April 26, 1993.

[37]As stated by one philosopher, "One will need to live with individuals' deciding with consenting others when to end their lives, not because such is good, but because one does not have the authority coercively to stop individuals from acting together in such ways." H. T. Engelhardt, Jr., "Fashioning an Ethics for Life and Death in a Post-Modern Society," *Hastings Center Report* 19, no. 1 (1989): S9. See also J. Rachels, *The End of Life* (New York: Oxford University Press, 1986), 181-82.

[38]Dworkin, 217.

[39]A. Quindlen, "Death: The Best Seller," *New York Times*, August 14, 1991, A19.

tance or direct killing, even with benevolent motives. Still others assert that seeking to end one's life intrinsically contradicts the value of autonomy. Like the "freedom" to sell oneself into slavery, the freedom to end one's life should be limited for the sake of freedom.

Many reject euthanasia because it violates the fundamental prohibition against killing. They understand this prohibition, except in defense of self or others, to be a basic moral and social principle. This view is expressed within the context of diverse religious, philosophical, and personal perspectives.[40] Rooted in religious beliefs about the value and meaning of human life, it also resonates to and informs secular values and attitudes, including our laws proscribing murder.

Assisted suicide is opposed by many for similar reasons; although it does not violate the ban against killing directly, it renders human life dispensable and implicates physicians or others in participating in the death of the patient. Some emphasize that assisted suicide and euthanasia are not simply nonintervention in the private choice of another person. The participation of a second person makes assisted suicide and euthanasia social and communal acts, ones in which social, moral, and legal principles must be considered.[41] A physician who assists a patient's death affirms, or at least accepts, the patient's choice, actively contributing to the outcome.[42] Some believe that one person

---

[40]See, e.g., R. M. Veatch, *Death, Dying, and the Biological Revolution*, rev. ed. (New Haven: Yale University Press, 1989), 69-72. Among the Biblical statements of this prohibition are Exodus 20:13, Deuteronomy 5:17, and Genesis 9:5-6. Many religious traditions understand these statements as prohibiting suicide and assisted suicide as well as direct killing. For an overview of the attitudes of diverse religious traditions, see R. Hamel, ed., *Active Euthanasia, Religion, and the Public Debate* (Chicago: Park Ridge Center, 1991); and C. S. Campbell, "Religious Ethics and Active Euthanasia in a Pluralistic Society," *Kennedy Institute of Ethics Journal* 2 (1992): 253-77. On the significance of religiously influenced views for public policy deliberations, see, e.g., S. Hauerwas, *Suffering Presence* (Notre Dame: University of Notre Dame Press, 1986), 105; Joseph Cardinal Bernadin, "Euthanasia: Ethical and Legal Challenge," *Origins* 18 (1988): 52; J. Stout, *Ethics After Babel* (Boston: Beacon Press, 1988); D. Callahan and C. S. Campbell, eds., "Theology, Religious Traditions, and Bioethics," *Hastings Center Report* 20, no. 4 suppl. (1990); S. L. Carter, *The Culture of Disbelief* (New York: Basic Books, 1993).

[41]See, e.g., Callahan, 52-53; T. L. Beauchamp and J. F. Childress, *Principles of Biomedical Ethics*, 3d ed. (New York: Oxford University Press, 1989), 227. Many religious traditions, including Roman Catholicism, challenge the notion of an autonomous right to end one's life, appealing to the social nature of human life and the mutual dependence of individuals in society. See, e.g., Bernadin, 55. This point is also advocated in secular terms.

[42]Opponents argue that the patient's request for suicide assistance is not just a way to obtain drugs: The request might represent a desire for companionship in pursuing a difficult course of action; a wish for confirmation of a decision about which the

should never be granted this power over the life and death of another, even a consenting other; it is intrinsically offensive to human dignity, in the way that consensual slavery would be.[43] Others are more pragmatically concerned about the influence physicians would exercise in the decision-making process.[44]

For some, assisted suicide and euthanasia are not inherently incompatible with self-determination, but they believe that the practices as applied in the daily routines of medical practice and family life would undermine the autonomy of many individuals. In many cases, a patient who requests euthanasia or assisted suicide may have undiagnosed major clinical depression or another psychiatric disorder that prevents him or her from formulating a rational, independent choice. Other patients may feel compelled to end their lives because they lack real alternatives, due to inadequate medical treatment or personal support.[45] Offering suicide assistance, but not good medical care, could be especially troubling for some segments of the population. As ex-

---

patient is unsure; inquiry of the physician's opinion on an issue about which the patient is ambivalent; an appeal for the physician's reassurance that he or she is committed to the patient and believes that the patient's life is worthwhile; or simply an expression of desperation and a cry for help. See, e.g., E. D. Caine and Y. C. Conwell, "Self-Determined Death, the Physician, and Medical Priorities: Is There Time to Talk," *Journal of the American Medical Association* 270 (1993): 875-76. See also Glover, 183.

[43] As stated by Daniel Callahan, "No human being, whatever the motives, should have that kind of ultimate power over the fate of another. It is to create the wrong kind of relationship between people, a community that sanctions private killings between and among its members in pursuit of their individual goals and values." D. Callahan, "Can We Return Death to Disease?" *Hastings Center Report* 19, no. 1 (1989): S5.

[44] Edmund D. Pellegrino argues that while the doctor appears to place the initiative in the patient's hands and be merely "open" to suicide under the right circumstances, the physician actually retains control: "Ultimately, the determination of the right circumstances is in the physician's hands. The physician controls the availability and timing of the means whereby the patient kills himself. Physicians also judge whether patients are clinically depressed, their suffering really unbearable, and their psychological and spiritual crises resolvable. Finally, the physician's assessment determines whether the patient is in the 'extreme' category that, per se, justifies suicide assistance." "Compassion Needs Reason Too," *Journal of the American Medical Association* 270 (1993): 874.

[45] See, e.g., Arras, 311-13; J. Teno and J. Lynn, "Voluntary Active Euthanasia: The Individual Case and Public Policy," *Journal of the American Geriatrics Society* 39 (1991): 827-30; H. Hendin and G. Klerman, "Physician-Assisted Suicide: The Dangers of Legalization," *American Journal of Psychiatry* 150 (1993): 143-45; D. W. McKinney, "Euthanasia as Public Policy: Rights and Risks," The Berry Street Essay, delivered in New Haven, Conn., June 22, 1989, Unitarian Universalist General Assembly, 9. See also the sections discussing suicide and depression in chapter 1.

pressed by one doctor who manages a Latino health clinic, legalizing assisted suicide would pose special dangers for members of minority populations whose primary concern is access to needed care, not assistance to die more quickly.

> In the abstract, it sounds like a wonderful idea, but in a practical sense it would be a disaster. My concern is for Latinos and other minority groups that might get disproportionately counseled to opt for physician-assisted suicide.[46]

Diverse religious traditions oppose assisted suicide and euthanasia because the practices violate the basic value of human life, seen as God's gift. From the perspective of many religions, suicide itself is not an ethically sanctioned choice. Many religious traditions reject assisted suicide and euthanasia based on their understanding of general values, including appreciation for the life and value of each individual, the individual's responsibility to the community, and society's obligations towards all of its members, especially the poor and vulnerable. Many religions understand life itself as something that is entrusted to persons by God, entailing a sense of individual responsibility that is often expressed in terms of "stewardship." Differing religious perspectives also share a commitment to compassion for patients and others who are suffering.[47] They believe that this compassion should be expressed by offering care and companionship, not assisted death or medical killing, to the severely ill.

As articulated in the 1980 Vatican Declaration on Euthanasia, and affirmed in recent speeches by Pope John Paul II, the Catholic Church firmly rejects assisted suicide and euthanasia.[48] Similar views are

---

[46]Dr. Nicolas Parkhurst Carballeira, Director of the Boston-based Latino Health Institute, in Lehr, April 26, 1993. A recent study found that patients treated at centers that serve predominantly minority patients were three times more likely than those treated elsewhere to receive inadequate pain treatment. Elderly individuals and women were also more likely than others to receive poor pain treatment. C. S. Cleeland et al., "Pain and Its Treatment in Outpatients With Metastatic Cancer," *New England Journal of Medicine* 330 (1994): 592-96.

[47]See, e.g., H. Arkes et al., "Always to Care, Never to Kill," *First Things* no. 18 (1992): 45-47; Hamel, ed., 45-77.

[48]Speaking in the United States in 1993, the Pope condemned euthanasia, stating: "In the modern metropolis, life — God's first gift, and the fundamental right of every individual, on which all other rights are based — is often treated as just one more commodity." "The Prayer Vigil," *Origins* 23 (1993): 184. See also "Contributors to the Formation of Society: Ad Limina Address," *Origins* 23 (1993): 486-87; "Veritatis Splendor," *Origins* 23 (1993): 321, par. 80.

expressed by representatives of all branches of Judaism.[49] Many Protestant denominations, such as the American Lutheran Church and the Episcopal Church, also oppose the practices as ethically unacceptable.[50] The Unitarian-Universalist Association, however, has expressed support for legalizing the practices.[51]

Benefiting the Patient

Individuals suffer from diverse causes. They may experience pain, physical discomfort, and psychological distress.[52] Relieving suffering is widely recognized as a basic moral value and a goal of medicine in particular.[53] The debate about euthanasia and assisted suicide turns in part on a judgment about how to help suffering individuals most effectively while protecting them and others from harm.

---

[49]For further discussion of Jewish views on assisted suicide and euthanasia, see, e.g., I. Bettan et al., "Euthanasia," in *American Reform Response*, ed. W. Jacob (New York: Central Conference of American Rabbis, 1983), 261-71; J. D. Bleich "Life as an Intrinsic Rather Than Instrumental Good: The 'Spiritual' Case Against Euthanasia," *Issues in Law and Medicine* 9 (1993): 139-49; B. A. Brody, "A Historical Introduction to Jewish Casuistry on Suicide and Euthanasia," in *Suicide and Euthanasia*, ed. Brody, 39-75; E. N. Dorff, "Rabbi, I Want to Die: Euthanasia and the Jewish Tradition," in *Choosing Death in America* (Philadelphia: Westminster/John Knox, forthcoming); D. M. Feldman and F. Rosner, ed., *Compendium on Medical Ethics*, 6th ed. (New York: Federation of Jewish Philanthropies of New York, 1984), 101-2; I. Jakobovits, *Jewish Medical Ethics*, 2d ed. (New York: Bloch, 1975).

[50]As stated in a report of the American Lutheran Church: "Some might maintain that active euthanasia can represent an appropriate course of action if motivated by the desire to end suffering. Christian stewardship of life, however, mandates treasuring and preserving the life which God has given, be it our own life or the life of some other person. This view is supported by the affirmation that meaning and hope are possible in all of life's situations, even those involving great suffering." "Death and Dying," 1982, in Hamel, ed., 63. See also Hamel, ed., 52-71.

[51]The 1988 Unitarian Universalist General Assembly issued a statement resolving "That Unitarian Universalists advocate the right to self-determination in dying, and the release from civil or criminal penalties of those who, under proper safeguards, act to honor the right of terminally ill patients to select the time of their own deaths." In Hamel, ed., 68-69. This resolution has been criticized by some within the Unitarian Universalist Association, including Donald McKinney. McKinney.

[52]See chapter 3 for discussion of current approaches in pain and palliative care. See also K. M. Foley, "The Relationship of Pain and Symptom Management to Patient Requests for Physician-Assisted Suicide," *Journal of Pain and Symptom Management* 6 (1991): 289-97.

[53]See, e.g., R. S. Smith, "Ethical Issues Surrounding Cancer Pain," in *Current and Emerging Issues in Cancer Pain: Research and Practice*, ed. C. R. Chapman and K. M. Foley (New York: Raven Press, 1993), 385-92.

In the debate about assisted suicide and euthanasia, compassion for patients in pain or with unrelieved suffering is a common moral and social ground. Disagreement centers on how society can best care for these patients, and the consequences for others if the practices are permitted. The debate hinges in part on assumptions about the number of patients affected, the availability of pain relief, and the effect of legalizing assisted suicide and euthanasia on the provision of palliative care. At the core are basic differences about what compassion demands for suffering individuals. Disagreement exists too about whether the availability of assisted suicide or euthanasia would reassure or threaten ill and disabled patients.

Proponents

Those who support euthanasia and/or physician-assisted suicide believe that such actions are the most effective way to help some patients experiencing intractable pain or intolerable psychological distress. They regard these actions as essential to fulfill a commitment to relieve suffering. Indeed, many feel that, in appropriate circumstances, a physician's desire to act compassionately towards his or her patient provides the strongest rationale for the practices.

Contemporary advocates argue that, despite advances in palliative medicine and hospice care, a small number of patients continue to suffer from severe pain and other physical symptoms that available medical therapies cannot reduce to a tolerable level.[54] Studies have shown that large numbers of patients receive poor palliative care; while state-of-the-art treatment could manage their pain and discomfort, they are not receiving and are unlikely to receive this care. In these cases, euthanasia or assisted suicide would directly end the patient's suffering.[55]

In addition to physical pain and discomfort, patients experience psychological and personal suffering, which is less amenable to medical treatment. As articulated by several doctors, "The most frightening aspect of death for many is not physical pain, but the prospect of losing control and independence and of dying in an undignified, un[a]esthetic, absurd, and existentially unacceptable condition."[56] Some patients suffer because of losses that have already occurred or because

---

[54] At least short of anesthetizing the patient to a sleep-like state; see p. 93, n. 60.

[55] G. A. Kasting, "The Nonnecessity of Euthanasia," in *Physician-Assisted Death*, ed. J. M. Humber, R. F. Almeder, and G. A. Kasting (Totowa, N.J.: Humana Press, 1993), 25-45; Weir, 123-24; Rachels, 152-54.

[56] Quill, Cassel, and Meier, 1383.

of anticipated losses and decline. Others may experience anxiety, loneliness, helplessness, anger, and despair. Proponents of assisted suicide and euthanasia assert that only the patient can determine when suffering renders continued life intolerable.[57]

The number of patients who would receive assistance to commit suicide or euthanasia is unknown. Most advocates assert that these actions would be appropriate only in rare cases, and that relatively few patients would be directly affected. They argue, however, that many individuals who never use the practices would benefit. Some patients would feel better cared for and more secure if they knew that their physician would provide a lethal injection or supply of pills if they requested these means to escape suffering.[58] Knowing that assisted suicide or euthanasia is available would also reassure members of society in general, including those who are not severely ill. "While relatively few might be likely to seek assistance with suicide if stricken with a debilitating illness, a substantial number might take solace knowing they could request such assistance."[59]

Opponents

Those who oppose legalizing assisted suicide and euthanasia are also deeply concerned about the needs of terminally and severely ill patients. They believe that society all too often abandons these patients, adding to their suffering and sense of despair. However, they reject assisted suicide and euthanasia as unacceptable or harmful responses to these patients in need. They also believe that the likely harm to many patients far exceeds the benefits that would be conferred. Advances in pain control have rendered cases of intolerable and untreatable pain extremely rare. In exceptional cases in which symptoms cannot be controlled adequately while the patient is alert, sedation to a sleep-like state would remain an option.[60] Allowing assisted suicide or

---

[57]Brock, 11; Weir, 123; Kasting.

[58]F. G. Miller and J. C. Fletcher, "The Case for Legalized Euthanasia," *Perspectives in Biology and Medicine* 36 (1993): 163-64; Quill, Cassel, and Meier, 1382.

[59]Watts and Howell, 1044-45.

[60]N. Coyle et al., "Character of Terminal Illness in the Advanced Cancer Patient: Pain and Other Symptoms During the Last Four Weeks of Life," *Journal of Pain and Symptom Management* 5 (1990): 83-93; Foley; Teno and Lynn. Watts and Howell (1045), in advocating assisted suicide, write: "We concede that there is another alternative: terminally ill patients who cannot avoid pain while awake may be given continuous anesthetic levels of medication. But this is exactly the sort of dying process we believe many in our society want to avoid." In contrast, Leon R. Kass states: "It will be pointed out [that] full analgesia induces drowsiness and blunts or distorts

euthanasia, especially given the current state of palliative care, would deny patients the treatment and support that should be a routine part of medical practice. It also would lead to the death of some patients whose pain could be alleviated.[61]

Health care professionals can do much to help relieve psychological suffering by providing humane care and personal support.[62] Opponents believe that assisting a patient's suicide or performing euthanasia in an attempt to relieve psychological anguish or despair will rarely serve the patient's interests. For some, this is an evident contradiction; causing death can never constitute a benefit.[63] Others maintain that assisted suicide and euthanasia could alleviate psychological suffering in rare cases, but believe that the advantages of allowing the practices are outweighed by the potential harm to many other patients.[64]

Significant too is the concern that suicide should not be pursued as a means to care for, or "treat," patients who suffer because of

---

awareness. How can that be a desired outcome of treatment? Fair enough. But then the rationale for requesting death begins to shift from relieving experienced suffering to ending a life no longer valued by its bearer or, let us be frank, by the onlookers." "Neither for Love nor Money: Why Doctors Must Not Kill," *Public Interest* 94 (1989): 33. Palliative care experts report that while sedation seems objectionable to many healthy individuals contemplating it in the abstract, most terminally ill patients and families find it acceptable. Nessa M. Coyle, R. N., Director, Supportive Care Program, Pain Service, Department of Neurology, Memorial Sloan-Kettering Cancer Center, oral communication, March 11, 1993. While continual sedation can be an important option for patients in severe and intractable physical pain, it is a less practical option for patients whose suffering is primarily psychological and who may have years to live. Quill, Cassel, and Meier.

[61]Reflecting on this danger in the United States, Alexander M. Capron writes: "The difficulties in developing caring and creative means of responding to suffering discourage society as well as health care providers from greater efforts. A policy of active euthanasia can become another means of such avoidance. . . I could not rid my mind of the images of care provided in our hard-pressed public hospitals and in many nursing homes, where compassionate professionals could easily regard a swift and painless death as the best alternative for a large number of patients." "Euthanasia in the Netherlands: American Observations," *Hastings Center Report* 22, no. 2 (1992): 32.

[62]See, e.g., N. Coyle, "The Euthanasia and Physician-Assisted Suicide Debate: Issues for Nursing," *Oncology Nursing Forum* 19, no. 7 suppl. (1992): 44-45; and discussion above, chapter 3. Most proponents of assisted suicide and euthanasia would agree with this statement but still believe that the practices should be available at the patient's option.

[63]As argued by Leon Kass: "To intend and to act for someone's good requires his continued existence to receive the benefit." Kass, 40.

[64]P. A. Singer and M. Siegler, "Euthanasia — A Critique," *New England Journal of Medicine* 322 (1990): 1881-83.

psychological reasons. Society has long discouraged suicide as a remedy for psychological suffering, even though many individuals who consider suicide are anguished and find relief in the prospect of death.[65] Even for patients who are suffering and seek assistance in ending life, complying with the request may provide the wrong kind of "assistance," causing some patients to end their lives prematurely. Two physicians report that, while many hospice patients at times express a desire for death, almost none make serious and persistent requests for active euthanasia. They write:

> New patients to hospice often state they want to "get it over with." At face value, this may seem a request for active euthanasia. However, these requests are often an expression of the patient's concerns regarding pain, suffering, and isolation, and their fears about whether their dying will be prolonged by technology. Furthermore, these requests may be attempts by the patient to see if anyone really cares whether he or she lives. Meeting such a request with ready acceptance could be disastrous for the patient who interprets the response as confirmation of his or her worthlessness.[66]

Others note that even if all patients are assumed to make rational and beneficial choices for themselves, giving patients the option of choosing to end life would change the way they and those around them perceive their lives. Specifically, a patient could no longer stay alive by default, without needing to justify his or her continued existence. The patient will be seen (by others and himself or herself) as responsible for the choice to stay alive, and as needing to justify that choice. Given societal attitudes about handicaps and dependence, "the burden of proof will lie heavily on the patient who thinks that his terminal illness or chronic disability is not a sufficient reason for dying."[67]

---

[65] As explained by one sociologist who studied suicide: "It is undeniable that all persons — 100 percent — who commit suicide are perturbed and experiencing unbearable psychological pain." E. S. Shneidman, "Rational Suicide and Psychiatric Disorders," *New England Journal of Medicine* 326 (1992): 889. Two psychiatrists offer a similar opinion; see Hendin and Klerman, 144.

[66] Teno and Lynn, 828.

[67] This argument is well developed by J. David Velleman, "Against the Right to Die," *Journal of Medicine and Philosophy* 17 (1992): 665-81. While Velleman argues against establishing a law or policy permitting euthanasia, he believes that some patients would benefit from death and welcome euthanasia and that in such cases rules against euthanasia should not be enforced.

Severely ill patients depend on others not only for physical care, but for conversation, respect, and meaningful human interaction. In some cases, family members may encourage patients to "choose" the option of dying.[68] More commonly, even without such pressure, a patient may assume that friends and family regard the choice to remain alive as irrational or selfish. As expressed by one commentator, "The patient may rationally judge that he's better off taking the option of euthanasia, even though he would have been best off not having the option at all. ... To offer the option of dying may be to give people new reasons for dying."[69]

Many opponents believe that establishing an option of assisted suicide or euthanasia would have negative consequences not only for patients who receive assisted dying, but for many others who would not use either practice. The option of assisted suicide or euthanasia could distract attention from the care that some patients might otherwise be offered. Especially if a patient's symptoms persist despite initial attempts to alleviate them, the effort and expense of more aggressive treatment and support may seem less compelling.[70] Officially sanctioning these practices might also provide an excuse for those wanting to spend less money and effort to treat severely and terminally ill patients, such as patients with acquired immunodeficiency syndrome (AIDS).[71]

Societal Consequences

Decisions about euthanasia and assisted suicide touch upon fundamental societal values and standards. They entail questions about why we value human life, when life may be taken, and what obligations we owe to others. Legalizing assisted suicide or euthanasia would represent a dramatic change, and is likely to cause both intended and unintended consequences.

Those who favor or oppose legalizing assisted suicide and euthanasia differ both in their prediction of societal consequences and

---

[68]See Kamisar, 37; and also the concerns noted in M. P. Battin, "Manipulated Suicide," in *Suicide: The Philosophical Issues*, ed. Battin and Mayo, 169-82.

[69]Velleman, 675-76.

[70]A. J. Dyck, "Physician-Assisted Suicide — Is It Ethical?" *Harvard Divinity Bulletin* 21, no. 4 (1992): 16.

[71]Donald McKinney argues that even if relatively few patients avail themselves of the choice, officially sanctioning the option may alter public perceptions, making improvement in palliative care and increased social support for suffering patients seem less urgent. McKinney, 7-8.

in the way that they evaluate possible outcomes.[72] They disagree, for example, about the effect of the practices on society's respect for the value of the lives of others, especially those who are most frail and ill. They also differ about whether expansion of a policy of voluntary euthanasia to include nonvoluntary euthanasia would benefit or threaten vulnerable members of society, and whether mistakes or abuses in a relatively small number of cases would constitute a moral outrage or the unfortunate but unavoidable imperfections of any human activity. Finally, proponents and opponents disagree about how the burden of proof should fall in deciding public policy. If the societal consequences of authorizing assisted suicide or euthanasia are uncertain, should society allow these practices until such time as harmful effects can be proven, or should the practices remain prohibited unless society can assure itself that they would not cause unacceptable social harm?[73]

Proponents

Proponents believe that legalizing assisted suicide and euthanasia would not produce harmful consequences for society as a whole, and that potential dangers can be minimized by appropriate safeguards. For example, some argue that, despite current prohibitions, assisted suicide now occurs. Openly permitting assisted suicide in accord with required safeguards might therefore encourage physicians to communicate more freely with their patients and to consult with professional colleagues. Mandated consultation with a licensed psychiatrist would improve the diagnosis and treatment of many patients who are depressed.[74] As a result, allowing the practice in carefully defined circumstances would lead to greater professional accountability and fewer cases of abuse.[75]

---

[72]See Brock, 14.

[73]Similar arguments about potential consequences and the "burden of proof" in the absence of unproven but probable risks have been raised in the debate on surrogate motherhood. See New York State Task Force on Life and the Law, *Surrogate Parenting: Analysis and Recommedations for Public Policy* (New York: New York State Task Force on Life and the Law, 1988) 73-74, 116-17.

[74]Some opponents, though, emphasize the difficulty of diagnosing depression among severely ill patients, and argue that mandated psychiatric consultation would fail to identify some cases of depression. See chapters 1 and 8.

[75]Cassel and Meier, 751. Data on the number of cases of assisted suicide and euthanasia currently occurring are difficult to obtain, especially because the practices are illegal. Information about cases of assisted suicide and euthanasia has largely been presented in anecdotal reports. See Lehr.

Many who favor legalizing physician-assisted suicide see little distinction between assisted suicide and euthanasia. Both practices rest on commitments to respect autonomy and prevent suffering. Some acknowledge that a practice of euthanasia with the patient's consent is likely to lead to euthanasia for patients incapable of expressing consent or refusal. They believe that nonvoluntary euthanasia would be appropriate when it reflects some information about the patient's own wishes or when it relieves the patient's suffering.[76] Others accept euthanasia for patients too ill or too young to decide for themselves because they see no value in continued life for severely disabled individuals who irreversibly lack the ability to experience life consciously or to relate to others. Essentially, some believe that these individuals do not "have a life" in the sense in which life is treasured.[77]

Advocates of legalizing assisted suicide and/or euthanasia maintain that although some abuses will occur, the number of inappropriate deaths would be small, and the opportunity to alleviate suffering in other cases outweighs this cost. The potential for abuse suggests the need for safeguards, but should not preclude legalizing assisted suicide and euthanasia. For them, claims about negative consequences for the medical profession or the broader society seem uncertain and speculative.[78]

Some advocates of legalizing assisted suicide or euthanasia favor prospective guidelines: for example, requiring that the attending

---

[76]Brock, 20.

[77]See, e.g., Rachels, 24-33, 64-67, 178-80; P. Singer, *Practical Ethics* (Cambridge: Cambridge University Press, 1979), 138-39.

[78]Concerns about the potential consequences of a change in policy are often discussed in terms of "slippery slope" arguments: allowing a given practice will tend to lead to acceptance of other actions that are objectionable. A logical or conceptual version of a slippery-slope argument would claim that there is no distinction in principle between two actions; for example, that if voluntary euthanasia is allowed, there would be no principled basis for not allowing nonvoluntary euthanasia. Causal or empirical versions of the argument maintain that allowing a certain type of action would tend to lead in practice to another, objectionable action; for example, that if voluntary euthanasia is allowed, society would be more likely to accept nonvoluntary euthanasia. The empirical version of the argument can rarely prove that a given result (e.g., nonvoluntary euthanasia) is certain to follow. Those utilizing such arguments maintain that they may nevertheless establish that allowing one type of action poses a significant or unacceptable risk that the problematic result will occur. See Arras; Beauchamp and Childress, 139-41; W. van der Burg, "The Slippery-Slope Argument," *Ethics* 102 (1991): 42-65; B. Freedman, "The Slippery-Slope Argument Reconstructed," *Journal of Clinical Ethics* 3 (1992): 293-97; B. Williams, "Which Slopes Are Slippery?" in *Moral Dilemmas in Modern Medicine*, ed. M. Lockwood (New York: Oxford University Press, 1985), 126-37.

physician consult with colleagues and that the patient voluntarily and repeatedly request assisted suicide or euthanasia, receive psychological evaluation and counseling, and experience intolerable suffering with no hope for relief.[79] Proposals also stipulate requirements for the patient's medical condition: for example, that assisted suicide or euthanasia would be allowed only if a patient is terminally ill or has an incurable disease. Others recommend that a panel or committee review the patient's request before assisted suicide or euthanasia is performed.[80]

Under some proposals, assisting suicide or performing euthanasia would remain a violation of criminal law, but guidelines would specify types of cases that would not subject physicians to any penalty. Physicians would be able to avoid punishment by proving that they acted appropriately in exceptional circumstances; a showing that the physician responded compassionately and competently to a voluntary request by a competent patient would constitute a defense to criminal prosecution.[81] Finally, some advocates have suggested a trial period of voluntary active euthanasia or measures to legalize the practice in a few states, in order to gain data on the consequences of the practice.[82]

Opponents

For many, the potential for error and abuse in particular cases, the risks to vulnerable individuals, and the profound effect on society's values present the most compelling reasons against allowing assisted suicide and euthanasia. Most immediately, the practices create enormous potential for abuse in particular cases. Some decisions to contribute to a patient's death may be well-intentioned but hasty and possibly mistaken. In other cases, patients may be pressured to consent to euthanasia when their care is expensive or burdensome to others. As one commentator has argued, "Advocating legal sanction of euthanasia at a time and in a society where access to care is so limited

---

[79]Various safeguards are suggested in Hemlock Society U.S.A., "Model Aid-in-Dying Act," 1993; M. Battin, "Voluntary Euthanasia and the Risks of Abuse;" Weir, "Morality," 124-25; H. Rigter, "Euthanasia and the Netherlands," *Hastings Center Report* 19, no. 1 (1989): S31-32; Quill, Cassel, and Meier, 1381-82. For a discussion and critique of guidelines proposed by Quill, Meier and Cassel, see chapter 6, pp. 142-45.

[80]See, e.g., Brody, 1387.

[81]This is the way the law is structured in the Netherlands, although most agree that physicians are not reporting many cases of euthanasia despite the legal requirement to do so.

[82]See, e.g., Brock, 20; Glover.

and its cost so critical, the so-called 'right to die' all too easily becomes a duty to die."[83]

Some warn that individuals who are disadvantaged or members of minority groups would be especially susceptible to such pressures. Others note the widely recognized failure of our health care system to provide minimally acceptable health care to the poor and disadvantaged. Especially in overburdened facilities serving the rural and urban poor, the lack of available options may effectively pressure patients into assisted suicide or euthanasia.[84] For some opponents, cases of abuse, even if relatively infrequent, would count decisively against a policy authorizing assisted suicide and euthanasia.[85]

Opponents also believe that the practice would expand, presenting even more profound dangers. A policy of allowing assisted suicide or euthanasia only when a patient voluntarily requests an assisted death, and a physician also judges that assisted suicide or euthanasia are appropriate to relieve suffering, is inherently unstable. The reasons for allowing these practices when supported by *both* a patient's request and a physician's judgment would lead to allowing the practices when *either* condition is met.[86] The value of self-determination supports compliance with any voluntary request by a patient with decision-making capacity. Moreover, any serious request would reflect psychological suffering that the patient considers unbearable. Suggested restrictions on the practices, such as requiring that patients have a terminal or degenerative illness, would be seen as arbitrary limits on patients' autonomy.[87] In particular cases, and more broadly over time,

---

[83]McKinney, 9. Similarly, David Velleman asserts that some patients will choose to die out of concern for the resources of family members or society, and that to accept such a "gift" can be problematic. "Establishing the right to die is tantamount to saying, to those who might contemplate dying for the social good, that such favors will never be refused." Velleman, 678-79.

[84]As argued by John Arras, "Insofar as we sustain unjust conditions, including profoundly inequitable systems of terminal health care, we thereby heighten the impoverished person's sense of being truly a 'dead end case.' By failing to alleviate or eliminate those social conditions that would make a quick death look relatively attractive, we become deeply implicated in this choice for death." Arras, 312.

[85]Singer and Siegler maintain, "Even one case of involuntary euthanasia would represent a great harm." Singer and Siegler, 1883.

[86]See Dyck; Kamisar.

[87]As argued by Benjamin Freedman (293), societal acceptance of decisions to forgo life-sustaining treatment began with decisions made directly by terminally ill patients; over time the courts and policymakers concluded that it is inappropriate or infeasible to make such criteria decisive for purposes of public policy. Daniel Callahan adds that

assisted suicide and euthanasia would be provided based on any serious voluntary request by a competent patient, regardless of his or her medical condition.[88]

Opponents similarly argue that restrictions requiring the patient's informed choice would be difficult to maintain. If intentionally contributing to or causing death is an appropriate course of treatment for suffering patients, then physicians should be able to provide this treatment to patients unable to make the request themselves.[89] The resulting policy of euthanasia for children and incompetent adults is regarded as intrinsically wrong, or as an option that poses an extraordinarily high risk of abuse.

Some believe that legalizing assisted suicide and euthanasia would have a subtle but widespread impact on society. They fear a general reduction of respect for human life if official barriers to killing are removed.[90] Others are especially fearful of the effect on the disabled and other vulnerable persons in society at large.

> Instead of the message a humane society sends to its members — "Everybody has the right to be around, we want to keep you with us, every one of you" — the society that embraces euthanasia, even the "mildest"

---

it would be difficult to enforce restrictions on euthanasia because of the privacy of the interaction between doctor and patient. Callahan, "When Self-Determination Runs Amok," 54.

Some express concern that legalizing assisted suicide and euthanasia would render it more difficult to forgo life-sustaining treatment. Restrictions on euthanasia might be applied to decisions to forgo treatment, and all decisions at life's end might become subject to overly intrusive review. S. M. Wolf, "Holding the Line on Euthanasia," *Hastings Center Report* 19, no. 1 (1989): S13-15; McKinney, 4-6.

[88] Among others, Yale Kamisar asserts that, if assisted suicide is allowed for patients with a terminal or degenerative illness, it would seem unfair to exclude others, such as a quadriplegic or severely injured accident victim. He continues: "Why stop there? If a competent person comes to the unhappy conclusion that his existence is unbearable and freely, clearly, and repeatedly requests assisted suicide, why should he be rebuffed because he does not 'qualify' under somebody else's standards?" Kamisar, 36-37. In a recent case in the Netherlands, a court approved a psychiatrist's assistance of suicide for a patient who was depressed and experiencing psychological suffering, but had no other medical illness. W. Drozdiak, "Dutch Seek Freer Mercy Killing;. Court Case Could Ease Limits on Assisted Suicide, Euthanasia," *Washington Post*, October 29, 1993, A29.

[89] Callahan, "When Self-Determination Runs Amok," 54; Dyck, 17; Capron, 31. Some point to the Dutch experience as evidence that the practice would expand. See the discussion in chapter 6, pp. 132-34.

[90] See, e.g., Beauchamp and Childress, 141; Dyck, 17.

and most "voluntary" forms of it, tells people: "We
wouldn't mind getting rid of you." This message
reaches not only the elderly and the sick, but all the
weak and dependent.[91]

Some who oppose legalizing euthanasia believe that acts of voluntary euthanasia are morally acceptable in exceptional cases, such as
when a terminally ill patient suffering from intolerable and untreatable
pain makes an informed request. On balance, however, they conclude
that conscientious objection and leniency in the judicial process would
be appropriate in these cases, but such exceptional cases cannot justify
explicit changes in the law or moral rules that bar active and intentional
killing. However strong our compassion for patients in these rare
circumstances, it cannot support fundamental changes to society's
moral code, with potentially disastrous and irreversible consequences.[92]

Similarly, some argue that even if actions of assisting suicide in
particular cases are morally justified or excusable, it would be difficult
or impossible to craft a policy that resulted in assisted suicide only in
those cases. A policy that allowed sensitive physicians to assist suicide
indirectly in exceptional cases, after lengthy discussions with a patient,
would also allow less thoughtful physicians to aid suicides after per-
functory conversations. Accordingly, a former president of Concern
for Dying, an advocacy organization for patients' rights, suggests:

> A deliberate act to assist someone in taking her/his
> life — however merciful the intent — should not be
> sanctioned by law. Rather it should be left a private
> act, with society able to be called in to judgment when
> and if the motive should be impugned. This is not

---

[91]R. Fenigsen, "A Case Against Dutch Euthanasia," *Hastings Center Report* 19, no. 1
(1989): S26. Richard Doerflinger similarly argues: "Elderly and disabled patients are
often invited by our achievement-oriented society to see themselves as useless
burdens. ... In this climate, simply offering the option of 'self-deliverance' shifts a
burden of proof, so that helpless patients must ask themselves why they are not
availing themselves of it." "Assisted Suicide: Pro-Choice or Anti-Life?" *Hastings
Center Report* 19, no. 1 (1989): S16-19. Hendin and Klerman assert that for society to
authorize assisted suicide would in effect endorse "the view of those who are
depressed and suicidal that death is the preferred solution to the problems of illness,
age, and depression." Hendin and Klerman, 145.

[92]See Veatch, 73-75; J. F. Childress, "Civil Disobedience, Conscientious Objection,
and Evasive Noncompliance: A Framework for the Analysis and Assessment of
Illegal Actions in Health Care," *Journal of Medical Philosophy* 10 (1985): 73-77.

a neat and precise system of justice to be sure, but one that continues to afford the least possibility of abuse.[93]

The Role and Responsibilities of Physicians

While any person can aid suicide or cause death, the current debate about assisted suicide and euthanasia generally centers on the actions of physicians. Long-standing medical tradition, exemplified by the Hippocratic Oath, enjoins physicians not to harm patients, and in particular not to "give a deadly drug to anybody if asked for it, nor ... make a suggestion to this effect."[94] The oath also commits the physician to employ therapeutic measures to benefit the patient.[95]

The issues of assisted suicide and euthanasia confront some physicians in a dramatic and deeply personal way, as they consider how best to respond to a patient's suffering, or to an explicit request for assistance in ending life. In these as in other cases, some physicians feel a conflict between their personal commitments and conscientious judgment in a particular case, and policies designed to prevent harm or abuse for patients generally.

The debate about assisted suicide and euthanasia raises complex questions about the duties of physicians and the goals of the medical profession. What is a physician's obligation when a patient requests assisted suicide or euthanasia? How does this obligation relate to the overall goals of medicine? What impact would the practices have on the social role of physicians and on the physician-patient relationship? In response to the growing public debate, the organized medical community has focused on the special questions posed for its profession.

---

[93]McKinney, 7.

[94]In T. L. Beauchamp and J. F. Childress, *Principles of Biomedical Ethics*, 2d ed. (New York: Oxford University Press, 1983), 330. The Hippocratic Oath dates back to approximately the fourth century B.C. Although doctors no longer swear by the god Apollo, the oath has been regarded as a central statement about the ethical responsibilities of physicians throughout the history of Western medicine. Nonetheless, not all aspects of the oath are universally honored as prescriptions in contemporary medical practice. For example, many physicians reject the oath's proscription against abortion.

[95]Ibid. The oath specifies, "I will apply dietetic measures for the benefit of the sick according to my ability and judgment."

Proponents

Physicians and others who advocate assisted suicide and euthanasia believe that the practices are consistent with the professional role and responsibilities of physicians. They assert that the physician's responsibility to care for patients should be understood broadly in terms of promoting patients' self-determination and enhancing their well-being. Accordingly, it would be appropriate for a physician to assist suicide or perform euthanasia when these actions are chosen by and would benefit a patient.[96] Others believe that "alleviating suffering, curing disease, and not causing death are important and simultaneous obligations."[97] If suffering can be eliminated only by causing death, a physician would face conflicting obligations, requiring a personal choice about which obligation is most compelling under the circumstances.

Some proponents regard assisted suicide as less threatening to professional integrity than euthanasia.[98] They believe that removing rules against physician-assisted suicide would offer physicians an important option in responding to the personal experiences and values of each patient. In appropriate cases, a physician's willingness to discuss this alternative and assist suicide would demonstrate commitment to the patient throughout the course of life, including the moment of death.

Some proponents maintain that physicians should have a special role in contributing to patients' deaths because they have access to drugs and the expertise to cause death quickly and painlessly.[99] Other individuals, such as family members and friends, may be reluctant to cause or contribute to a patient's death. In addition, the moral authority of physicians enables them to aid patients seeking to end their lives in less tangible ways.

> Historically, in the United States suicide has carried a strong negative stigma that many today believe unwarranted. Seeking a physician's assistance, or what can almost seem a physician's blessing, may be a way of trying to remove that stigma and show others

---

[96]Brock, 16-17.

[97]Loewy, 31.

[98]Diane E. Meier argues that euthanasia and assisted suicide "would likely have a substantially different impact on the ethos of the medical profession." Meier, 35.

[99]See, e.g., Brock, 21.

that the decision for suicide was made with due seriousness and was justified under the circumstances. The physician's involvement provides a kind of social approval, or more accurately helps counter what would otherwise be unwarranted social disapproval.[100]

Some urge that only physicians should be authorized to assist suicide or perform euthanasia. Physicians can discuss the patient's medical condition, explore alternative means for alleviating pain and suffering, and determine whether the patient's judgment is significantly impaired by psychiatric conditions. Physicians can also use their technical skills to provide or administer a lethal dose that leads to a rapid and painless death. Finally, limiting the number of people authorized to assist suicide or perform euthanasia would enhance accountability and protect against abuse.[101]

Others frame the argument for assisted suicide and euthanasia more broadly. Another person, such as a family member, might be best able to help the patient achieve relief through death. The patient may not have an established relationship with a physician, or the patient's physician may be unwilling to comply with the patient's request. In several prominent cases, family members or friends, motivated by compassion, have assisted suicide or caused death. According to some advocates, "mercy-killing" should be established in general as an acceptable defense to criminal prosecution.[102]

Opponents

Many physicians and others who oppose assisted suicide and euthanasia believe that the practices undermine the integrity of medicine and the patient-physician relationship. Medicine is devoted to healing and the promotion of human wholeness; to use medical techniques in order to achieve death violates its fundamental values. Even in the absence of widespread abuse, some argue that allowing physicians to act as "beneficent executioners" would undermine patients' trust, and change the way that both the public and physicians view medicine.[103]

---

[100] Ibid.

[101] See, e.g., Weir, 125.

[102] Rachels, 2-6, 28-33, 168-70.

[103] As expressed by a group of four physicians: "If physicians become killers or are even merely licensed to kill, the profession — and, therewith, each individual

Some believe that, while physicians may be motivated by compassion in some cases, a physician abandons the patient in a profound sense when he or she deliberately causes the patient's death.[104] Others note that professionals such as physicians have great power and enjoy significant discretion to use that power prudently. Strict boundaries to prevent the misuse of power are therefore necessary. General professional limits may in some cases impinge on an individual physician's personal sense of vocation, but are needed to maintain public confidence in the profession and guard against abuse.[105]

Some object that assisted suicide and euthanasia would be used as a "quick fix" of the kind that is too prevalent in contemporary medical practice.

> Having adopted a largely technical approach to healing, having medicalized so much of the end of life, doctors are being asked ... to provide a final technical solution for the evil of human finitude and for their own technical failure: If you cannot cure me, kill me.[106]

Others note that relying on medical practices to assist suicide removes a natural psychological barrier to the act, leading some individuals to end their lives without facing the full implications of the act.[107] Some believe that a judgment about whether to assist suicide or

---

physician — will never again be worthy of trust and respect as healer and comforter and protector of life in all its frailty." W. Gaylin et al., "Doctors Must Not Kill," *Journal of the American Medical Association* 259 (1988): 2139-40. See also McKinney, 6-8; D. Orentlicher, "Physician Participation in Assisted Suicide," *Journal of the American Medical Association* 262 (1989): 1844-45. Some physicians writing near the beginning of the century expressed similar concerns. If part of the doctor's role was to cause death in specified cases, "his very presence would necessarily be associated with the idea of death. He would enter the sick room, into which he should bring life and hope, with the dark shadow of death behind him." "The Right to Die," in Reiser, Dyck, and Curran. 491

[104] See P. Ramsey. *The Patient as Person* (New Haven: Yale University Press, 1970).

[105] Kass, 35.

[106] Ibid.

[107] A. Alvarez writes that "Modern drugs not only have made suicide more or less painless, they have also made it seem magical. A man who takes a knife and slices deliberately across his throat is murdering himself. But when someone lies down in front of an unlit gas oven or swallows sleeping pills, he seems not so much to be dying as merely seeking oblivion for a while." Alvarez, 137. Writing about ancient Greece, Paul Carrick notes that the development of hemlock contributed to a change in the conception of suicide. and to an increase in the suicide rate. Carrick, 130.

perform euthanasia is not essentially a medical judgment, and falls outside the parameters of the patient-physician relationship.[108] They object to the notion that physicians would be granted special authority to assist suicide or perform euthanasia.

Some believe that assisted suicide or euthanasia performed by physicians would be more problematic than similar actions by other individuals. Because of the risks of abuse and threats to the integrity of the medical profession, it would be particularly objectionable for physicians to participate in these actions. A group of four physicians writes: "We must say to the broader community that if it insists on tolerating or legalizing active euthanasia, it will have to find non-physicians to do its killing."[109]

Finally, some object in particular to the concept of killing as a form of healing or death as cure, arguing that such views resonate with periods in history when the medical profession was used to end human life. While the practice of mass murder in Nazi Germany differs from contemporary proposals for euthanasia, it began with the active killing of the severely ill, and built on earlier proposals advanced by leading German physicians and academics in the 1920s, before the Nazis took power. Like policies currently advocated in the United States, these proposals were limited to the incurably ill, and mandated safeguards such as review panels.[110]

---

[108] "Are doctors now to be given the right to make judgments about the kinds of life worth living and to give their blessing to suicide for those they judge wanting? What conceivable competence, technical or moral, could doctors claim to play such a role?" Callahan, "When Self-Determination Runs Amok," 55.

[109] Gaylin et al., 2140. For some, physician participation in assisted suicide and euthanasia raises similar concerns to physician participation in capital punishment: whatever an individual physician's personal beliefs about the practice, to act as a physician in a way that contributes to a person's death would violate one's professional responsibilities. For a recent statement on participation in capital punishment, see American Medical Association, Council on Ethical and Judicial Affairs, "Physician Participation in Capital Punishment," *Journal of the American Medical Association* 270 (1993): 365-68. An argument for distinguishing between physician involvement in capital punishment and physician involvement in euthanasia may be found in Loewy, 29-34.

[110] Capron, 32-33; R. J. Lifton, *The Nazi Doctors: Medical Killing and the Psychology of Genocide* (New York: Basic Books, 1986), 45-50; Veatch, 66-67. Lifton, while distinguishing Nazi "euthanasia" from euthanasia in the Anglo-American context, traces the significance of concepts such as "life unworthy of life" and "killing as a therapeutic imperative" in removing social and psychological barriers against killing and advancing the Nazi program of genocide. "The medicalization of killing — the imagery of killing in the name of healing — was crucial to that terrible step." Lifton, 14-15, 46. See also the recent translation of Karl Binding and Alfred Hoche's 1920

The Views of Medical Organizations

In recent years, professional organizations — including the American Medical Association, the American College of Physicians, and the American Geriatrics Society — have joined the public debate about assisted suicide and euthanasia. The positions embraced by these organizations share several elements. The organizations consistently distinguish assisted suicide and euthanasia from the withdrawing or withholding of treatment, and from the provision of palliative treatments or other medical care that risk fatal side effects.[111]

Professional organizations report that most pain and suffering can be alleviated, but that some patients find their situation so intolerable that they request assisted suicide or euthanasia. Physicians should respond to these patients by exploring their concerns, investigating whether the patient is suffering from depression, and improving palliative care when needed. The organizations generally recognize that assisted suicide or euthanasia might be beneficial to a small number of patients. They note, however, that such actions are illegal, and they express concern that allowing these practices could damage the physician-patient relationship and pose serious risks to vulnerable members of society.[112]

Within the framework of this consensus, medical societies have offered somewhat differing views. While not supporting assisted suicide and euthanasia, the *American College of Physicians Ethics Manual* does not explicitly reject all such actions. The manual recommends that physicians respond to patient requests for euthanasia or assisted suicide by seeking to ascertain and respond to the patient's concerns.[113] In contrast, the American Geriatrics Society strongly

---

work, "Permitting the Destruction of Unworthy Life: Its Extent and Form," trans. W. E. Wright, P. G. Derr, and R. Salomon, *Issues in Law and Medicine* 8 (1992): 231-65.

[111]American Medical Association; American College of Physicians, "American College of Physicians Ethics Manual," 3d ed., *Annals of Internal Medicine* 117 (1992): 953-54; American Geriatrics Society, Public Policy Committee, "Voluntary Active Euthanasia," *Journal of the American Geriatrics Society* 39 (1991): 826.

[112]Ibid.

[113]As stated in the ACP manual: "In most cases, the patient will withdraw the request when pain management, depression, and other concerns have been addressed, but occasionally the issue of physician-assisted suicide needs to be explored in depth. However, our society has not yet arrived at a consensus on assisted suicide and most jurisdictions have specific laws prohibiting such action. Physicians and patients must continue to search together for answers to these problems without violating the physician's personal and professional values and without abandoning the patient to struggle alone." American College of Physicians, 955.

urges physicians not to provide interventions that directly and intentionally cause the patient's death. It also recommends that the current legal prohibition of physician assistance to commit suicide and euthanasia should not be changed.[114]

The Council on Ethical and Judicial Affairs of the American Medical Association similarly states that "physicians must not perform euthanasia or participate in assisted suicide." While these actions may seem beneficial for patients in some sympathetic cases, authorizing physicians to perform them would pose unacceptable risks of allowing mistaken or coerced deaths. It could also gradually distort both public perceptions of medical practice and the practice of medicine itself.[115]

Killing and Allowing to Die

The debate about euthanasia and assisted suicide takes place against the backdrop of changes in medical practice. Medical developments have increased the number and range of treatment decisions that must be made near the end of life. Decisions to withhold and withdraw life-sustaining treatment in accord with the patient's wishes and interests have become widely accepted in principle, and to an increasing extent in practice. As a result, many physicians have participated in decisions and actions to end life-sustaining treatment, giving them a sense of control over the timing and manner of a patient's death.

Some believe that such actions are essentially similar to assisted suicide and euthanasia. They challenge the commonly accepted dis-

---

[114] As set forth in the organization's policy statement, "Active euthanasia might reasonably be preferred by a few patients with intractable pain or other overwhelming symptoms; however, the benefit of allowing this choice must be weighed against possible abuse of euthanasia on the frail, disabled, and economically disadvantaged members of society." The American Geriatrics Society also expressed its concern that allowing euthanasia could also lessen patients' trust in physicians, and further weaken society's commitment to provide adequate resources for supportive care. American Geriatrics Society, 826.

[115] American Medical Association. The Committee on Bioethical Issues of the Medical Society of the State of New York articulates a similar position in "Physician-Assisted Suicide," *New York State Journal of Medicine* 92 (1992): 391. The National Hospice Organization has adopted a resolution rejecting the practice of euthanasia and assisted suicide. The resolution "reaffirms the hospice philosophy that hospice care neither hastens nor postpones death," and advocates hospice care as an alternative to euthanasia and assisted suicide. Resolution approved by the delegates of the National Hospice Organization, Annual Meeting, November 8, 1990, Detroit, Michigan.

The American Nurses Association has not issued a formal position statement on assisted suicide and euthanasia. Some nurses have argued that ANA position papers would suggest a position opposing euthanasia. N. Coyle, 44.

tinction between intentional killing, which is viewed as always wrong, and allowing to die, which is accepted in many cases. Many of those who reject this distinction support policies authorizing assisted suicide and euthanasia.[116] The current debate about assisted suicide and euthanasia poses questions about whether killing and allowing to die are intrinsically different on ethical grounds, and whether the practices should be distinguished for purposes of social policy.

Against the Distinction

Some claim that forgoing treatment cannot be distinguished in principle from taking affirmative steps to end a patient's life because the intentions, motives, and outcomes are identical in both cases. They argue that in each instance, the decision maker seeks the patient's death and is motivated by compassion, and the same result occurs.[117] Some supporters of assisted suicide and euthanasia assert that society currently accepts decisions to forgo life-sustaining treatment that effectively constitute killing; for example, withdrawing a respirator or failing to provide artificial nutrition and hydration.

Even if this characterization of current practice is rejected, they argue, killing (or more generally, contributing to a person's death) should not be seen as intrinsically immoral. Ending a person's life is wrong in most cases because it deprives a person of the benefit of

---

[116]Others who reject the distinction oppose decisions to forgo life-sustaining treatment, as well as assisted suicide and euthanasia. Discussion about distinguishing between killing and allowing to die may be found in R. F. Weir, *Abating Treatment with Critically Ill Patients: Ethical and Legal Limits to the Medical Prolongation of Life* (New York: Oxford University Press, 1989), 228-32, 261-68; J. McMahan, "Killing, Letting Die, and Withdrawing Aid," *Ethics* 103 (1993): 250-79; J. Feinberg, *Harm to Others* (New York: Oxford University Press, 1984), 159-63, 171-86, 257-59n; P. Foot, "Morality, Action and Outcome," in *Morality and Objectivity: A Tribute to J. L. Mackie*, ed. T. Hondreich (London: Routledge and Kegan Paul, 1985), 23-25.

[117]Rachels, 106-28, 139-43; Rachels, "Active and Passive Euthanasia," *New England Journal of Medicine*, 78-80. See also J. Fletcher, *Humanhood: Essays in Biomedical Ethics* (Buffalo: Prometheus Press, 1979), 149-58. Rachels describes two cases: Smith, who kills his 6-year-old cousin, and Jones, who intentionally lets his cousin die, both in order to gain an inheritance. He argues that as both acts are equally reprehensible, the "bare difference" between killing and letting die is morally insignificant.

Others have criticized such arguments as inconclusive at best. Even if the two cases in the example are equally objectionable, the difference between killing and letting die is significant in other cases. For instance, a person is not morally obligated to endanger his or her own health or spend a large sum of money to save another person, but it would be morally wrong for a person to kill someone actively in order to safeguard his or her health or save that sum of money. Beauchamp and Childress, 136-38; Feinberg, 167-68, citing H. Malm, "Good Samaritan Laws and the Concept of Personal Sovereignty," typescript, University of Arizona (1983), 11.

continued life, and violates the individual's rights. However, in appropriate cases of assisted suicide or voluntary euthanasia, the patient believes that continued life would not provide a benefit (and, with euthanasia, waives his or her right not to be killed).[118] Some patients decide to stop or withhold life-sustaining treatment because they perceive life as a burden and wish to die. In these cases, assisted suicide or euthanasia would end the patient's life and suffering more quickly and effectively than withdrawing or withholding treatment. As one philosopher argues:

> If one simply withholds treatment, it may take the patient longer to die, and so he may suffer more than he would if more direct action were taken and a lethal injection given. This fact provides strong reason for thinking that, once the initial decision not to prolong his agony has been made, active euthanasia is actually preferable to passive euthanasia, rather than the reverse.[119]

Finally, proponents of assisted suicide and euthanasia point out that the potential for mistake or abuse exists for withdrawing and withholding treatment as well. They argue that society has addressed this problem with appropriate safeguards, and could do the same for assisted suicide and euthanasia.

For the Distinction

Despite such claims, the distinction between killing and letting die, in general and in the context of medical decisions, is widely accepted and supported. Many insist that the nature of the action in each case is different. Decisions to withhold or withdraw treatment allow the natural course of the disease to continue. The decision maker determines that certain treatments are not medically appropriate or morally obligatory, and the physician refrains from imposing interventions that legally would constitute battery. Moreover, forgoing treatment does not always result in a patient's immediate death; the patient may continue to live, as in cases of an inaccurate prognosis.[120]

---

[118]Rachels, *End of Life*, 39-59.

[119]Rachels, "Active and Passive Euthanasia," 78-80.

[120]Beauchamp and Childress, 144; Weir, *Abating Treatment*, 316-18; Ramsey, 153. See also G. R. Scofield "Privacy (or Liberty) and Assisted Suicide," *Journal of Pain and Symptom Management* 6 (1991): 283.

This distinction in the nature of the acts of killing and allowing to die is accompanied by a difference in causation. In one case, the decision maker seeks to cause death and employs direct means to achieve this result. In the other, the decision maker accepts but does not cause the person's death, which is caused by the underlying illness or condition. Paul Ramsey, for example, argues that forgoing treatment is not simply an indirect means of killing. "In omission no human agent causes the patient's death, directly or indirectly. He dies his own death from causes that it is no longer merciful or reasonable to fight by means of possible medical interventions."[121]

For many, the prohibition against actively and intentionally killing innocent persons represents a basic moral and social norm. Diverse philosophical and religious perspectives affirm this view.[122] Some also contend that the psychological effect on professionals and family are different in cases of killing and allowing to die.[123]

For others, the crucial distinction lies in the different consequences of policies of killing and of allowing to die. A practice of accepted killing is more vulnerable to abuse in particular cases, and poses a greater risk of harm to others in society. Some focus on the role of the distinction in the context of law and public policy. As articulated by the President's Commission for the Study of Ethical Problems in Medicine and Biomedical and Behavioral Research, the prohibition of active killing is part of "an accommodation that adequately protects human life while not resulting in officious overtreatment of dying patients," and "helps to produce the correct decision in the great majority of cases."[124]

Some argue that the negative effects of active killing on those involved and on society are stronger, and the potential scope of abuse

---

[121]Ramsey, 151. See also Callahan, "When Self-Determination Runs Amok," 53-54; McMahan, 263, 271. The two types of cases also tend to be characterized by different intentions. See Weir, *Abating Treatment*, 310-11; G. Meilaender, "The Distinction Between Killing and Allowing to Die," *Theological Studies* 37 (1976): 468-69.

[122]See pp. 88-91.

[123]This argument was put forward as early as 1884 in an editorial in the *Boston Medical and Surgical Journal*: "Perhaps logically it is difficult to justify a passive more than an active attempt at euthanasia; but certainly it is less abhorrent to our feelings. To surrender to superior forces is not the same thing as to lead the attack of the enemy upon one's friends. May there not come a time when it is a duty in the interest of the survivors to stop a fight which is only prolonging a useless and hopeless struggle?" "Permissive Euthanasia," in Fye, 501-2.

[124]President's Commission, 70-73.

wider, than with allowing patients to die.[125] Additionally, patients have a strong moral and legal right to refuse treatment. Respecting decisions to forgo treatment recognizes this right to be let alone and the moral obligation not to impose treatment coercively. In contrast, people do not have the same basic right to active participation by others in achieving their death. Society's refusal to allow another person to assist suicide or to cause death directly does not impose the same burden on the patient that would result from forced medical interventions.[126]

---

[125]See the discussion of risks posed by euthanasia throughout this chapter and in chapter 6.

[126]See, e.g., Veatch, 67.

Part II

Deliberations and Recommendations of the Task Force

6

Crafting Public Policy on Assisted Suicide and Euthanasia

Modern medical advances have posed unprecedented dilemmas. The introduction of new medical procedures such as life-sustaining treatment, in vitro fertilization, and organ transplantation has forced us to examine our most basic values and relationships. Often the issues are presented in stark human terms by highly publicized cases. They are frequently unavoidable; society must either abandon use of the technology or find its way to some solution.

The current debate about assisted suicide and euthanasia is different in this regard. Dr. Jack Kevorkian's machine was not a technological breakthrough. Morphine, barbiturates, and other drugs prescribed to assist a suicide were developed long ago and have long been employed in medical practice for other purposes. Indeed, suicide is a practice with ancient roots, although often achieved with messier and more painful, nonmedical means.

Suicide, then, is not a new phenomenon, arising in the wake of medical advances. What is new about the current debate in the United States is the serious consideration of placing suicide and direct killing under the stewardship of medicine in accord with policies devised and sanctioned by the state.

The issue arises today in part because the advent of life-sustaining treatment and other aggressive treatments to prolong life has generated the need to make choices about the timing and manner of death. Medical advances have also spurred public fear about losing control over the dying process. Undoubtedly, many Americans have now cared for loved ones whose dying was protracted by unwanted medical interventions. At the same time, public policies about medical treatments to sustain life have promoted patient autonomy and choice. Starting in 1976 with the landmark case of Karen Ann Quinlan, respect for autonomy has been a critical guidepost for court decisions and legislation about life-sustaining measures. The personal nature of

117

treatment choices and the emphasis on individual rights in other spheres of public life have contributed to this trend.

In its recommendations for public policy on decisions about life-sustaining treatment, the Task Force on Life and the Law has consistently promoted autonomy as a fundamental principle in choices about medical treatment. Prized in its own right for its connection to human freedom and identity, autonomy has also been advocated by the Task Force as a means to understand and attain the patient's best interests. In the absence of an identified consensus about what is best for patients in diverse medical circumstances, the patient's own values offer important guidance. The Task Force also regards respect for the personal, moral, and religious beliefs of each person as crucial in a pluralist, diverse society such as ours.

Based on recommendations by the Task Force, many of New York's laws on treatment decisions reflect this judgment. The health care proxy and do-not-resuscitate laws seek to further the patient's wishes and best interests, looking to guidance from the patient whenever possible.[1] Pending legislation on treatment decisions for incapacitated patients also relies on the patient's own wishes as the preferred benchmark for treatment decisions.[2]

Although cherished, autonomy has never been the only value embraced by the Task Force. Nor has it always been paramount. In devising recommendations on organ transplantation, the Task Force considered whether patients in need of a transplant should be allowed to place themselves on a waiting list at more than one transplant center, thereby giving themselves an advantage over others waiting for a scarce donated organ. The Task Force concluded that fairness should override autonomy in the distribution of organs, and proposed a ban on the practice of multiple listing.[3] That ban became law in 1991, along with other policies to promote equity of access to transplantation.[4]

Similarly, the issue of surrogate parenting called for judgments about the scope of individual liberty when weighed against other social concerns. Proponents of surrogacy urged that both women who wished

---

[1]N.Y. Public Health Law, Article 29-C (McKinney 1993); N.Y. Public Health Law, Article 29-B (McKinney 1993).

[2]New York State Assembly Bill No. 7166.

[3]New York State Task Force on Life and the Law, *Transplantation in New York State: The Procurement and Distribution of Organs and Tissues*, 2d ed. (New York: New York State Task Force on Life and the Law), 1989.

[4]N.Y. Public Health Law, § 4363 (McKinney 1993).

to serve as surrogates and intended parents should be granted the right to engage freely in the arrangements as an extension of the right to reproduce. The Task Force disagreed, concluding that other values — the best interests of children, the prohibition against the sale of human beings, the commercialization of reproduction, and the dignity of women — should not be sacrificed.[5] It proposed that surrogacy contracts should be declared void and that fees to surrogate brokers and to surrogates should be banned. These policies now provide the basis for New York law on surrogate parenting.[6]

Suicide is not prohibited by law in New York or in any other state in the nation. However, assistance to commit suicide is legally barred by New York's criminal law, while direct measures to end the patient's life, such as a lethal injection, would constitute second-degree murder.[7] Although some doctors, protected by a promise of confidentiality, report that they and an uncertain number of their colleagues now provide these alternatives to patients, their actions are not legally sanctioned.

Legalization of assisted suicide and/or euthanasia would be a profound shift in public policy and professional standards. Nonetheless, public support for legalizing the practices appears to be significant. This support rests on an appeal to the two basic prongs of the argument favoring legalization — the rights of individuals and compassion or mercy for those who are suffering. For many individuals, the issue is best captured by a single question: are these options they might want for themselves at some future time? If so, many people assume that government should support, or at least not hamper, access to medical assistance to achieve death.

The Question of Legal Change

In the course of their deliberations, it became clear that the Task Force members hold different views about the ethical acceptability of assisted suicide and euthanasia. These differences persisted throughout the many months of their inquiry and discussion. Some of the members believe that it is always wrong for one human being to assist the suicide of another or to take another person's life — they

---

[5] New York State Task Force on Life and the Law, *Surrogate Parenting: Analysis and Recommendations for Public Policy* (New York: New York State Task Force on Life and the Law, 1988).

[6] N.Y. Domestic Relations Law, Article 8 (McKinney 1993).

[7] For a discussion of New York law on assisted suicide and euthanasia, see chapter 4.

regard both actions as a violation of principles fundamental to our social fabric and to the medical profession.[8] Other members believe that assisted suicide is ethically acceptable in certain cases, although they consider the circumstances that would justify the practice as rare. A few members believe that euthanasia might also be ethically acceptable in even more exceptional circumstances. Despite these differences about the underlying ethical questions, the Task Force members unanimously recommend that existing law should not be changed to permit assisted suicide or euthanasia. Legalizing assisted suicide and euthanasia would pose profound risks to many individuals who are ill and vulnerable. The Task Force members concluded that the potential dangers of this dramatic change in public policy would outweigh any benefit that might be achieved.

The risk of harm is greatest for the many individuals in our society whose autonomy and well-being are already compromised by poverty, lack of access to good medical care, advanced age, or membership in a stigmatized social group. The risks of legalizing assisted suicide and euthanasia for these individuals, in a health care system and society that cannot effectively protect against the impact of inadequate resources and ingrained social disadvantages, would be extraordinary.

For purposes of public debate, one can posit "ideal" cases in which all the recommended safeguards would be satisfied: patients would be screened for depression and offered treatment, effective pain medication would be available, and all patients would have a supportive, committed family and doctor. Yet the reality of existing medical practice in doctors' offices and hospitals across the state generally cannot match these expectations, however any guidelines or safeguards might be framed. These realities render legislation to legalize assisted suicide and euthanasia vulnerable to error and abuse for all members of society, not only for those who are disadvantaged. The argument for mercy or compassion then is complex. Constructing an ideal or "good" case is not sufficient for public policy, if it bears little relation to prevalent medical practice.

The appeal to autonomy is also far more complex in practice. From the perspective of good health, many individuals may believe that they would opt for suicide or euthanasia rather than endure a vastly diminished quality of life. Yet, once patients are confronted by illness, continued life often becomes more precious; it is not so readily discarded. Given access to appropriate relief from pain and other

---

[8]These members would, however, recognize the legitimacy of killing in certain well-identified exceptions such as self-defense or as a participant in a just war.

debilitating symptoms, many of those who consider suicide during the course of a terminal illness abandon their desire for a quicker death in favor of a longer life made more tolerable with effective treatment.

Undoubtedly, the desire for "control" at life's end is widely shared and deeply felt. Yet, as a society, we have better ways to give people greater control and relief from suffering than by making it easier for patients to commit suicide or to obtain a lethal injection. In particular, we must help patients and their families realize the opportunity to refuse life-sustaining measures in accord with policies that are humane and thoughtful. We must also make good pain relief and palliative care standard, not exceptional, treatment for all patients. In Chapter Eight the Task Force presents specific recommendations to achieve these goals.

Evaluating the Risks

Pressure and Persuasion

Physicians who provide suicide assistance or euthanasia despite existing legal prohibitions report that they do so in response to repeated requests for help from patients. The request, and the ensuing dialogue with the physician, are patient-initiated. This will change if assisted suicide and euthanasia are legalized. Both practices would become options in the panoply of alternatives that physicians offer their patients. As with other "treatments," judgments about when and for whom assisted suicide and euthanasia are provided would be managed principally by physicians, not their patients. While we advocate patient autonomy and accept something far short of this ideal for other treatments, the consequences of doing so for assisted suicide and euthanasia are too severe.

Illness is a quintessential state of vulnerability; it entails a loss of confidence in one's body and one's future. Serious illness also brings with it a loss of physical freedom and the ability to engage in the activities by which we define ourselves. Patients bring this vulnerability to their relationship with physicians. Physicians in turn hold the knowledge and expertise patients may desperately need, adding to the profound dependence that characterizes the doctor-patient relationship.

This dependence is manifested in many aspects of the doctor-patient relationship. Patients turn to their doctors for information about their diagnosis and prognosis, the likely symptoms of illness, and treatment alternatives. Through their tone, the encouragement they provide or withhold, and the way they present the information available, physicians can often determine the patient's choice. A 25 percent chance of survival, with good supportive care, sounds quite different from a 75 percent chance of failure, with significant disability and pain.

For all medical treatments, ranging from simple procedures such as blood tests to surgical procedures and treatments such as chemotherapy, physicians also decide which patients are candidates for the treatment. If assisted suicide and euthanasia were accepted as "therapy," physicians would make a medical judgment about which patients are "good" candidates for the practices. Physicians would also do what is routinely called for in good medical practice — they would make a recommendation. Even assuming that all physicians would act in good faith, never attempting to pressure their patients to commit suicide or to accept euthanasia, physicians' recommendations would be a powerful factor in their patients' choices. Indeed, patients generally do what their doctors recommend.[9]

Once the physician suggests assisted suicide or euthanasia, some patients will feel that they have few, if any, alternatives but to accept the recommendation. Most patients are unaware of the options to relieve pain and minimize symptoms. Even those who are more sophisticated about the options for continued care may fear that if they embrace the decision to live, they will do so without the medical support and care needed to make that decision tolerable. In an outpatient setting, patients can change physicians, although not all feel empowered to do so. For hospital patients, this option is harder to attain and more remote.

It is also significant that "neutrality" about the course of treatment is neither encouraged nor prevalent in medical practice. Physicians generally seek to persuade patients to accept treatment they have recommended.[10] Physicians do so out of a sense of benevolence and

---

[9]This dependence gives rise to some of the same concerns for decisions about life-sustaining treatment. However, as discussed below, decisions to forgo treatment are an integral part of medical practice. The risks and benefits of these decisions lead to a different assessment for public policy.

[10]As described in the conclusion of a major study of informed consent, "In addition to making a recommendation, the doctor's self-perceived role is to get the patient to go along with this recommendation if there is any hesitancy on the patient's part. This is done by some explanation about the need for the recommended treatment and the consequences of not heeding the recommendation. But in the doctor's view there is no decision for the patient to make, except whether or not to get proper medical care." C. W. Lida and A. Meisel, "Informed Consent and the Structure of Medical Care," in President's

confidence in their own judgments; they often believe that they know what is best for their patients. Yet, physicians' judgments about the value of continued life for the patient will be shaped by the physician's own attitudes about illness, physical dependence, pain, and disability. The patient's social and personal circumstances will also influence how some physicians respond to the patient and to the value of continued life for the patient.[11] Moreover, in some cases, offering assisted suicide and euthanasia may reflect physicians' own frustration in situations when medicine can provide care but not cure.

Physicians are also increasingly aware of and subject to pressures generated by the need to control costs. Limits on hospital reimbursement based on length of stay and diagnostic group, falling hospital revenues, and the social need to allocate health dollars may all influence physicians' decisions at the bedside. In many respects, physicians serve as gatekeepers in medical practice. Risk managers, administrators, and third-party payers also now have a less visible, but still significant role in treatment decisions. The growing concern about health care costs will not be diminished by health care reform. Under any new system of health care delivery, as at present, it will be far less costly to give a lethal injection than to care for a patient throughout the dying process.[12]

The current debate about medical futility reflects, in part, the extent to which the cost of treatment is viewed as relevant to decisions at the bedside. Some physicians have argued that they should determine when the benefits of treatment are too low to justify the cost in order to allocate health care resources. To date, the futility debate has focused on certain aggressive treatments, such as cardiopulmonary resuscitation, or on continued treatment for certain patients, such as those who are permanently unconscious. But once a decision is made not to pursue cure or treatment, and assisted suicide and euthanasia are available, the economic logic will be inescapable. The care provided to dying or very ill patients, not just their treatment, is

Commission for the Study of Ethical Problems in Medicine and Biomedical and Behavioral Research, *Making Health Care Decisions* (Washington D. C.: U.S. Government Printing Office, 1982), vol. 2, p. 400.

[11]Several studies have demonstrated that factors independent of clinical considerations, including race, economic status, and age, affect physicians' judgments about the course of treatment. See p. 125, n. 14.

[12]The 6.6% of medicare beneficiaries who died in 1990 accounted for 21.5% of all medicare expenditures. *Health Care Financing Review*, 1992 Annual Supplement (Baltimore: U.S. Department of Health and Human Services, Health Care Financing Administration, Office of Research and Demonstrations, 1993), 34.

expensive and demanding for health care professionals. The extra weeks or months of caring for patients who do not opt for assisted suicide or euthanasia will seem all the more "futile" and costly.

Nor will the commitment to care or treat remain unaffected by the existence of a neat, fast solution to medicine's hardest or least satisfying cases. Physicians who determine that a patient is a suitable candidate for assisted suicide or euthanasia may be far less inclined to present treatment alternatives, especially if the treatment requires intensive efforts by health care professionals. Nurses, social workers, and other health care professionals, crucial to the emotional support and day-to-day care of patients, may also be more likely to experience the survival of some patients — and their refusal to die more quickly — as a heavier burden.

Care and support for terminally and chronically ill patients also impose serious burdens on family members and other caregivers. The burdens are both financial and emotional. Family members may be drained by these demands or may conclude, based on their own perspective, that the patient's life is no longer worth living. Out of this benevolence, or from sheer frustration or exhaustion, family members may suggest or encourage the patient to accept assisted suicide or euthanasia. Motivated by a sense of guilt or abandonment, many patients will feel that they have no choice once the option is presented. Indeed, if assisted suicide and euthanasia are widely available, patients may feel obligated to consider these options to alleviate the burden their illness and continued life imposes on those closest to them.

These subtle but potentially pervasive changes will have the most significant impact on certain groups of patients — patients most likely to be considered "hopeless," such as those with acquired immunodeficiency syndrome (AIDS); patients who pose a risk to health care providers and family members, including those with multidrug-resistant tuberculosis; or patients who are least compliant, such as those who are mentally ill or drug addicted. Some health care professionals already regard caring for these patients as a special burden. Given the overall life circumstances of some of these patients, both health care professionals and family members may find it easy to rationalize that euthanasia or assisted suicide would be in these patients' best interests.[13] Establishing a quick, painless death as a state-sanctioned option may also mean that society becomes less committed to creating ways for patients, especially those who are socially disadvantaged, to live longer and better.

Finally, it must be recognized that assisted suicide and euthanasia will be practiced through the prism of social inequality and prejudice that characterizes the delivery of services in all segments of society, including health care. Those who will be most vulnerable to abuse, error, or indifference are the poor, minorities, and those who are least educated and least empowered. This risk does not reflect a judgment that physicians are more prejudiced or influenced by race and class than the rest of society — only that they are not exempt from the prejudices manifest in other areas of our collective life.[14]

While our society aspires to eradicate discrimination and the most punishing effects of poverty in employment practices, housing, education, and law enforcement, we consistently fall short of our goals. The costs of this failure with assisted suicide and euthanasia would be extreme. Nor is there any reason to believe that the practices, whatever safeguards are erected, will be unaffected by the broader social and medical context in which they will be operating. This assumption is naive and unsupportable.

Even our system for administering the death penalty, which includes the stringent safeguards of due process and years of judicial scrutiny, has not been freed of error or prejudice. For example, blacks who kill whites are sentenced to death at nearly 22 times the rate of blacks who kill blacks and more than seven times the rate of whites who kill

---

[13]As Leon Kass has argued, the option of suicide or euthanasia will influence physicians profoundly. "How easily will they be able to care for patients when it is always possible to think of killing them as a 'therapeutic' option? ... Physicians get tired of treating patients who are on their way down — 'gorks,' 'gomers,' and 'vegetables' — are only some of the less than affectionate names they receive from house officers." Leon Kass, "Why Doctors Must Not Kill," *Commonweal* 118, no. 14, suppl. (1991): 473.

[14] Studies have found that some physicians make treatment decisions based on criteria that are independent of the patient's medical needs, including age, race, and mental disability. Other studies have found broad patterns of inequality in access to treatment depending on race. See, e.g., N. J. Farber et al., "Cardiopulmonary Resuscitation (CPR) Patient Factors and Decision Making," *Archives of Internal Medicine* 144 (1984): 2229-32; R. M. Wachter et al., "Decisions About Resuscitation: Inequities Among Patients with Different Diseases but Similar Prognoses," *Annals of Internal Medicine* 111 (1989): 525-32; American Medical Association, Council on Ethical and Judicial Affairs, "Black-white Disparities in Health Care," *Journal of the American Medical Association* 263 (1990): 2344-46.

blacks.[15] Euthanasia is not a death sentence — it is not imposed on an individual by the state but administered with consent. The process for obtaining consent, however, will be blanketed in the privacy of the doctor-patient relationship. In that relationship, blatant prejudice may not be prevalent, but the more subtle biases that operate in our health care system will shape the consent process and the decisions made by patients.[16]

The Fallibility of Medical Practice

Diagnosing and Treating Depression. All proposals for assisted suicide and euthanasia implicitly assume or explicitly require the patient's primary physician to determine whether the patient has capacity to make an informed decision. For other medical decisions, this requirement has been interpreted to mean that the patient is capable of understanding and appreciating the risks and benefits of the proposed treatment, assessing the alternatives, and reaching an informed judgment. The notion of competence to make treatment decisions, or the capacity to make a particular decision, also presumes that the patient is not clinically depressed. Depression can impair a patient's ability to understand information, to weigh alternatives, and to make a judgment that is stable over time and consistent with the patient's values.

Depression accompanied by feelings of hopelessness is the strongest predictor of suicide for both individuals who are terminally ill and those who are not. Studies that have examined the psychological profile of individuals who commit suicide indicate that more than 95 percent had a major psychiatric illness at the time of death. Significantly, the majority of individuals who kill themselves suffer from depression that is treatable with appropriate clinical care.[17] Among terminally and incurably ill patients, uncontrolled pain is also an important risk factor for suicide because it contributes to hopelessness and depression.

---

[15] *McKlesky v. Kemp*, 481 U.S. 279, 327 (1987) (Brennan, J., dissenting). As Justice Blackmun recently observed, "It should not be surprising that the biases and prejudices that infect society generally would influence the determination of who is sentenced to death, even within the narrower pool of death-eligible defendants selected according to objective standards." *Callins v. Collins*, 62 U.S.L.W. 3546, 3549 (1994) (Blackmun, J., dissenting from denial of certiorari).

[16] See discussion of racial disparities in health care delivery, p. 125, n. 14.

[17] See discussion of suicide and depression in chapter 1.

Theoretically, contact with a physician or other health care professional provides the opportunity to screen patients for depression and offer appropriate treatment. In practice, however, this kind of screening and the subsequent offer of effective treatment are not standard care. Most doctors are not adequately trained to diagnose depression, especially in complex cases such as patients who are terminally ill. When an assessment is performed, the medical illness may obscure indicia of depression, rendering the diagnosis difficult. Even if diagnosed, undertreatment for depression is pervasive. In elderly patients as well as the terminally and chronically ill — those groups who would be the likeliest candidates for assisted suicide and euthanasia — depression is grossly underdiagnosed and undertreated.

If assisted suicide and euthanasia are legalized, internists, family physicians, geriatricians, and specialists in certain fields such as oncology would be most likely to receive requests by patients or to initiate discussion about assisted suicide and euthanasia. They would be responsible for screening patients for eligibility, including an assessment of decision-making capacity. Physicians in these areas of practice rarely have extensive training in treating or diagnosing depression.

Too often, clinicians fail to detect treatable depression or other psychiatric illness, assuming that the depression is expected or beyond treatment.[18] Frequently in the elderly, the symptoms of depression, such as loss of appetite and disrupted sleeping patterns, are mistaken for signs of old age, dementia, or a response to life in a nursing home. One study found that depression was diagnosed in only 15 percent of the depressed elderly, and was treated in only 25 percent of those cases. Another found that 75 percent of elderly patients who committed suicide had seen a primary care physician during the month before dying, but their psychiatric disturbances had been largely undetected.[19]

Even psychologists and psychiatrists who routinely treat and diagnose depression may have limited experience doing so for patients who

---

[18]As two geriatric psychiatrists recently noted in the *New England Journal of Medicine*, "Furthermore, research and our clinical work have made it clear to us that many doctors on the front lines, who would be responsible for implementing any policy that allowed assisted suicide, are ill equipped to assess the presence and effect of depressive illness in older patients. In the absence of that sophisticated understanding, the determination of a suicidal person's 'rationality' can be no more than speculation, subject to the influence of personal biases about aging, old age, and the psychological effects of chronic disease." Y. Conwell and E. D. Caine, "Rational Suicide and the Right to Die," *New England Journal of Medicine* 325 (1991): 1101.

[19]See discussion in chapter 1.

are terminally or chronically ill. For these patients, clinicians must be able to distinguish the realistic sadness and sense of loss that accompanies such illness from severe clinical depression or the psychiatric disorders that impair decision-making capacity. These disorders are prevalent in those patients who ultimately choose to commit or attempt suicide.

The presence of unrelieved pain also increases susceptibility to suicide. The experience of pain is closely linked to physical disability, depression, and feelings of hopelessness. Depression and anxiety in turn often augment the patient's experience of pain.[20] The widespread undertreatment of pain in current clinical practice therefore has far-reaching implications for the depression experienced by terminally and incurably ill patients, as well as for the choices they make about assisted suicide and euthanasia. As shown by studies of cancer and AIDS patients, the interplay of physical pain, depression, and suicide is complex. Undeniably, however, the failure to relieve physical pain creates vulnerability to depression and despair, both of which predispose patients to consider or to commit suicide.[21]

This problem is well-illustrated by a recent reported case involving a 70-year-old woman suffering from rheumatoid arthritis. On a video she sent to Jack Kevorkian seeking his help to end her life, she stated, "I'm in total despair because the pain cannot be controlled. I would like an out." As reported by Kevorkian's lawyer, her doctor offered her a morphine patch only after Kevorkian made clear that he might help her to die. Kevorkian in turn did not offer her pain relief, but assistance to commit suicide.[22]

Exploring the Meaning of Suicide. Many patients who are terminally or severely ill have suicidal ideation. When patients express suicidal thoughts to their physician, it may be a plea for help, a statement of their despair, or a search for guidance. The discussion itself can often be therapeutic, helping the patient feel less isolated or frightened. A physician's response, including the offer of pain relief, referral for psychiatric care, social work counseling to address family tension,

---

[20]Ibid.

[21]The failure to relieve pain may influence health care professionals' judgment as well as the patient's. A recent study showed that lack of knowledge about pain relief correlated with the willingness to endorse assisted suicide. R. K. Portenoy et al., "Determinants of the Willingness to Endorse Assisted Suicide: A Survey of Physicians, Nurses, and Social Workers," unpublished study, 1994.

[22]G. Golightly, "Pain Specialist Offers to Aid Kevorkian Client," *Houston Chronicle*, March 31, 1994, A16.

reassurance that the patient is not an undue burden on others, or palliative care to alleviate other symptoms, including depression, often diminishes or removes the desire for suicide. Each of these steps can lessen a patient's sense of helplessness, a critical factor of both depression and suicidal ideation.[23]

Few patients who express suicidal ideation actually commit suicide. Indeed, patients often prove remarkably resilient. Although some individuals speak about suicide when they first learn of their diagnosis, they adjust to their situation, even as their medical condition deteriorates. This phenomenon is often observed with AIDS patients and others suffering from terminal illness. Given time, many patients, even the most severely ill, adapt to their circumstances if they have sufficient support and care.

Just as a physician's response can forestall or prevent suicide, a physician's ready acceptance of the patient's decision to accept suicide or euthanasia can encourage that outcome. If the physician quickly accepts the patient's choice, the patient may feel abandoned. The physician's acceptance may also contribute to a sense of hopelessness or to feelings of guilt about burdening family and care givers. For this reason, those who advocate allowing assisted suicide or euthanasia recognize the importance of the patient-physician relationship and dialogue. They urge that physicians must carefully consider all other alternatives, and offer available palliative care and social support. They call for a dialogue in which the physician seeks to understand the meaning of the request for each patient and responds with care and concern, ultimately accepting but not encouraging the patient's decision to opt for suicide or euthanasia.

This dialogue requires commitment and compassion. The physician must listen attentively to the patient, engaging in an intensely personal exploration of the patient's feelings, of his or her relationship with others, and of the reasons why the patient has made this choice. It is a demanding and time-consuming process. In short, the qualities needed for this sensitive discussion are an ideal for medical practice and the physician-patient relationship. This ideal, if ever the norm, is less and

---

[23]As Edwin Shneidman observed, "What we fear is something worse than what we have. Oftentimes, persons literally on the ledge of committing suicide would be willing to live if things, life, were only just a little bit better, a just noticeable difference more tolerable. The common fear is that the Inferno is bottomless and that the line on internal suffering must be drawn *somewhere*. Every suicide makes this statement: This far and no further — even though he would have been willing to live on the brink." E. S. Shneidman, "Some Essentials of Suicide and Some Implications for Response," in *Suicide*, ed. A. Roy (Baltimore: Williams and Wilkins, 1986), 4.

less common in an age of high-tech medicine. In fact, the dearth of such qualities in medical practice — the willingness to listen, the openness to exploring the patient's wishes and feelings about treatment, and the ability to talk sensitively about dying — has contributed substantially to problems in making decisions about life-sustaining treatment.

Timothy Quill's article in the *New England Journal of Medicine* about how he assisted his patient to die caused such a stir in part because many believed that he presented all the "right" ingredients — a sensitive doctor with a long-standing relationship with his patient, efforts to persuade her to accept treatment, familiarity with her past struggles and her present reality, the ability to listen, and a firm belief in its importance as part of his duty to his patient.[24] One "good" case, however, is not a sufficient basis for public policy. Any law permitting assisted suicide and euthanasia will authorize doctors like Kevorkian as well as those like Quill to assist or cause their patients' deaths. While the shortcomings of Kevorkian's methods are glaring,[25] the problems generated by the practice in the hands of other doctors will be less obvious and more pervasive — doctors who are caring but harried, those who are uncomfortable talking about dying, those unable to distinguish their views from the values and needs of their patients, and those who are not ill-intentioned but perhaps indifferent to the fate of some patients with whom they have had little contact and for whom they hold no hope for recovery.[26]

Like the availability of pain relief or the skills needed to diagnose depression, the kind of doctor-patient relationship envisioned by those who advocate legalizing suicide will simply be unavailable to many

---

[24] T. E. Quill, "Death and Dignity: A Case of Individualized Decision Making," *New England Journal of Medicine* 324 (1991): 691-94. Even in this case, many have challenged the ethical and clinical acceptability of Dr. Quill's actions. See e.g., P. Wesley, "Dying Safely," *Issues in Law and Medicine* 8 (1993): 467-85; E. D. Pellegrino, "Compassion Needs Reason Too," *Journal of the American Medical Association* 270 (1993): 874-75.

[25] Kevorkian appears to have had little, if any, prior relationship with the 20 individuals whose deaths he assisted. Nor does it appear from public accounts that he counseled them about treatment alternatives, conducted an in-depth psychological evaluation, or offered palliative care. Indeed, as a retired pathologist, it is unlikely that he has any experience in treating patients who are depressed or chronically or terminally ill.

[26] In this regard, it is notable that a recent study found that "burn-out" among health care professionals correlated strongly with the willingness to endorse assisted suicide. Portenoy et al.

patients.[27] Public policy cannot be predicated on an ideal when the reality will often be quite different, with serious, irreversible consequences for patients.

Prognosticating at Life's End. One cornerstone of good medical practice is an accurate diagnosis and prognosis for the patient. In many cases, prognostication at the end of life is highly uncertain, even in the hands of the best clinicians. Some diagnoses are clear cut. Many others are not. Once the diagnosis is made, estimating the patient's life expectancy is typically more art than science. It is neither precise nor entirely predictable.

The patient's diagnosis, his or her life expectancy, and the outcome of treatment will be critical to all patients as they consider the option of an immediate death. Euthanasia and assisted suicide leave no opportunity to recognize or correct a diagnosis that is negligently provided, or provided competently, but proves incorrect over time. In contrast, when life-sustaining treatment is withdrawn or withheld, certain death does not follow if the underlying diagnosis is mistaken. Moreover, assisted suicide and euthanasia could be used for patients without an immediate life-threatening condition, including those who may have many more years of life ahead.

Overall, the risk of misdiagnosis of the patient's medical or psychiatric condition, the undertreatment of pain, and the risks of abuse must be weighed in relation to their consequences. With assisted suicide and euthanasia, the result will be the patient's death. How many instances of error or abuse render the risk unjustifiable in light of these consequences? The number of such errors or cases of abuse cannot be quantified. But given the state of the art of diagnosing and treating depression, as well as the inherent fallibility of medicine, such cases will not be rare. Taken together, the risk and the consequences yield a remarkably high price in human life for policies allowing assisted suicide and euthanasia.

An Option Without Limits

The prohibition against assisted suicide and euthanasia carries intense symbolic and practical significance. While suicide is no longer prohibited or penalized, the ban against assisted suicide and euthanasia shores up the notion of limits in human relationships. It reflects the gravity with which we view the decision to take one's own

---

[27]For further discussion of the practical problems of proposed guidelines or safeguards, see pp. 142-45.

life or the life of another, and our reluctance to encourage or promote these decisions.

If assisted suicide and euthanasia are legalized, it will reflect changed attitudes about the practices. Just as significant, it will prompt further change. Social attitudes will evolve in part because our laws convey acceptance and sanction. More far reaching will be the shift in attitude as assisted suicide or direct killing become more frequent and more widely practiced. If the practices become a standard part of the arsenal of medical treatments, it would profoundly affect our response to those cases that are sanctioned and to those that are not. The momentous nature of the actions, and the sense of caution or gravity with which they are pursued, would naturally lessen for both health care professionals and for the public. By legalizing the practices, we will blunt our moral sensibilities and perceptions.

Once assisted suicide and euthanasia are integrated into medical practice, the criteria now proposed as safeguards will prove elastic and unstable. One important criterion now rests on compassion for those who are suffering. But pain, and to a greater extent suffering, are inherently subjective. The experience of physical pain and the degree of suffering it causes depend on psychological and other personal factors. If policies on assisted suicide or euthanasia do not make the practices universally available at the request of any competent adult, the policies must define the class of eligible individuals.

Most proposals to legalize assisted suicide have rejected terminal illness as the dividing line because it would not respond to many circumstances that can cause the same degree or pain and suffering. Yet as long as the policies hinge on notions of pain or suffering they are uncontainable; neither pain nor suffering can be gauged objectively or subjected to the kind of judgments needed to fashion coherent public policy. Moreover, even if the more narrow category of terminal illness is chosen at the outset, the line is unlikely to hold for the very reason that it has not been selected by advocates of assisted suicide — the logic of suicide as a compassionate choice for patients who are in pain or suffering suggests no such limit.[28]

---

[28]While euthanasia and assisted suicide were originally proposed in the Netherlands as options for patients suffering from an incurable disease, a recent court decision approved the use of these practices for a suicidal patient suffering from depression but not any underlying physical illness. In that case, a psychiatrist assisted in the suicide of a physically healthy 50-year-old woman who was depressed following the loss of her two sons and recent divorce. W. Drozdiak, "Dutch Seek Freer Mercy Killing: Court Case Could East Limits on Assisted Suicide, Euthanasia," *Washington Post*, October 29, 1993, A 29.

Nor does the emphasis on autonomy in current debates provide an enduring or effective restraint, although to date the proposals to legalize euthanasia would allow euthanasia based solely on the consent of a competent adult. For many physicians, as well as for the public, patients incapable of consenting will, in certain respects, seem the "best" candidates for the practice — patients who are permanently unconscious, severely demented, or otherwise incapacitated. Once euthanasia becomes an accepted "therapy," the expansion to include those who are incapable of consenting would be a logical, if not inevitable, progression.

Even if the law is never changed to sanction involuntary euthanasia, the potential for abuse would be profound. This risk does not presume that physicians will act malevolently. On the contrary, this risk is substantial precisely because physicians will act with benevolent motives. Once euthanasia is established as a "therapeutic" alternative, the line between patients competent to consent and those who are not will seem arbitrary to some doctors. To others, it will seem outright discriminatory or unjust to deny a therapy because of the patient's incapacity to consent.[29] As with other medical decisions, some doctors will feel that they can and should make a decision in their patient's best interests, for patients clearly incapable of consenting and for those with marginal or uncertain capacity to consent.[30]

Experience in the Netherlands suggests that this type of abuse or expansion, resulting in nonvoluntary euthanasia, would be significant. Since 1984, guidelines have tacitly allowed euthanasia in response to a repeated and voluntary request from a suffering, competent patient. Although nonvoluntary euthanasia performed without the patient's request is prohibited, nonvoluntary euthanasia has been conducted in a substantial number of cases. The most extensive study of euthanasia

---

[29]As described by one Dutch physician who consented to euthanasia for his severely impaired newborn son, "I concur that autonomy ought to be the point of departure in euthanasia decisions, but it should not be the only principle considered. Because newborns cannot exercise autonomy does not mean that they should be denied beneficence. There are many less important decisions we make in their behalf, why should they be denied perhaps the most caring choice of all?" C. Spreeuwenberg, "The Story of Laurens," *Cambridge Quarterly* 2 (1993): A261-63.

[30]The much publicized article "It's Over, Debbie" that appeared anonymously in the *Journal of the American Medical Association* illustrates this point well. In that case, the physician had no prior relationship with the patient and no knowledge of her capacity to consent to euthanasia. He decided that she was suffering and responded to her mumbled words "Let's get this over with," by returning to her room several minutes later and giving her a lethal dose of morphine. "It's Over, Debbie," *Journal of the American Medical Association* 259 (1988): 272.

in the Netherlands reported that in 1990 approximately 1.8 percent of all deaths resulted from voluntary euthanasia. An additional 0.8 percent of all deaths represented euthanasia performed without a contemporaneous request from the patient.[31] If euthanasia were practiced in a comparable percentage of cases in the United States, voluntary euthanasia would account for about 36,000 deaths each year, and euthanasia without the patient's consent would occur in an additional 16,000 deaths.

The Task Force members regard this risk as unacceptable. They also believe that the risk of such abuse is neither speculative nor distant, but an inevitable byproduct of the transition from policy to practice in the diverse circumstances in which the practices would be employed.

The Alternatives for Public Policy

Support for legalizing assisted suicide and euthanasia rests in part on the belief that individuals should have the right to assistance to end their lives at a time and in a manner they choose. None of the Task Force members believes that respect for autonomy dictates the legalization of assisted suicide and euthanasia. The moral claim to autonomy is weakened by both the overall risks of the practice and the extraordinary nature of the remedy sought. Moreover, if assisted suicide and euthanasia are legalized, the autonomy of some patients would be extended while the autonomy of others would be compromised by the pressures to exercise these new options.

The legalization of assisted suicide and euthanasia is also urged on grounds of mercy and the alleviation of suffering. Some of the Task Force members believe that the practices offer clear benefits to certain patients who are dying or otherwise suffering greatly. They recognize that providing a quick, less prolonged death for some patients can be a compassionate act. These members, however, regard the number of cases when assisted suicide or euthanasia are medically and ethically appropriate as extremely rare. They do not believe that the benefits incurred for this small number of

---

[31]An alternative measure used in the study suggests that nonvoluntary euthanasia occurred in 1.6% of all deaths. P. J. Van der Maas et al., "Euthanasia and Other Medical Decisions Concerning the End of Life," *Lancet* 338 (1991): 669-74. A more recent study asked the physicians who performed nonvoluntary euthanasia for further information. Only 56% of nonvoluntary euthanasia cases involved patients who lacked decision-making capacity at the time of death; in the remaining 44% of cases, euthanasia was performed on competent (36%) or possibly competent (8%) patients without an explicit request. L. Pijnenborg et al., "Life-Terminating Acts Without Explicit Request," *Lancet* 341 (1993): 1196-99.

patients can justify a major shift in public policy or the serious risks that legalizing the practice would entail.

Public support for legalizing assisted suicide and euthanasia can be attributed in part to fear of the dying process — fear of losing control in the face of modern medical technologies and fear of dying in pain. Both fears arise from the failure of clinical practice to use modern medical advances well. In the one case, medical technologies to sustain life have been overused, subjecting patients to unwanted and burdensome treatment. In the other, medical techniques to relieve pain are remarkably underutilized.

Many patients now experience a more protracted and more painful death than could be provided if existing medical alternatives were applied well. In particular, modern pain relief and palliative care, appropriately used, can relieve pain in all but very rare cases. These techniques, such as a self-administered opioid drip, can give patients direct control over their treatment. With effective pain relief, the disability and suffering associated with severe pain can also be ameliorated for the vast majority of patients. In fact, although many patients express suicidal ideation at some time in the course of their illness, few commit or attempt suicide when offered appropriate support.

The Task Force urges steps to enhance pain relief and improve the psychological treatment available to terminally and severely ill patients. The members recognize that such remedies, even when implemented well, will not relieve the pain of all patients. They feel deep compassion for patients in those rare cases when pain cannot be alleviated even with the most aggressive palliative care. They believe, however, that legalizing assisted suicide or euthanasia to make the practices readily available to these patients would create widespread and unjustified risks for many others.

Enhanced pain relief, no matter how well or widely administered, will not offer a panacea for the broader problem of human suffering. Inherently subjective, the experience of suffering covers a wide range of human situations — individuals who are disabled or fear the onset of disability; those who are terminally or chronically ill but free of severe pain; and individuals who are isolated and alone, as well as those who face the despair imposed by poverty and deprivation. In some cases, such as quadriplegia, the disability and associated dependence may be almost total. In others, it is not physical pain or impairment that causes despair, but anticipated physical decline and loss of control. For some individuals, suffering arises from mental illness that is either long-standing and somatic such as schizophrenia or from severe symptoms of depression.

Caring health care professionals can sometimes relieve the patient's suffering: a disabled person may benefit from physical therapy or equipment to increase functioning; clinical depression is often treatable, even in the presence of chronic or terminal illness; and social work support or psychological counseling can improve personal relationships and help to minimize social isolation. But suffering also often stems from causes that lie totally outside the realm of physical symptoms and medical cures. Indeed, suicides by terminally ill persons are a small fraction of the suicide attempts and suicides committed each year in the United States.

The Task Force members believe that medically assisted dying and direct medical killing are unacceptable societal responses to the problem of human suffering. Compared to the resources, caring, and compassion needed to respond to suffering individuals, a lethal prescription or injection would offer a simple solution for profoundly human and complex dilemmas. It would also extend medicine from the realm of care or cure to dispensing death for problems endemic to the human condition.

Apart from the number of patients who would actually seek assisted death or euthanasia, those who advocate legalizing the practices maintain that many individuals would benefit from knowing that these options are available, even if they never use them. Clearly, whatever other meanings they may carry, the practices have become a potent symbol of control. For some segment of the public, assisted suicide and euthanasia represent a sense of empowerment and a certain means of escape from a painful, intolerable death. Given the data showing how few terminally ill patients actually commit suicide if adequate pain relief and support are provided, this desire for an assisted death appears to appeal most to those who are healthy, not to those who are ill.

The Task Force members believe that it is important for individuals to have a sense of control over their medical destiny at life's end. Instead of assistance to commit suicide or laws that would make a lethal injection available upon request, they advocate enhanced pain relief and palliative care and improvement in our laws and practices for decisions about life-sustaining treatment. Effective implementation of existing laws on treatment decisions would enable patients and those close to them to refuse life-sustaining treatment that prolonged the patient's suffering. Experience with many of these laws, such as the health care proxy law in New York State, is still relatively limited. However, an estimated 10 to 15 percent of the population has already signed a health care proxy. Available studies also show that most people are convinced of the importance of advance planning. These data point to the potential success of further outreach as public habits evolve. In addition, laws that allow family members and others to decide about treatment in the absence of an advance directive are newly enacted in many states. Some states like New York are considering, but have not passed, this kind of legislation.[32] These laws also promise significant change, and a greater sense of control for patients and those closest to them. Finally, it appears that professional practices and attitudes are changing, reflecting more willingness by physicians to talk with patients about treatment options.

All in all, it is too early to declare policies on decisions for life-sustaining treatment a failure and move on to more drastic remedies. Instead, health care professionals and other segments of society must be committed to translating existing legal alternatives into effective and compassionate practice at the bedside.

The debate on assisted suicide and euthanasia has also highlighted the severe shortcomings of current pain relief practices and palliative care.[33] Although some health care professionals and others had commented on this problem previously and sought to promote change, awareness of the problem was not widespread. Nor has the medical community made the commitment needed to give pain relief and palliative care a higher priority in medical training and practice. Extensive measures to educate the public about pain relief have also not been undertaken. In short, the lack of effective pain relief and palliative care is a problem that society has just started to tackle.

These steps will not eliminate all support for legalizing assisted suicide and euthanasia. Nor will they respond to all cases or reasons why patients might seek relief through these practices. Yet, they might address the public concern that seems to underlie support for assisted suicide and euthanasia. Press coverage of end-of-life choices has long obscured the distinction between refusing treatment and euthanasia — both practices have been labeled with the "right-to-die" rubric. Public opinion polls are imprecise and unclear, providing no sense of whether

---

[32]Assembly Bill No. 7166. The surrogate decisions legislation was proposed by the Task Force and is part of Governor Cuomo's legislative program for 1994. Many professional and civic organizations testified in support of the bill at public hearings.

[33]For specific recommendations by the Task Force to change existing law, regulations, and clinical practice to enhance pain relief, see chapter 8.

the public understands the distinctions between stopping treatment, assisted suicide, and euthanasia. The polls have also yielded little insight about the public's real concerns about the dying process.

If the refusal of treatment and effective pain relief became available alternatives, the public might assess the need for assisted suicide and euthanasia quite differently. The plea for autonomy would still retain an intuitive appeal, but the felt need for the options might diminish significantly if we used our existing clinical and legal resources more wisely and effectively.

Inherent Ethical Objections

Our laws prohibiting assisted suicide and euthanasia are long-standing. Historically, they have rested on both an assessment of consequences and a judgment that it is intrinsically wrong for one person to assist another to commit suicide or to take another person's life, even with the best or most benevolent of motives. Our society has long regarded this proscription against killing or aiding a suicide, except in defense of self or others, as fundamental to our social fabric and to the boundaries established in our relationships with one another.

Some of the Task Force members believe that assisted suicide and euthanasia are inherently wrong. The practices presume an absolute dominion over human life, by both the person who commits suicide or consents to be killed and the person who acts to make that possible. Fear of death, the discomfort of disability, anxiety about aging, or despair at personal failures, among other reasons, may have rendered this control appealing throughout human history. But American society has never obliged; it has never affirmatively sanctioned suicide or set forth rules for those who assist or kill another. Embedded in that judgment has been a sense of the limits of human power and control. These Task Force members believe that this limit should not be abandoned.

These Task Force members are also deeply concerned that assisted suicide and euthanasia will foster disrespect for human life. Both practices render human life dispensable; death becomes another problem to be mastered or managed, rather than a distinct and inviolable part of our humanness. The dignity of human life itself precludes policies that would allow it to be disposed of so easily. Respect for human life also makes an agreement that aims at death ethically unacceptable as a basis for human relationships.

Some Task Force members are most troubled by the prospect of medicalizing the practices — they believe that physicians should neither assist their patients to commit suicide nor kill them, even with benevolent motives. Many of the physicians, as well as others on the Task Force, embrace this view. They regard both assisted suicide and euthanasia as inherently and irreconcilably incompatible with medical practice.[34]

These Task Force members, like the Task Force as a whole, believe that physicians have an ethical duty to alleviate pain. They strongly endorse public and professional programs that would enhance effective pain relief and give pain relief a higher priority in medical education, training, and practice. But they do not believe that the professional obligation to alleviate suffering can justify allowing physicians to kill their patients or to assist suicide. In their view, physicians cannot assist their patients' suicide or perform euthanasia without violating values that are intrinsic to the practice of medicine and to the patient-physician relationship.

Physicians wield enormous power in their relationship with patients. This power itself demands clear boundaries. Policies and laws allowing physicians to withhold or withdraw life-sustaining treatment, in consultation with patients or others close to the patient, recognize the limits of what medicine can achieve. This sense of limits should not suggest, nor should it support, the medicalization of assisted suicide or direct killing.

Finally, these members believe that granting physicians authority to assist suicide and perform euthanasia would have deeply troubling consequences for the patient-physician relationship. It would erode the commitment of physicians and other health care professionals to care for dying and incurably ill patients. Patients in turn might be fearful that they would become candidates for these "treatments," or might worry about the consequences of refusing these options once they are presented by their physician. Most significant, those members believe that once physicians are licensed to kill as a therapeutic alternative, the public image of the medical profession and the medical art will be

---

[34] This conflation of healing and killing was in fact central to the medicalization of euthanasia in the Nazi regime. In sharp contrast to the current euthanasia movement, which espouses the practice for the good of patients, the Nazi medical vision focused on the health and good of the nation, or *Volk*, not the patient's own wishes to die. Nonetheless, as Robert Jay Lifton describes in the introduction to his powerful, meticulously documented book, *The Nazi Doctors*, "My argument in this study is that the medicalization of killing — the imagery of killing in the name of healing — was crucial to that terrible step. At the heart of the Nazi enterprise, then, is the destruction of the boundary between healing and killing." R. J. Lifton, *The Nazi Doctors: Medical Killing and the Psychology of Genocide* (New York: Basic Books, 1986), 14.

damaged irrevocably. For all these reasons, some of the Task Force members have concluded not only that the nature and goals of medicine offer no special reason that doctors should be exempted from the general prohibition against killing, but that it would be especially inappropriate and harmful to make doctors the repository of legally sanctioned killing or suicide assistance.

Private Acts and Public Policy

Other Task Force members do not share the conclusion that assisted suicide is inherently unethical or incompatible with medical practice. On the contrary, some members believe that it is not intrinsically wrong for doctors or others to assist suicide in some cases. In fact, they believe that in appropriate circumstances, this assistance would manifest a physician's commitment and duty to his or her patient. Nonetheless, these members believe that legalizing assisted suicide would be unwise and dangerous public policy for the reasons discussed above. Essentially, they concluded that ethical, compassionate actions by thoughtful individuals in some cases cannot be translated into good public policy.

These members can envision rare cases when assisted suicide offers patients relief from pain and a prolonged dying that cannot be ameliorated by currently available medical practice. They believe that in such cases suicide can be an ethically acceptable choice for both the patient and for the physician or others who assist the patient. They think that this option can be a rational response to an intolerable situation. They would, however, oppose any change in existing law to make such assistance legal.

Several facts played a critical role in the judgment reached by these members. They recognize that in extreme cases when assistance to commit suicide is most compelling, patients may now find a physician willing to provide medication and information. It is highly unlikely that physicians who are thoughtful and responsible in providing this assistance will face criminal sanctions; given the sympathies of juries and the difficulties of proving intention in the private interaction between doctor and patient, prosecutors have not been eager to bring these cases.

Although the law barring assisted suicide and euthanasia is rarely enforced, these Task Force members believe that this legal prohibition serves important purposes. In addition to regulating and restraining behavior, our laws also serve a highly symbolic function. These members regard the consequences of quietly tolerating assisted suicide as a private act of agreement between two individuals in extreme cases as profoundly different from the consequences of legalizing the practice. The legal prohibition, while not uniformly honored, preserves the gravity of conduct to assist suicide. It demands caution and reflection. It maintains the decision by both patient and physician as a solemn, private act and prevents abuse. It also requires a deep commitment by health care professionals who must violate the law to offer this assistance to patients.

These Task Force members acknowledge the inherent tension and discomfort of a position that prohibits actions they believe are ethically justifiable. They recognize the problems of a policy that renders relief for patients, albeit in rare cases, contingent on the moral courage of health care professionals and on their willingness to violate the law. Significant too is the fact that some physicians now provide suicide assistance without the benefit of guidelines that would be established if the state and the medical profession sanctioned and regulated the practice.[35] Finally, they recognize the shortcomings of a policy that leaves physicians who act responsibly and with the best of motives subject to possible criminal or professional sanctions for conduct that is legally proscribed but caring and appropriate.

On balance, even considering these reasons to legalize assisted suicide, these members unanimously concluded that the prohibition against assisted suicide should not be changed. While not a tidy or perfect resolution, it serves the interests of patients far better than legalizing the practice. By curtailing the autonomy of patients in a very small number of cases when assisted suicide is a compelling and justifiable response, it preserves the autonomy and well-being of many others. It also prevents the widespread abuses that would be likely to occur if assisted suicide were legalized.

Some Further Thoughts About Euthanasia

With a few exceptions, the Task Force members believe that euthanasia is ethically unacceptable under any circumstances. They regard euthanasia as morally more objectionable and socially more dangerous than assisted suicide. The ethical distinction arises because the moral agency of the person who performs euthanasia, whether it is a physician, family member, or other person, is more

---

[35] The number of physicians willing to assist suicides without the benefit of protection from liability is far smaller than the number who would participate if the practice were legal. The fact that physicians must take some risk and act out of commitment to their patients is itself a valuable safeguard.

direct. Euthanasia is another form of killing, albeit with consent and for benevolent motives.

With assisted suicide, the patient takes his or her own life, although those who assist also bear moral responsibility for their actions. This difference in moral agency, and the fact that it is the patient, not another person, who takes the final step, has significant implications for the risks posed by the practices. Most important, assisted suicide always involves a patient who is competent, or who at least has the capacity to take the medication provided or to perform any other last act required to achieve death. In contrast, as discussed above, euthanasia need not distinguish between the competent and the incompetent. Indeed, any such distinction is unlikely to hold either in medical practice or public policy. The notion of medical killing of individuals without consent under guidelines sanctioned or un-sanctioned by the state, even for the most benevolent of motives, is profoundly disquieting.

Euthanasia is more troubling even for patients who are competent to consent to their deaths. Many individuals may feel ambivalent and uncertain when confronting their own imminent death. The willingness of their physician or family members to perform euthanasia may overcome that ambivalence, or leave people feeling that the momentum toward their death cannot be forestalled or reversed. The potential to abuse the practice by causing death without the patient's consent is also far stronger with euthanasia than with assisted suicide. Given the private nature of the doctor-patient relationship and medical decisions, this kind of abuse would be difficult to prevent and to identify.

Response to Proposed Guidelines to Legalize Assisted Suicide

The Task Force examined, and ultimately rejected, proposals to legalize assisted suicide. One of the most thoughtful of these proposals was presented in a 1992 article entitled "Care of the Hopelessly Ill: Proposed Criteria for Physician-Assisted Suicide," by three doctors.[36] The authors recommend that physician-assisted suicide should be legalized. They also propose criteria to guide physicians in determining when to comply with a patient's request for suicide assistance: the patient must suffer from an incurable condition; the patient must

---

[36] T. E. Quill, C. K. Cassel, and D. E. Meier, "Care of the Hopelessly Ill: Proposed Clinical Criteria for Physician-Assisted Suicide," *New England Journal of Medicine* 327 (1992): 1380-84.

repeatedly request suicide assistance; his or her judgment must not be distorted by reversible depression; the doctor-patient relationship must be meaningful; the physician should insure that the patient receives good palliative care; and the physician should consult with another doctor and document the decision-making process. The authors suggest that in appropriate cases, physicians should prescribe a lethal dose of medication, which "should ideally be taken in the physician's presence." They argue that legalizing physician-assisted suicide would help suffering patients who wish to end their lives, and would allow physicians and loved ones to remain with them at the end of life without facing legal liability.[37]

The Task Force believes that such a policy poses severe risks to large numbers of patients, especially those who are most disadvantaged. Some of the members also reject this policy because they believe that assisted suicide is morally unacceptable even with the "best" of practices. The care of many patients currently fails to meet generally accepted standards of high-quality clinical practice. These failures are most egregious for poor and socially disadvantaged individuals, and for patients in large, overburdened facilities serving the urban and rural poor. Many will not have the benefit of skilled pain management and comfort care. Indeed, a recent study found that patients treated for cancer at centers that care predominantly for minority individuals were three times more likely to receive inadequate therapy to relieve pain.[38] Many patients will also lack access to psychiatric services. Furthermore, for most patients who are terminally or severely ill, routine psychiatric consultation would be inadequate to diagnose reliably whether the patient is suffering from depression.[39]

Many patients from all sectors of society cannot rely on a physician-patient relationship marked by good communication, personal concern, and respect. It is unlikely that patients who now face difficulties in obtaining minimally acceptable treatment would receive the excellent care and personal support essential to the proposal.[40] Efforts to

---

[37]Ibid.

[38]C. S. Cleeland et al., "Pain and Its Treatment in Outpatients with Metastatic Cancer," *New England Journal of Medicine* 320 (1994): 592-96.

[39]See the discussion in chapters 1 and 8 on the difficulty of diagnosing depression in this group of patients.

[40]Two psychiatrists write: "The guidelines of Quill and colleagues require effective, collaborative, and committed doctor-patient relationships. They rely on the abilities of physicians to detect or determine when contemplation is rational and not 'distorted.' Such relationships between patients and skilled physicians exist, no doubt,

increase access and assure quality have had uneven results at best. In short, it is improbable that the proposed clinical criteria will serve as effective safeguards for vulnerable patients.

It is unclear to what extent the authors of the guidelines intend their recommendations to provide legal safeguards that could be enforced to prevent poor practices or abuse. The proposal instead seems to suggest guidance for physicians confronted with a request for assistance in suicide. The safeguards proposed depend on the conscientious and largely subjective judgment of each physician. For example, the criteria suggest that the physician determine that the doctor patient relationship is "meaningful," and that he or she has been able to "get to know the patient in order to understand fully the reasons for the request."[41] Physicians will interpret this requirement in entirely different ways. To date, both Quill and Kevorkian have stated that they were able effectively to evaluate patients' requests for assistance to commit suicide.

Other criteria proposed are necessarily subjective, but for that reason would be an elastic and ineffective guidepost for public policy and sanctioned private behavior. For example, the patient need not be terminally ill but must "have a condition that is incurable and associated with severe, unrelenting suffering." The physician's own judgments about the reasonableness of the patient's request would be decisive, a judgment that would depend almost entirely on the personal views of each physician and the way he or she values the patient's life.

The impetus to expand these or other stipulated criteria is especially strong under the proposed guidelines because the guidelines present assisted suicide as a medical treatment. Some advocates have portrayed assisted suicide as an exceptional action when treatment fails.[42] However, the authors present physician-assisted suicide as "part of the continuum of options for comfort care,"[43] although one that should be available only when alternatives fail. Some physicians

---

but how common are they in 1993? Indeed, current social and economic pressures make these qualities more precarious, not less. Managed competition and cost control are necessary and likely, but they will not encourage leisurely interactions or time to 'just talk.'" E. D. Caine and Y. C. Conwell, "Self-determined Death, the Physician, and Medical Priorities: Is There Time to Talk?" *Journal of the American Medical Association* 270 (1993): 875-76.

[41]Quill, Cassel, and Meier, 1382.

[42]S. H. Wanzer et al., "The Physician's Responsibility Toward Hopelessly Ill Patients: A Second Look," *New England Journal of Medicine* 327 (1992): 1384-88.

[43]Quill, Cassel and Meier, 1381.

will undoubtedly feel that requirements that they may find arbitrary should not prevent them from offering a suffering patient a "treatment" to end life.

Permitting physicians to assist the suicide of patients physically capable of committing suicide, and characterizing this action as a "treatment," would also lead to acceptance of voluntary euthanasia for patients physically unable to perform the final act. In individual cases, the line between assisted suicide and euthanasia may be blurred. This risk is especially great because the proposal permits, and in fact encourages, the physician's presence when the patient commits suicide. As others have argued, the physician's presence raises additional concerns because patients who are ambivalent or hesitant may find it harder to delay or change the decision to die.

The authors of the guidelines on assisted suicide reject legalizing euthanasia because of the risks the practice would entail. They also acknowledge that continued prohibition of euthanasia carries a cost to some incurably ill patients who wish to end their lives:

> Such persons ... must not be abandoned to their suffering; a combination of decisions to forgo life-sustaining treatment (including food and fluids) with aggressive comfort measures (such as analgesics and sedatives) could be offered, along with a commitment to search for creative alternatives. We acknowledge that this solution is less than ideal, but we also recognize that in the United States access to medical care is currently too inequitable, and many doctor-patient relationships too impersonal, for us to tolerate the risks of permitting active voluntary euthanasia.[44]

The Task Force agrees. These same risks render assisted suicide unacceptable. While euthanasia is socially more dangerous, the same systemic problems undermine the reliability of any proposed safeguards for assisted suicide. Moreover, assisted suicide and euthanasia are closely linked; as experience in the Netherlands has shown, once assisted suicide is embraced, euthanasia will seem only a neater and simpler option to doctors and their patients.[45]

---

[44]Quill, Cassel, and Meier, 1381.

[45]In the Netherlands, assisted suicide and voluntary euthanasia are both legally sanctioned. A lethal injection is preferred by both doctors and patients as a simpler option. Only a small percentage of cases are assisted suicides; a recent study reported that of all voluntary euthanasia and assisted suicide deaths, 85% are attributed to voluntary euthanasia and 15% to assisted suicide. Van Der Maas et al.

Distinguishing Decisions to
Forgo Life-Sustaining Treatment

Promoting patient autonomy has been central to public policies on life-sustaining treatment over the past two decades. The Task Force has proposed four laws that enhance autonomy and the well-being of patients in decisions about life-sustaining treatment. Three of those laws have been enacted and one is pending. A distinction between decisions to forgo life-sustaining measures and assisted suicide and euthanasia is crucial to the Task Force's position on both issues, and to the coherence of the policies it has proposed for New York State.

Some of the Task Force members believe that intention provides a moral dividing line between forgoing treatment and assisting suicide or performing euthanasia. With the former, the patient and physician accept the patient's death as a consequence of stopping or withholding treatment that is unwanted or unduly burdensome. They do not, however, aim to achieve the patient's death. Other members do not distinguish the two practices based on intention, but believe that the difference between allowing the patient to die a natural death and intervening to cause death directly is ethically significant. All the Task Force members agree that allowing decisions to forgo life-sustaining treatment and allowing assisted suicide or euthanasia have radically different consequences and meanings for public policy.

Existing law prohibits assisted suicide and euthanasia in all cases. A similar ban for all decisions to stop or to withhold life-sustaining treatment would be unthinkable. It would lead to inhumane and abusive medical treatment. It would also be an extraordinary intrusion on individual liberty.

If a patient is denied medically assisted suicide or euthanasia, he or she is likely to die more slowly of natural causes. When a competent patient is denied the option of refusing treatment, he or she will not only have life prolonged, but must be physically forced to undergo unwanted treatment. Whether the treatments are highly invasive such as chemotherapy or a respirator, or are generally regarded as less intrusive such as antibiotics, the patient's body is physically invaded without consent. Under the common law, this is called battery.

In many cases, the patient must also be physically restrained to accept the treatment; for example, when resisting patients are force fed because they are demented or unable to consent to the removal of treatment, the patient's hands are sometimes tied to the bed to prevent the patient from removing the feeding tube. For patients who are competent and physically mobile, the restraint on freedom would be even harsher, since imposing treatment would require involuntary detention. While such detention is now practiced in some cases to force patients to undergo treatment for contagious diseases such as multi-drug-resistant tuberculosis, this extreme denial of individual freedom is tolerated only because of the immediate danger of contagion and life-threatening harm to others.

Even the firmest supporters of assisted suicide and euthanasia would acknowledge that only a relatively small percentage of patients in hospitals and nursing homes today would use the practices, if legal. In contrast, a significant percentage of those cared for in modern medical facilities undergo life-sustaining treatment. It is estimated that approximately 70 percent of the deaths in hospitals today involve some decision to withhold or to stop treatment. In many cases, the decision to initiate treatment is often acceptable to the patient and to health care professionals because treatment can be withdrawn or withheld if the patient's condition worsens or the treatment proves intolerable for the patient.

Years of experience with life-sustaining treatment have yielded hard lessons about the burden that such treatment can impose on dying and severely ill patients. A policy that uniformly prohibited decisions to stop such treatments once they had begun would result in incalculable harm. In short, use of the treatments is inconceivable without policies that allow their discontinuance in appropriate circumstances. Those policies entail some of the same risks posed by assisted suicide and euthanasia — the possibility that physicians will not diagnose depression, treat pain adequately, or explore other alternatives with the patient and family. However, the benefits of the treatments, and the corresponding need to allow decisions to forgo them in many cases, far outweigh those risks. Indeed, it renders the willingness to undertake the risks a moral and social imperative.

Under current policies, the appropriateness of stopping or withholding treatment for competent patients has been tied to autonomy — to the patient's own values and preferences. This is not just sound public policy, but the only acceptable alternative in a pluralist society. Decisions to accept or to refuse treatment call for choices about the value and nature of human life, tolerance for disability and dependence, and our relationships to family members and to others. As a society, we share no single belief about these profoundly personal questions. Even if held by a majority, one response could not be imposed on those who disagreed.

The decision to commit suicide or to consent to a lethal injection is also tied to personal values and beliefs. But embracing autonomy in the sphere of decisions about life-sustaining treatment does not mandate recognition of a right to assisted suicide and euthanasia. Among individual rights, only the right to believe is absolute. All the others are qualified; they are calibrated depending on the strength of the claim to freedom and the consequences for society as a whole. Our constitutional law as well as our broader structure of civil laws and policies are built on this foundation of social judgments. In the arena of medical choices, as in other spheres of our collective life, autonomy is not all or nothing. Even if the lines are hard to draw, the necessity for doing so is no less compelling.

While the Task Force members are concerned about the movement to legalize assisted suicide and euthanasia, they have consistently rejected any arguments to deny the right to refuse life-sustaining treatment based on notions of a slippery slope to assisted suicide and euthanasia. Grounding policies for life-sustaining treatment on such fears would lead to serious harm to patients. It would also fuel the movement for assisted suicide and euthanasia, a movement that draws considerable strength from public fears of an intolerable death prolonged by medical advances. Those fears are not baseless; they are unfortunately now grounded in experience. Policies and laws that deny individuals and those close to them the option of refusing unwanted burdensome treatment will not dampen the public desire for control, but will only heighten demands for more drastic and absolute steps.[46]

---

[46]As Joseph Cardinal Bernadin argued in discussing policies about withdrawing and withholding artificial nutrition and hydration, "The challenge is to develop a nuanced public policy to protect against an attitude that could erode respect for the inviolable dignity of human life. If we do not resolve this critical issue in a way that agrees with the common sense of people of good will, we may contribute to the sense of desperation that will lead people to accept euthanasia as an alternative solution to the problem." Joseph Cardinal Bernardin, "Context for and Moral Principles Guiding Catholic Conference of Illinois' Position on Senate Bill 2213," Meeting of Pro-Life Department, Catholic Conference of Illinois, Sept. 11, 1990, p.8.

7

Developing Professional Medical Standards

The medical profession has traditionally established standards of conduct that govern its members. The standards are set in a variety of ways, including statements by professional bodies such as the American Medical Association, the actual practice of physicians, expert opinion by physicians, and clinical research findings. The standards also generally adhere to parameters or policies established by the criminal and civil law. By delineating the boundaries of appropriate medical conduct, professional standards provide guidance to physicians on many aspects of clinical practice, including physicians' duties to patients, the patient-physician relationship, and ethical dilemmas posed by treatment decisions.

Ultimately, the responsibility for establishing guidelines for medical practice rests with the medical profession itself. However, certain ethical principles have emerged from the Task Force's deliberations on assisted suicide and euthanasia that provide a useful framework within which such guidelines can be formed. The Task Force believes that professional standards should recognize the provision of effective pain relief and palliative care, including treatment for depression or referral for treatment, as a basic obligation all physicians owe to their patients. The Task Force has also concluded that the legal prohibitions against euthanasia and intentional or reckless suicide assistance provide valuable guidance for professional standards of conduct.

The medical profession should not simply restate legal principles in setting professional standards on these sensitive issues. In particular, concepts such as "intention" and "recklessness" must be applied in the context of the profession's own standards of accepted medical care. By addressing these concepts in ways that are relevant to concerns that routinely arise in clinical practice, the medical profession can assist physicians who care for seriously and terminally ill patients and enhance the care provided to these patients.

The principles identified by the Task Force are set forth below. The Task Force believes that these principles will offer important guidance for physicians while respecting the need for professional judgment in formulating treatment recommendations.

- Physicians have a professional obligation to provide appropriate pain relief and palliative care.

- Physicians have a professional obligation to assess and treat depression or refer patients for treatment.

- Physicians should not refrain from discussing a patient's suicidal thoughts, and indeed should explore, discuss, and respond to a patient's indications of suicidal thinking. This is an important aspect of care and also may facilitate prevention of suicide.

- Physicians should not perform euthanasia or assist a patient to commit suicide. However, the provision of medication that may hasten a patient's death is ethically and professionally acceptable, provided the medication is not intended to cause the patient's death or to assist the patient to commit suicide, and the medication is provided in accord with accepted medical standards.

- A physician may appropriately provide medication in the face of a known risk of suicide, provided that the benefits of the medication outweigh the risk and the physician has considered the comparable benefits and risks of alternative treatment options.

- The provision of medication used by a patient to commit suicide does not, in itself, establish that the physician intended to assist the patient to commit suicide. Rather, an evaluation of the physician's intent must take into account a range of factors, such as the physician's reasons for providing the specific amount and type of medication, and whether the amount and type of medication could have served a legitimate medical purpose for the particular patient in light of identified treatment goals.

The Task Force encourages professional medical societies to expand on these principles by formulating guidelines for the care and treatment of seriously ill patients. Such guidelines should recognize that suicide assistance and euthanasia are not permitted, but must also seek to promote the appropriate provision of pain relief. Reducing misunderstanding and unwarranted fears of professional sanctions for providing pain medication should be a central goal of professional standards. The guidelines should recognize that, as with other treatments, physicians should document their decisions about pain medication and the reasons for those decisions.

In New York State, the State Board for Professional Medical Conduct has a special obligation to apply professional medical standards in particular cases to determine whether a physician has breached accepted standards of care and, if so, to determine the penalty that should result. The board should determine the penalty from the full range of penalties available, weighing the particular circumstances of each case.

8

Caring for Severely Ill Patients

The debate about euthanasia and assisted suicide has highlighted pervasive and serious shortcomings in the care of terminally ill and chronically ill patients. These patients, as well as others who experience pain and suffering, often receive inadequate relief from pain and other debilitating symptoms despite the fact that effective treatments are available.[1] In addition, many physicians fail to discuss treatment options and the possibility of forgoing treatment with patients in a timely and appropriate manner, leading to overtreatment and a sense of isolation and powerlessness on the part of patients and those close to them.

The Task Force believes that improving care for terminally and severely ill patients is critically important. It is crucial not just as a response to those who seek assisted suicide and euthanasia, but as a basic obligation to all patients whose pain and suffering could be alleviated with responsible medical care. The Task Force's recommendations for improving the provision of pain relief and care for severely ill patients are set forth below.

Decisions About Life-Sustaining Treatment

Patients' participation in treatment decisions contributes to their sense of self and well-being. Physicians should seek patients' participation in decisions about withdrawing or withholding life-sustaining treatment early enough in the course of illness to give patients a meaningful opportunity to have their wishes and values respected.

Competent adults have a firmly established legal right to decide about treatment. Unfortunately, this right often is not realized in clinical practice, leaving patients feeling helpless and fearful about the dying process. Advance planning and discussion about treatment al-

---

[1]See chapter 3.

ternatives is the best way to give patients greater control over the course of their treatment.

When health care professionals engage in a dialogue with patients about treatment, they manifest respect and care for patients and enhance patients' sense of dignity and self-worth. In addition, patients' participation in the decision-making process fosters decisions that promote their interests and personal values, enabling them to guide their course of treatment and to refuse unwanted medical interventions.[2] Advance planning for decisions about life-sustaining treatment is especially important. In addition to giving patients a greater role in the treatment process, advance discussions about life-sustaining treatment offer health care professionals the opportunity to assure patients that they will continue to receive care to alleviate pain and maximize their quality of life, even if they decide to forgo life-sustaining measures or aggressive medical treatments.

Two types of advance directives are widely used: a living will, which specifies treatment wishes, and a health care proxy, which appoints someone (an "agent") to decide about treatment on the patient's behalf.[3] Given the difficulties of anticipating in advance the patient's medical condition and treatments that will be available at some future time, the Task Force on Life and the Law strongly endorses the health care proxy as the better approach.[4] Individuals can leave treatment instructions to guide their health care agent, but they are not required to do so. However, all those who sign a health care proxy should be encouraged to discuss their treatment goals and general preferences with their agent. When advising patients, health care professionals should also stress that the proxy is not just a way to refuse treatment, but a way to choose someone the patient trusts to consent to treatment

---

[2]See, e.g., New York State Task Force on Life and the Law, *When Others Must Choose: Deciding for Patients Without Capacity* (New York: New York State Task Force on Life and the Law, 1992); President's Commission for the Study of Ethical Problems in Medicine and Biomedical and Behavioral Research, *Deciding to Forego Life-Sustaining Treatment* (Washington: U.S. Government Printing Office, 1983); R. R. Faden and T. L. Beauchamp, *A History and Theory of Informed Consent* (New York: Oxford University Press, 1986); E. D. Pellegrino and D. C. Thomasma, *For the Patient's Good* (New York: Oxford University Press, 1988).

[3]For discussion of law on advance directives see chapter 4, pp. 50-52.

[4]New York State Task Force on Life and the Law, *Life-Sustaining Treatment: Making Decisions and Appointing a Health Care Agent* (New York: New York State Task Force on Life and the Law, 1987); T. E. Miller, "Public Policy in the Wake of Cruzan: A Case Study of New York's Health Care Proxy Law," *Law, Medicine and Health Care* 18 (1990): 360-67.

and decide about the course of treatment in consultation with physicians.

The majority of patients and the public are already convinced about the importance of advance planning for medical decisions.[5] Studies consistently show that patients would like to discuss life-sustaining treatment and advance directives with their physician. Furthermore, many patients expect their physician to initiate the conversation. Relatively few patients, however, have actually discussed life-sustaining measures with their doctor.[6]

Physicians are often reluctant to discuss life-sustaining treatment or advance directives with patients, and wait for patients to raise the issue. This failure to talk with patients appears to stem from diverse reasons. These include unjustified concerns by some physicians that the discussion itself will harm the patient, discomfort and lack of experience in talking about dying, and a failure to recognize the conversation as an integral part of caring for dying and severely ill patients. However, studies show that patients do not respond negatively to discussions about forgoing treatment or advance directives, nor do they experience an increased sense of anxiety or depression.[7] In fact, many patients are relieved to discuss the topic, even if they find the conversation difficult.

Some physicians do not talk with patients about treatment wishes or advance directives because of a paternalistic belief that physicians can best determine the course of treatment. However, decisions about which treatments would be worthwhile or unacceptably burdensome reflect deeply held personal preferences and values. Studies have shown that physicians' judgments are influenced by their own personal

---

[5] L. L. Emanuel et al., "Advance Directives for Medical Care — A Case for Greater Use," *New England Journal of Medicine* 324 (1991): 889-95.

[6] E. R. Gamble, P. J. McDonald, and P. R. Lichstein, "Knowledge, Attitudes, and Behavior of Elderly Persons Regarding Living Wills," *Archives of Internal Medicine* 151 (1991): 277-80; B. Lo, G. A. McLeod, and G. Saika, "Patient Attitudes to Discussing Life-Sustaining Treatment," *Archives of Internal Medicine* 146 (1988): 1613-15; T. E. Finucane et al., "Planning with Elderly Outpatients for Contingencies of Severe Illness," *Journal of General Internal Medicine*, 3 (1988): 322-35; R. H. Shmerling et al., "Discussing Cardiopulmonary Resuscitation: A Study of Elderly Outpatients," *Journal of General Internal Medicine* 3 (1988): 317-21; J. S. Haas et al., "Discussion of Preferences for Life-Sustaining Care by Persons with AIDS — Predictors of Failure in Patient-Physician Communication," *Archives of Internal Medicine* 153 (1993): 1241-48; Emanuel et al.

[7] P. Cotton, "Talk to People About Dying — They Can Handle It, Say Geriatricians and Patients," *Journal of the American Medical Association* 269 (1993): 321-22; Lo, McLeod, and Saika.

views about the value of life with mental or physical impairment.[8] More generally, physicians are often poor judges of the choices that patients would make for themselves. In several studies, physicians fared no better than chance alone at predicting their patients' wishes about treatment.[9]

Talking to patients about forgoing treatment and advance planning should be understood as an essential part of medical care. Ideally these conversations should take place within the context of an ongoing patient-physician relationship, beginning when patients are healthy. In general, patients would prefer to talk with their physician about advance directives as part of a routine office visit in advance of illness.[10] The Patient Self-Determination Act, which requires health care facilities to inform patients about their right to decide about treatment and to prepare advance directives, also presents an opportunity to discuss advance planning as a routine matter. In New York State, all patients admitted to a hospital, nursing home, or mental health facility, as well as those enrolled in numerous outpatient settings, must receive a copy of the health care proxy form. The health care proxy can serve as a springboard for a dialogue between physicians and their patients.

Physicians should talk about treatment options and facilitate advance planning as soon as possible after serious illness has been diagnosed if the discussion has not occurred earlier. Unfortunately, physicians often wait until the end stages of illness to talk about withdrawing or withholding treatment.[11] This is too late — many

---

[8]N. J. Farber et al., "Cardiopulmonary Resuscitation (CPR): Patient Factors and Decision Making," *Archives of Internal Medicine* 144 (1984): 2229-32; L. J. Schneiderman et al., "Do Physicians' Own Preferences for Life-Sustaining Treatment Influence Their Perceptions of Patients' Preferences?" *Journal of Clinical Ethics* 4 (1993): 28-33.

[9]R. F. Uhlmann, R. A. Pearlman, and K. C. Cain, "Physicians' and Spouses' Predictions of Elderly Patients' Resuscitation Preferences," *Journal of Gerontology* 43 (1988): M115-21; J. Ouslander, A. Tymchuk, and B. Rahbar, "Health Care Decisions Among Elderly Long-Term Care Residents and Their Potential Proxies," *Archives of Internal Medicine* 149 (1989): 1367-72.

[10]Shmerling et al., 317-21; Finucane et al., 322-35.

[11]For example, a review of patient deaths over two months at a major center for cancer treatment in New York City showed that while DNR orders had been entered for 86% of patients who died of cancer and all patients who died of AIDS, many orders had been entered in the last days of life. The median interval between entry of the DNR order and death was only six days, despite the fact that treatment for cancer and AIDS usually offers an extended opportunity to discuss treatment options with patients. R. I. Misbin et al., "Compliance with New York State's Do-Not-Resuscitate Law at Memorial Sloan-Kettering Cancer Center: A Review of Patient Deaths," *New*

patients lose decision-making capacity as their illness progresses. The discussion may also be more threatening to some patients if delayed too late in the course of illness. Physicians should discuss treatment decisions at a time that is sensitive to patients' needs, and early enough to give patients a meaningful opportunity to think about and express their wishes or appoint someone they trust to act as their health care agent.

Talking to patients about advance decisions, illness, and dying should be addressed in medical education at all stages of training and practice. A 1987 conference on the intellectual basis of medicine and its future called for significant changes in the medical school curriculum, decrying the failure of medical schools to train doctors adequately to conduct a medical interview and to talk to patients.[12] According to the American Medical Association (AMA), only three of 126 accredited medical schools in the United Sates require a class about death and dying.[13] At its 1993 annual meeting, the AMA adopted a resolution calling for a curriculum on "end-of-life care" for medical schools and residencies. Recently developed courses for medical students and residents include role playing, group discussions, and individual conversations with dying patients.[14]

Health care providers and other segments of society should also conduct public education about advance directives. Physicians are most directly responsible for informing their patients. Other health care professionals can also assist patients to learn about these options. Organizations outside the health care setting should contribute to

---

York State Journal of Medicine 93 (1993): 165-68. A study at a university hospital in Massachusetts of 389 patients with a DNR order who had a cardiac arrest found that 76% of patients lacked decision-making capacity when the order was entered, even though only 11% lacked capacity when admitted to the hospital. S. E. Bedell et al., "Do-Not-Resuscitate Orders for Critically Ill Patients in the Hospital: How Are They Used and What Is Their Impact?" *Journal of the American Medical Association* 256 (1986): 233-37.

[12] The conference report described a "persistent inability or unwillingness on the part of what is alleged to be a majority of physicians to converse, to listen, to try to understand, to learn about the patient's 'lifeworld,' the natural history of the illness and the search for help, and about the circumstances under which the illness arose and the meaning to the individual of his or her symptoms and illness. If this is not a medical disgrace, it must be close to it. Indeed, lack of interviewing and communication skills is probably the root cause of our malaise vis-a-vis the public and our patients." K. L. White, *The Task of Medicine* (Menlo Park, Cal.: The Henry J. Kaiser Family Foundation, 1988), 33.

[13] B. Clements, "Final Journey," *American Medical News*, August 16, 1993, 9-12.

[14] Ibid.

public education; diverse groups in New York State now distribute information about advance directives and sample forms, including Choice in Dying, the American Association of Retired Persons, the New York State Catholic Conference, and Agudath Israel. The Task Force and the New York State Department of Health have distributed tens of thousands of health care proxy forms. Social groups, religious congregations, and community organizations should also sponsor discussions about treatment decisions and encourage advance planning.

Improving Palliative Care

Health care professionals have a duty to offer effective pain relief and symptom palliation to patients when necessary, in accord with sound medical judgment and the most advanced approaches available.

Alleviation of pain and the symptoms of illness or disease makes a powerful contribution to the patient's quality of life. It can also speed recovery and provide other tangible medical benefits.[15] Physicians and nurses have an ethical and professional responsibility to offer effective pain and symptom management. This responsibility must be understood as central to the art of medicine and the delivery of medical care.[16] Attention to patients' symptoms should not be reserved for the end of life, nor should it be a sign that curative efforts have been abandoned. Palliative care should be understood to include symptom control at all stages of disease.

The failure to provide pain relief is a pervasive fault of current clinical practice. It is also one of the most amenable to change. Physicians and nurses who care for terminally ill patients have a special responsibility to develop the ability to provide effective pain and symptom management. Hospitals and other health care facilities must

---

[15] Acute Pain Management Guideline Panel, *Acute Pain Management: Operative or Medical Procedures and Trauma, Clinical Practice Guideline*, AHCPR pub. no. 92-0032 (Rockville, Md.: Agency for Health Care Policy and Research, U. S. Department of Health and Human Services, Public Health Service, Feb. 1992), 5-6.

[16] See American Medical Association, Council on Ethical and Judicial Affairs, "Decisions near the End of Life," *Journal of the American Medical Association* 267 (1992): 2231. The American Nursing Association states: "The main goal of nursing intervention for dying patients should be maximizing comfort through adequate management of pain and discomfort as this is consistent with the expressed desires of the patient." "Position Statement on Promotion of Comfort and Relief of Pain in Dying Patients," 1991. See also R. S. Smith, "Ethical Issues Surrounding Cancer Pain," in *Current and Emerging Issues in Cancer Pain: Research and Practice*, ed. C. R. Chapman and K. M. Foley (New York: Raven Press, 1993), 385-92.

create an environment in which patients and health care professionals regard pain relief as a priority of medical care.

Skill in prescribing and administering medications is essential for palliative care, but it is not sufficient. In order to assess pain, the symptoms caused by illness, and the side effects of treatment, health care professionals must communicate with patients and listen carefully to their needs. A patient's personal and social outlook as well as the pathological processes of disease will affect the patient's experience of pain. Caring, communication, and support are important to patients in any state of health or illness. For terminally and chronically ill patients, they are especially vital.

For these patients in particular, physicians and nurses must seek to provide comprehensive continuing care: "a system of intensive and flexible care, focusing on symptom management, pain control, and the changing psychological and social state of the ... patient and family."[17] Pain relief is one of the first elements that should be addressed in the continuing care of a patient.[18] It is also a logical focus for society's initial efforts to improve palliative care. The effective implementation of existing clinical knowledge and programs for pain management is almost certain to have an immediate impact on relieving suffering. At the same time, pain relief should not be seen as a technical panacea, sufficient to respond to the suffering of all patients. Pain relief is one discrete aspect of a larger problem. The ways in which the health care system treats patients and responds to their suffering and despair more generally must also be improved, although these are admittedly broader and less concrete goals.

---

[17]N. Coyle, "Continuing Care for the Cancer Patient with Chronic Pain," in *Why Do We Care?*, Syllabus of the Postgraduate Course, Memorial Sloan-Kettering Cancer Center, New York City, April 2-4, 1992, 371.

[18]V. Ventafridda, "Continuing Care: A Major Issue in Cancer Pain Management," *Pain* 36 (1989): 138.

Physicians and nurses must be aware that psychological dependence on pain medication rarely occurs in terminally ill patients. While physical dependence is somewhat more common, proper adjustment of medication can minimize any negative effects. Concerns about psychological or physical dependence should not prevent patients from receiving appropriate palliative treatments.

Failure to provide adequate pain relief stems from diverse causes. One significant reason for the inadequacy of current practices is that health care professionals are ill-informed about and overly fearful of addiction. These fears are often shared by patients and family members, making them reluctant to seek pain relief.

Palliative care experts stress the importance of distinguishing among tolerance, physical dependence, and psychological dependence on drugs. Tolerance and physical dependence are both common physiological responses to prolonged administration of a medication such as morphine. If tolerance develops, a patient requires larger or more frequent doses to achieve the same level of analgesia. In most cases, a patient's need for increased amounts of opioids reflects increasing pain from the progression of the disease, not ongoing exposure to opioids. If physical dependence occurs, the dosage of opioids must be reduced gradually to avoid symptoms of withdrawal when the patient no longer requires pain medication.[19] Health care professionals who are aware of these phenomena can adjust medication to provide adequate pain relief while minimizing and managing side effects. Neither tolerance nor physical dependence should prevent patients from receiving needed pain medication.

Both tolerance and physical dependence are distinct from psychological dependence, or addiction. Patients receiving opioid medications to relieve pain almost never develop psychological dependence.[20] In fact, they display responses to opioids that differ markedly from those of people who abuse such drugs for "recreational" or nonmedical purposes.[21] Psychological dependence can repre-

---

[19]American Pain Society, *Principles of Analgesic Use in the Treatment of Acute Pain and Cancer Pain*, 3d ed. (Skokie, Ill.: American Pain Society, 1992), 25-26.

[20]One study of over 10,000 patients without a prior history of substance abuse who received opioids to treat pain revealed only four documented cases of psychological dependence; another study of similar size reported no such cases. R. K. Portenoy, "Chronic Opioid Therapy in Nonmalignant Pain," *Journal of Pain and Symptom Management* 5 (1990): S55.

[21]K. M. Foley, "The Relationship of Pain and Symptom Management to Patient

sent a significant issue for one group of patients — those who have a history of substance abuse. Nonetheless, steps can be taken to minimize the risk of psychological dependence with these patients.[22]

Even if the risk of psychological dependence were much higher than it actually is, opioid medications would still be appropriate therapy for some patients suffering significant pain, especially those who are terminally ill. For most patients, opioids such as morphine represent the most effective means to relieve severe pain. While psychological dependence would be an unwelcome side effect, it would not outweigh the benefits these medications can provide for terminally ill patients.

Health care professionals must be educated about both the rarity of psychological dependence and the vital importance of palliation for patients in severe pain.[23] Misunderstanding about the risk of addiction, and corresponding reluctance to provide pain medication, deny patients needed and appropriate therapy. Many patients and family members also have an exaggerated sense of the likelihood of "addiction" and the harm of psychological or physical dependence. A 1993 study of public opinion about pain relief found that 87 percent of respondents expressed concern that they would become over-reliant on pain medication, and 82 percent feared that they would become addicted.[24] These considerations are extremely important to some individuals and will shape their willingness to seek or to accept pain relief. Health care professionals should explore these concerns with patients and family members to dispel misunderstanding and encourage their acceptance of appropriate pain medication.

Requests for Physician-Assisted Suicide," *Journal of Pain and Symptom Management* 6 (1991): 291; Portenoy, S54.

[22]See A. Jacox et al., *Management of Cancer Pain, Clinical Practice Guideline* no. 9, AHCPR pub. no. 94-0592 (Rockville, Md.: U. S. Department of Health and Human Services, Public Health Service, Agency for Health Care Policy and Research, March 1994), 134-38; Acute Pain Management Guideline Panel, 60-62. If the risk of psychological dependence is minimized as far as possible consistent with adequate palliation, but remains significant, a prudent judgment weighing the risks and benefits of treatment could still support the provision of needed treatment. See the discussion regarding the risk of hastening a patient's death, pp. 162-65.

[23]Many health care professionals have an inflated sense of the risk of psychological dependence. See, e.g., R. M. Marks and E. J. Sachar, "Undertreatment of Medical Patients with Narcotic Analgesics," *Annals of Internal Medicine* 78 (1973): 173-81; M. Angell, "The Quality of Mercy," *New England Journal of Medicine* 306 (1982): 98-99; and the discussion in chapter 3.

[24]Mellman Lazarus Lake, "Presentation of Findings: Mayday Fund," September 1993.

Patients and family members may also believe that if they receive opioids at one stage of the disease, the drugs will be less effective at a later stage when the pain is more severe. While patients do develop tolerance to some pain relief medications, including opioids, there is no ceiling dosage. If carefully adjusted to minimize side effects, doses can be increased substantially to maintain or increase palliation. Furthermore, the physiology of pain is such that smaller doses of analgesia are required to prevent pain or treat moderate pain than are needed to treat pain that has become severe.[25]

The provision of appropriate pain relief rarely poses a serious risk of respiratory depression. Moreover, the provision of pain medication is ethically and professionally acceptable even when such treatment may hasten the patient's death, if the medication is intended to alleviate pain and severe discomfort, not to cause death.

One commonly identified barrier to adequate pain relief is the fear of health care professionals that pain medications such as opioids may hasten a patient's death. In a major study of 687 physicians and 759 nurses, 41 percent of respondents agreed with the statement that "clinicians give inadequate pain medication most often out of fear of hastening a patient's death."[26]

Opioids represent the primary means of pain relief for most patients in severe pain.[27] While these medications can slow the patient's breathing, when properly used the risk of respiratory depression that harms the patient or hastens death is minimal. According to one estimate, the risk of respiratory distress with the use of opioids is no more than one percent.[28] The risk is low because patients develop tolerance that lessens the potential side effects of opioids, such as respiratory depression or mental cloudiness. Like other aspects of palliative care, providing opioids requires care and continual reassessment of the patient's condition. When the level of medication is carefully adjusted, large doses of opioids can be provided safely in any health care setting, including a patient's home.

---

[25]See chapter 3.

[26]M. Z. Solomon et al., "Decisions Near the End of Life: Professional Views on Life-Sustaining Treatments," *American Journal of Public Health* 83 (1993): 14-23.

[27]See chapter 3.

[28]Angell.

It is widely recognized that the provision of pain medication is ethically and professionally acceptable even when the treatment may hasten the patient's death, if the medication is intended to alleviate pain and severe discomfort, not to cause death.[29] In an unusual case, a dying patient who had not received opioids previously might require a large dose to relieve sudden severe pain, posing a significant risk of hastening death. Health care professionals should seek to minimize this risk, consistent with adequate treatment for pain and other symptoms. Even if significant risk remains, the benefits of treatment will outweigh that risk in some cases.

Some Task Force members analyze such cases in terms of the principle of double effect. According to this principle, an action with both good and evil effects is permitted if the action is not intrinsically wrong the agent intends only the good and not the evil effect, the evil effect is not the means to the good effect, and there is a favorable balance between the good and evil effects.[30] A decision to provide pain medication in the case described above would be ethically acceptable under this analysis. The administration of medication is not intrinsically wrong and is intended to alleviate the patient's pain, not to hasten the patient's death, although the risk of death could be anticipated. Respiratory failure is not intended, nor is it necessary to relieve pain. In addition, because the patient is terminally ill and experiencing severe pain, the good achieved would outweigh the risk of harm.

---

[29]American Medical Association, Council on Ethical and Judicial Affairs, *Current Opinions* (Chicago: American Medical Association, 1989), sec. 2.20, p. 13. A Catholic directive states that "it is not euthanasia to give a dying person sedatives and analgesics for the alleviation of pain, when such a measure is judged necessary, even though they may deprive the patient of the use of reason, or shorten his life." National Conference of Catholic Bishops, *Ethical and Religious Directives for Catholic Health Facilities* (St. Louis: Catholic Health Association of the United States, 1975), 13-14, par. 29. See similarly the Vatican's 1980 "Declaration on Euthanasia," in President's Commission, 304-5.

A Jewish authority agrees that "relief of pain is adequate reason to assure palliation therapy, even with attendant risk." D. M. Feldman and F. Rosner, ed., *Compendium on Medical Ethics*, 6th ed. (New York: Federation of Jewish Philanthropies, 1984). See similarly I. Jakobovits, *Jewish Medical Ethics*, 2d ed. (New York: Bloch, 1975), 276. See also New York State Task Force on Life and the Law, *When Others Must Choose*, 208-11; President's Commission, 77-82.

[30]T. L. Beauchamp and J. F. Childress, *Principles of Biomedical Ethics*, 3d ed. (New York: Oxford University Press, 1989), 127-28. Evaluation of the balance of good and evil effects is classically phrased in terms of proportionality. Most instances of causing unintended but foreseeable deaths would be judged as morally wrong on this basis because the negative effect of the patient's death would outweigh any good effects, but exceptions are possible in cases such as the one described.

Other Task Force members do not accept all elements of this principle of double effect but agree that intentions can be a significant and decisive factor in evaluating actions. They note that many medical interventions, including high-risk surgery, intend to cure the patient or to relieve pain, but entail some identifiable and foreseeable risk to life. Society has granted physicians the authority to evaluate the risks and benefits of treatment, to recommend a course of treatment, and to provide treatments chosen by a patient or a surrogate in pursuit of accepted medical goals. Judgments about potentially risky and life-threatening interventions undertaken to cure the patient or relieve pain fall squarely within the scope of the physician's professional role.[31]

Whether a given dose of morphine is appropriate for pain relief cannot be determined simply by looking at the number of milligrams prescribed, but must be assessed on a case-by-case basis using prudent medical judgment. Large doses may be required to relieve pain for some patients, and can be administered without undue risk. If the patient has received increasing doses of morphine over time, for example, he or she may sustain a larger dose without significant likelihood of harm.

A greater risk of side effects, including depressed respiration and the possibility of death, would be acceptable for a dying patient in severe pain, provided that the patient or those deciding on his or her behalf have been informed of and accept this risk. For the rare patient who requires sedation that renders him or her unconscious in order to avoid intolerable suffering during the end stage of the dying process, the administration of morphine to maintain a state of unconsciousness may be medically necessary and appropriate.[32] Physicians should discuss these decisions with the patient and with other health care professionals caring for the patient. Open discussion of these and other alternatives promotes good medical care and can prevent misunderstanding.

Similar considerations apply when health care providers do not administer medications directly, but write a prescription or give patients medicine to use at home. Physicians regularly provide patients with a supply of pain medication that can last for 30 to 90 days. In some cases, a physician may perceive a risk that the patient will use the medication to commit suicide. As discussed below, when health care

---

[31]President's Commission, 77-82.

[32]In these cases, sedative drugs often are used in combination with the opioid that is being administered to manage pain.

professionals believe that a patient may be considering suicide, they should encourage the patient to talk about his or her suicidal thoughts, and respond to concerns that may be causing distress, such as inadequate symptom control or clinical depression.[33]

For patients who express suicidal ideation or pose a risk of suicide, the physician must formulate an individualized judgment, weighing the potential benefits of palliation in the home setting against the risk of suicide. He or she should consider several factors, including the likelihood of suicide, the severity of the patient's pain or symptomatic distress, and the possibility of alternative treatments or means of providing the medication that minimize the risk of suicide. Physicians must also consider the benefit of and need for psychiatric counseling and treatment.

A physician may decide that the risk of providing large doses of pain medication is too great, given the circumstances of a particular case. In some cases, however, a physician may appropriately determine that the benefit of or need for pain medication outweighs a risk that the patient will commit suicide. These cases are legally and ethically distinct from situations when a physician provides drugs with the intention of assisting the patient to commit suicide.

The education of health care professionals about pain relief and palliative care must be improved. Training in pain relief and palliative care should be included in the curriculum of nursing schools, medical schools, residencies, and continuing education for health care professionals. In addition, biomedical research facilities should engage in further research in the physiology of pain and its appropriate relief, both at the basic and the clinical levels.

Health care professionals often lack the clinical knowledge and experience needed to provide effective palliative care. These deficiencies must be addressed in all contexts in which professional education occurs. In recent years, curricula have been developed that can serve as valuable resources. The most extensive document is the *Core Curriculum for Professional Education in Pain*, developed by the International Association for the Study of Pain.[34] The American Society of

---

[33]See pp. 177-81

[34]International Association for the Study of Pain, Task Force on Professional Education, *Core Curriculum for Professional Education in Pain* (Seattle: IASP Publications, 1991). Information on obtaining this document and other resources appears in Appendix G.

Clinical Oncology and the International Society of Nurses in Cancer Care have also developed curricula.[35]

Perhaps most importantly, educators must convey to nursing and medical students that pain and symptom management are a basic and essential component of medical care for professionals in all areas of medical practice. Too often, education about pain relief takes place only within departments of anesthesia, where study is focused largely on the treatment of post-operative pain. The relief of pain related to terminal and chronic illnesses must also be integrated into the medical and nursing curriculum, particularly in specialties such as oncology, where the treatment of pain should be a central concern. The importance of pain and symptom management must be stressed during medical and nursing school as well as during clinical training. For medical students, education during residency is especially important in shaping their future orientation for medical practice. Palliative care must be an integral part of residency training.

Continuing education for health care professionals is also vital. Many practicing physicians and nurses require continuing education about pain relief to remedy deficiencies in their initial professional training. Health care professionals should also be regularly informed about advances in the field. All means of continuing education should be used to educate doctors and nurses about palliative care, including professional workshops and grand rounds in hospitals.

In recent years, general guidelines for the treatment of pain have been issued by organizations such as the Agency for Health Care Policy and Research and the American Pain Society (APS).[36] These guidelines offer a valuable framework and resource for improving palliative care. Physicians and nurses may also benefit from several easy-to-use references on pain relief that are now available.[37] These

---

[35] American Society of Clinical Oncology, "Cancer Pain Assessment and Treatment Curriculum Guidelines," *Journal of Clinical Oncology* 10 (1992): 1976-82; R. Tiffany, "A Core Curriculum for a Post Basic Course in Palliative Nursing Care," *Palliative Medicine* 4 (1990): 261-70. Other resources include textbooks, such as J. J. Bonica, *The Management of Pain*, 2d ed. (Philadelphia: Lea and Febiger, 1990). See also the many references provided in the curricula and in the American Pain Society's *Principles of Analgesic Use*. Medical and nursing educators must consider the adequacy of presentation of pain and palliative care in textbooks and introduce alternative resources when necessary. See, e.g., B. R. Ferrell, "Pain and Addiction: An Urgent Need for Change in Nursing Education," *Journal of Pain and Symptom Management* 7 (1992): 117-24.

[36] Acute Pain Management Guideline Panel: Jacox et al.; American Pain Society.

[37] These include the American Pain Society's *Principles of Analgesic Use*; D. E.

resources will not be effective, however, without both institutional commitment to implement the guidelines and effective programs to educate health care professionals.

Activities at the state level can also enhance public and professional education about pain relief. For example, in Wisconsin, as part of a comprehensive statewide approach to improve pain management, the Wisconsin Cancer Pain Initiative has sponsored meetings and workshops for professional education and has devised a curriculum on cancer pain management. The Initiative has developed a network of almost 300 health care professionals to serve as informal resources in their community and as advocates for improved pain control.[38]

New York's extensive network of biomedical research facilities can also play a critical role in improving pain relief and palliative care. These institutions should devote greater resources to researching the physiology of pain and its appropriate relief, at both the basic and the clinical levels. Such research is particularly important for individuals suffering from chronic pain, for whom existing pharmacological treatments may not be appropriate.

Hospitals and other health care institutions should explore ways to promote effective pain relief and palliative care and to remove existing barriers to this care.

Hospitals and other health care facilities have the responsibility to promote high quality medical care within their institutions. This responsibility should encompass the delivery of adequate pain and

---

Weissman et al., *Handbook of Cancer Pain Management*, 3d ed. (Madison: Wisconsin Pain Initiative, 1992); and Washington State Medical Association, *Pain Management and Care of the Terminal Patient* (Seattle: Washington State Medical Association, 1992).

[38] J. L. Dahl and D. E. Joranson, "The Wisconsin Cancer Pain Initiative," in *Advances in Pain Research and Therapy*, ed. K. M. Foley et al., vol. 16 (New York: Raven Press, 1990), 499-503; D. E. Weissman, M. Gutmann, and J. L. Dahl, "Physician Cancer Pain Education: A Report from the Wisconsin Cancer Pain Initiative," *Journal of Pain and Symptom Management* 6 (1991): 445-48. One innovation of the Wisconsin Cancer Pain Initiative is the Cancer Pain Role Model program, established in 1990. D. E. Weissman, J. L. Dahl, and J. W. Beasley, "The Cancer Pain Role Model Program of the Wisconsin Cancer Pain Initiative," *Journal of Pain and Symptom Management* 8 (1993): 29-35.

The Mayday Fund, a private foundation devoted to relieving pain and associated suffering, funds professional educational programs, including a one-day role model training program for social workers, a two-day course for primary care faculty physicians, and training programs for physicians and nurses ranging from one to four weeks to a one-year fellowship. Mayday Fund, "1993 Role Model Program."

symptom management. Institutions must clearly identify pain and symptom management as a professional responsibility of physicians and nurses.[39] They also must provide the resources needed for such care, including reference materials, in-service training, and the availability of clinicians with expertise in palliative care.

Facilities also can improve pain management by making patients' pain more "visible" for health care professionals. One basic way to achieve this goal is to train nurses and physicians to ask patients about their pain on a regular basis. Measures of pain intensity and relief should then be recorded in the medical record and prominently displayed.

Hospitals and nursing facilities should also address palliative care in their quality-assurance procedures. In 1991, the American Pain Society proposed "Quality Assurance Standards for Relief of Acute Pain and Cancer Pain."[40] Its recommendations are designed to improve the treatment of all types of pain. The APS emphasizes the need for systems "to assure that the occurrence of pain is recognized and that when pain persists, there is rapid feedback to modify treatment." Among other steps, the standards recommend that: (1) health care professionals should record pain and pain relief in the medical chart; (2) each clinical unit should identify levels of pain and relief that would trigger a review of current pain therapy, and should survey patient satisfaction; (3) institutions should make information about analgesics readily available; (4) facilities should inform patients that they will receive attentive analgesic care; and (5) facilities should monitor adherence to these practices.

---

[39] A statement by a Task Force on Practitioner-Assisted Suicide at the University of Rochester Medical Center could provide a model for other institutions. Rejecting the options of assisted suicide and euthanasia, the group unanimously recommended "that greater attention be paid to the clinical problems of the dying patient. Although these issues are presently covered within the Medical and Nursing School curriculum, [we] would like to see increased attention to these matters at all levels of educational development for our students, staff, residents and faculty." January 25, 1994.

[40] The proposal appears as Appendix C below. American Pain Society, Committee on Quality Assurance Standards, "American Pain Society Quality Assurance Standards for Relief of Acute Pain and Cancer Pain," in *Proceedings of the VIth World Congress on Pain*, ed. M. R. Bond, J. E. Charlton, and C. J. Woolf (New York: Elsevier Science Publishers, 1991).

Public education is essential to improve pain relief practices. Nurses and physicians should create an atmosphere that will encourage patients to seek relief of pain. To the extent possible, strategies for pain relief should give patients a maximal sense of involvement and control.

Many patients believe that they should not discuss their pain and symptoms with health care professionals. They do not realize the extent to which symptom palliation is possible, and may feel that talking to their doctor or nurse about pain and symptoms would be pointless or would be perceived as complaining or weakness.[41]

Health care professionals should encourage patients to report their symptoms and seek relief from pain. Awareness of patient symptoms, like physical findings and laboratory tests, can contribute to formulating a diagnosis and assessing a patient's condition. Alleviating pain and suffering often facilitates the healing process and markedly improves the patient's quality of life. Health care professionals should also seek the participation of family members or others close to the patient in pain relief efforts. While individuals are often reluctant to seek pain relief for themselves, they do so more readily for family members. [42]

Whenever possible, pain and symptom management should involve patients and give them a sense of control. For many patients, behavioral techniques are helpful. In some cases in which oral medications do not relieve pain sufficiently, patient-controlled analgesia using an infusion pump may be possible. Patient participation can contribute to effective analgesia and add to the patient's feeling of independence.

Materials and programs have been developed to educate patients and help them to seek pain relief effectively. These can serve to complement discussions with health care professionals, or compensate in part for the failure of health care professionals to provide information and encourage patients to talk about their pain and

---

[41]Mellman Lazarus Lake.

[42]Ibid.

symptoms.[43] Several organizations are also available to provide information and assistance to patients.[44]

Insurance companies and others responsible for health care financing should promote effective pain and symptom management and address barriers that exist for some patients.

While the personal and financial resources required for effective palliative care are more modest than those used for some forms of curative therapy, they can be significant. Some insurance companies will pay only for a supply of medication lasting 21 or 30 days, even when larger quantities are appropriate and it is difficult for the patient to obtain a new supply.[45] Some policies do not pay for hospitalization required to alleviate pain or for appropriate palliative care in the home.[46] Patients without medical insurance face far more imposing barriers to receiving palliative treatment. While deficiencies in the provision of palliative care are widespread, disadvantaged patients receive the least support and care during the dying process as well as other stages of illness.

The World Health Organization has recommended that health care resources for palliative care should be increased, and that resources for curative treatments, especially those of questionable effectiveness,

---

[43]The Agency for Health Care Policy and Research has produced two booklets for patients: Acute Pain Management Guideline Panel, *Pain Control After Surgery: A Patient's Guide*, AHCPR pub. no. 92-0021 (Rockville, Md.: U. S. Department of Health and Human Services, Public Health Service, Agency for Health Care Policy and Research, 1992); and Agency for Health Care Policy and Research, *Managing Cancer Pain*, AHCPR pub. no. 94-0595 (Rockville, Md.: U. S. Department of Health and Human Services, Public Health Service, Agency for Health Care Policy and Research, 1994). The American Cancer Society and National Cancer Institute have prepared a clear and comprehensive booklet entitled *Questions and Answers About Pain Control: A Guide for People with Cancer and Their Families* (1992). Shorter booklets on cancer pain relief, directed to adult patients, adolescents, and parents of children with cancer, are available from the Wisconsin Pain Initiative.

[44]In the New York City metropolitan area, Cancer Care promotes education about pain relief. The organization also provides guidance, social services, and financial assistance to cancer patients and loved ones. The Cancer Information Service of the National Cancer Institute also offers information about pain management and other cancer-related issues to patients, families, health care professionals, and the general public. See list of resources in Appendix G.

[45]Federal regulations do not allow prescriptions for certain drugs such as morphine to be refilled.

[46]Foley, 292.

could be reduced.[47] Others believe that the resources needed for effective palliative care could be provided without significantly diminishing the provision of curative therapy.

Access to palliative care and pain relief must no doubt be addressed as part of the broader question of access to health care — in particular, in the context of current deliberations on health care reform. The complex issues of access to health care and allocation of health care resources are beyond the scope of this report. Nevertheless, it appears that much can and should be done to remove financial barriers and to promote effective pain and symptom management.

New York State statutes and regulations should be modified to improve the availability of medically necessary analgesic medications, including opioids. This should be done in a balanced manner that acknowledges the importance of avoiding drug diversion.

Statutes and regulations governing controlled substances must strike a careful balance between two important public health goals. On the one hand, the law must encourage the availability of analgesic medications, including opioids, for individuals who need them for legitimate medical uses. On the other hand, the law should prevent diversion of these same drugs to persons who will abuse them.

Experience has shown that certain provisions of current New York law pose obstacles to the availability of medication to relieve pain or severe discomfort. The Task Force believes that these provisions should be modified to enhance the appropriate care and treatment of seriously ill patients. Specifically, the Task Force recommends the following changes to New York statutes and regulations.

First, statutes and regulations governing controlled substances should include a positive statement that opioids and similar drugs have a useful and legitimate medical purpose and that they must be available to patients whenever medically appropriate. Such a statement — which is already present in federal statutes and regulations — would undercut the prevailing public perception that controlled substances are in-herently harmful, and would provide legal support for policies that

---

[47]World Health Organization, *Cancer Pain Relief and Palliative Care: Report of a WHO Expert Committee*, WHO Technical Report Series 804 (Geneva: World Health Organization, 1990).

actively encourage medical use of these drugs.[48] In addition, an affirmative statement supporting the use of controlled substances in the medical context might lessen the stigma attached to the provision and use of analgesic medications, further reducing impediments to the legitimate use of these medications.

Second, the Task Force urges the legislature to eliminate the requirement that health care practitioners report addicts and habitual users to the Department of Health.[49] This requirement stigmatizes individuals who use controlled substances for medical purposes. In addition, it places physicians in an awkward position in relation to patients they must report, and may cause some individuals to refuse needed pain relief. The Task Force also recommends that the legislature modify the definition of the terms "addict" and "habitual user" in the Public Health Law to exclude patients who use controlled substances in a medically appropriate manner.[50] By applying such labels to patients who use controlled substances for the relief of pain or severe discomfort, the law unjustifiably gives credence to physicians' and patients' fears that patients will become dependent on medically necessary drugs.[51] As discussed above, these fears are largely unfounded.[52] It is also inappropriate to apply a term so charged with negative connotations to patients who use drugs for legitimate medical purposes.[53]

Third, the Task Force proposes that barriers to obtaining long-term supplies of medically necessary controlled substances should be modified. These barriers in existing statutes and regulations can im-

---

[48]See Controlled Substances Act, 21 U.S.C. 801 (1993) ("Many of the drugs included within this title have a useful and legitimate medical purpose and are necessary to maintain the health and general welfare of the American people."); 21 C.F.R. Part 1306.07(c) (1993) ("This section is not intended to impose any limitation on a physician or authorized hospital staff to ... administer or dispense (including prescribe) narcotic drugs to persons with intractable pain in which no relief or cure is possible or none has been found after reasonable efforts.).

[49]N.Y. Public Health Law § 3372 (McKinney 1985); 10 N.Y.C.R.R. § 80.108.

[50]N.Y. Public Health Law § 3302(1) & (17) (McKinney 1985).

[51]According to a 1993 national survey, 82% of all Americans fear that they would become addicted to pain medication, and 87% fear that they would become over-reliant on it. Mellman Lazarus Lake.

[52]See the discussion in this chapter and in chapter 1.

[53]Significantly, the federal definition of the term "addict" does not include patients who use controlled substances to relieve chronic pain. See D. E. Joranson, "Federal and State Regulation of Opioids," *Journal of Pain and Symptom Management* 5 (1990): S12, S14.

pose severe burdens on patients who live far away from a pharmacy that stocks controlled substances, or whose insurance plans require the use of mail-order pharmacies that delay access to the medication.[54] For example, although physicians may prescribe a three-month supply of certain controlled substances to relieve pain for patients over 65 who suffer from chronic and incurable diseases,[55] chronically and incurably ill patients under age 65 must obtain a new prescription for pain medication every 30 days.[56] This regulation should be eliminated.[57] Likewise, current regulations permit a physician to issue an additional prescription for Schedule II substances only when the patient has exhausted all but a seven-day supply of the previous prescription.[58] The Department of Health should modify this prohibition to permit the earlier issuance of second prescriptions in hospital pharmacies, or prescriptions for particular patients based on specified medical criteria.

Fourth, the Task Force urges the Department of Health to consider regulations that would facilitate the use of controlled substances on a trial basis. Patients react differently to pain medications, and often physicians can determine the appropriate medication for a patient only after trial and error with a variety of dosages or drugs. If patients must purchase a full prescription of each medication they try, the costs can be prohibitive. The Department of Health should therefore evaluate the benefits of permitting pharmacies to fill prescriptions partially for controlled substances, as is currently permitted in the hospice setting.[59] This policy would allow patients to try a drug for a short time period without purchasing the full prescription.

Finally, the legislature and the Department of Health should assess the administrative and economic feasibility of eliminating the triplicate prescription system for controlled substances. Under this system,

---

[54] R. K. Portenoy, "The Effect of Drugs Regulation on the Management of Cancer Pain," *New York State Journal of Medicine* 91 (1991): 16S.

[55] 10 N.Y.C.R.R. § 80.67(d)(1)(iii) & 80.69(d)(1)(iii).

[56] 10 N.Y.C.R.R. § 80.67(c).

[57] The Department of Health should also study the need and appropriateness of explicitly allowing a three-month supply of controlled substances for the relief of severe discomfort, as well as pain.

[58] 10 N.Y.C.R.R. §§ 80.67(c); 80.69. Patients may refill prescriptions for other medications earlier than seven days prior to the date the previously dispensed supply would be exhausted only if specifically authorized by the prescriber. N.Y. Public Health Law § 3339 (McKinney 1985).

[59] 10 N.Y.C.R.R. § 80.73.

copies of each prescription are retained by the physician and the pharmacy and an additional copy is sent to the Department of Health. Many physicians have criticized the triplicate prescription program as unnecessarily intrusive and as a deterrent to the prescription of medically useful controlled substances.[60] Although these criticisms are not supported by empirical data,[61] a simplified system might assuage physicians' concerns while retaining the record-keeping benefits that the triplicate system provides. One alternative to the triplicate forms would be a single serialized form that pharmacies could transmit electronically to the Department of Health. The Department of Health and others should study the feasibility of this and other reporting systems with the goal of replacing the current triplicate system.

While statutory and regulatory reform is important, changes in the law will not, in themselves, eliminate the underutilization of medically necessary controlled substances. Barriers to effective pain relief arise from many sources, including lack of information on the part of health care professionals and insufficient professional commitment to palliative care. Along with the modification of statutes and regulations, education and outreach will be essential to eradicate these barriers. To this end, professional organizations should play an active role in clarifying the ethical and legal acceptability of prescribing controlled substances for medical purposes. In particular, the perceived risk of sanctions often bears little relation to the actual "risks" of prescribing medications in accord with accepted medical standards. While clarification from the Department of Health and an affirmative statement of the value of narcotic analgesics will be valuable, these steps will have little affirmative impact unless health care professionals are informed and responsible about any clarification that is offered.

[60] See P. B. Farnsworth, "Triplicate Prescription in New York: History and Review," *New York State Journal of Medicine* 91 (1991): 5S; Portenoy, 16S ("The multiple copy prescription is a tangible reminder to the physician of the intense scrutiny that accompanies the prescription of these drugs, and awareness of this scrutiny may ... increase the clinician's perception that some personal risk accrues from the administration of these agents to patients.").

[61] Criticisms of the triplicate prescription program tend to focus on the Department of Health's 1987 investigation of an oncologist who had failed to write dates and patient ages on all of his forms. See, e.g., Joranson, S17. This investigation appears to have been an isolated incident and does not provide evidence of a systematic problem. In fact, data compiled by the Department of Health suggest that the triplicate prescription system has not deterred physicians from prescribing controlled substances for medical purposes. Between 1980 and 1991, for example, annual prescriptions for morphine increased from 5,555 to 40,164. J. D. Eadie, Director, Division of Public Health Protection, New York State Department of Health, "Memorandum to the New York State Task Force on Life and the Law," August 13, 1993.

Pharmacists must also be educated about the importance of providing controlled substances for pain relief and their responsibility to do so. At a minimum, they should be encouraged to stock medically necessary controlled substances routinely. If encouragement fails, the Department of Health should consider regulations aimed at promoting availability, such as a requirement that pharmacies provide controlled substances within 24 hours of a patient's request.

Diagnosing and Treating Depression

Health care professionals should be familiar with the characteristics of major depression and other common psychiatric illnesses, as well as the possibility for treatment. They must be sensitive to the special factors complicating the diagnosis of these conditions among the elderly and the terminally ill. Physicians must also be trained to distinguish major clinical depression from the sadness and temporary reactive depression that often accompany terminal illness. Major clinical depression is generally treatable and can be treated effectively even in the absence of improvement in the underlying disease. Patients should also receive appropriate treatment for less severe depression that often accompanies terminal illness.

Depression is frequently underdiagnosed and undertreated, especially for the elderly and for patients with chronic or terminal medical conditions.[62] Health care professionals must be aware of the risk factors for depression and the common symptoms that patients experience when suffering from depression. Risk factors for major depression include personal or family history of depressive disorder, prior suicide attempts, female gender, lack of social supports, stressful life events, and current substance abuse.[63]

Major depression is marked by the presence of symptoms for at least two weeks, almost every day, all day. These symptoms include either depressed mood (feeling sad or blue) or loss of interest in activities that are normally pleasurable. In addition, patients with depression experience at least three of the following symptoms: (1) significant weight loss/gain, (2) insomnia/hypersomnia, (3) psychomotor agita-

---

[62]See chapter 1 for complete discussion.

[63]Depression Guideline Panel, *Depression in Primary Care*, vol. 2, *Treatment of Major Depression, Clinical Practice Guideline*, no. 5, AHCPR pub. no. 93-0551, (Rockville, Md.: U. S. Department of Health and Human Services, Public Health Service, Agency for Health Care Policy and Research, April 1993), 1.

tion/retardation, (4) fatigue, (5) feelings of worthlessness (guilt), (6) impaired concentration (indecisiveness), (7) recurrent thoughts of death or suicide. Other physical or psychological symptoms such as headaches, aches and pains, digestive problems, sexual problems, pessimistic or hopeless feelings, and anxiety may also accompany depression.

Patients with serious medical conditions, especially terminal illnesses, may develop a range of depressive symptoms short of major depression. Experience with cancer patients indicates that with the initial diagnosis, patients often respond with shock and disbelief or denial of the diagnosis. Subsequently, patients may experience sad or depressed moods, anxiety, and other symptoms commonly associated with depression. Symptoms usually dissipate within two to three weeks once the patient is receiving treatment or has adjusted to his or her situation. These episodes, referred to as "reactive depressive symptoms" or "adjustment disorder with depressed symptoms," can reoccur at various times during the course of an illness.[64]

Physicians and other health care professionals must be able to assess depression and the risk of suicide. Since many individuals do not seek out mental health professionals to treat depression, primary care physicians and physicians treating patients with terminal and chronic illness should evaluate patients for depression during a regular medical visit.[65] Diagnosing the physical symptoms of depression may be especially difficult for patients with coexisting medical conditions because some physical symptoms associated with depression may be caused by the illness or medications.

More than 80 percent of patients diagnosed with major depression can be effectively treated.[66] The National Institutes of Health (NIH) Consensus Panel on Depression in Late Life lists five goals for treating depression: (1) decreasing symptoms of depression, (2) reducing risk of relapse and recurrence, (3) increasing quality of life, (4) improving medical health status, and (5) decreasing health care costs and

---

[64] A. J. Roth and J. C. Holland, "Treatment of Depression," *Primary Care in Cancer* 14 (1994): 24-29.

[65] Appendix E contains a series of questions that can assist physicians in evaluating the patient and determining the presence and severity of depression.

[66] Dr. William S. Breitbart, Assistant Attending Psychiatrist, Psychiatry Service, Department of Neurology, Memorial Sloan-Kettering Cancer Center, presentation to the New York State Task Force on Life and the Law, May 13, 1992.

mortality.[67] The initial phase of treatment should attempt to bring about a remission of the symptoms. Following remission, therapy should ordinarily be continued for the next six to nine months to prevent relapse and recurrence. Finally, for some patients, a third phase of maintenance therapy will be necessary beyond the first year of treatment to prevent further relapse.[68]

Health care professionals must understand that even in patients with coexisting medical conditions, major depression can be successfully treated through pharmacological treatments and psychotherapy. In fact, experts contend that cancer patients often respond to lower dosages of antidepressants and in a shorter interval of time than physically healthy patients with depression.[69] In contrast, most elderly patients who are depressed respond to treatment more slowly than younger patients. Patients diagnosed with major depression should be referred to a psychiatrist for appropriate treatment. The primary care physician and other professionals such as social workers, psychologists, and clergy, may provide critical support to patients who experience depressive symptoms without major depression.

Responding When a Patient Requests Assisted Suicide or Euthanasia

It is common for terminally ill patients to have suicidal ideation, although patients rarely act on such thoughts. Physicians should create an atmosphere within which patients feel comfortable expressing suicidal thoughts. Discussion with a physician or other health care professional about suicide does not prompt suicide; on the contrary, talking with health care professionals often decreases the risk of suicide.

Suicidal thoughts and suicidal actions represent distinct phenomena, especially for terminally ill patients such as those with acquired immunodeficiency syndrome (AIDS) or cancer. Many patients with advanced disease think about suicide at some point in the course of their illness. These thoughts usually stem from suffering, depression, and an overwhelming sense of hopelessness or helpless-

---

[67]NIH Consensus Development Panel on Depression in Late Life, "Diagnosis and Treatment of Depression in Late Life," *Journal of the American Medical Association* 268(1992): 1018-24.

[68]G. J. Kennedy, "Depression in the Elderly," in *Psychiatry 1993*, ed. R. Michaels et al., vol. 2 (Philadelphia: J. P. Lippincott, 1993), 1-11.

[69]Roth and Holland.

ness. For some patients, framing the option of suicide may provide a sense of control: "If it gets too bad, I always have a way out." However, few patients who experience suicidal ideation actually attempt or complete suicide. When offered personal support and palliative care, most patients adapt and continue life in ways they might not have anticipated. Clinicians often observe that patients are able to sustain and cope with tremendous suffering as they approach death. Life often becomes more precious as it becomes shorter.[70]

Nevertheless, suicidal thoughts must be taken seriously. They reflect deep personal suffering. A patient's suicidal thoughts may indicate a worsening of disease or insufficiencies in current therapy. In many cases they are accompanied by treatable psychiatric conditions. Health care professionals should actively explore indications of suicidal thinking and should respond appropriately when a patient expresses such thoughts.

It is well-established that talking about suicidal thoughts does not increase the risk of suicide and, indeed, generally decreases that risk. A physician or nurse who learns of a patient's suicidal thoughts can often help the patient address the factors leading to those thoughts. Acknowledging the patient's concerns and manifesting empathy and care can itself be therapeutic. Conversely, the failure of health care professionals to create an environment in which patients feel comfortable talking about suicide can increase the patient's suffering and sense of isolation, making suicide more likely in some cases.[71]

Some health care professionals, like other people, find it extremely difficult to talk about suicide with patients. Medical and nursing training often does little to prepare them for this responsibility. Physicians and nurses who feel unable to discuss suicide with a patient must involve another health care professional who can provide this critical aspect of patient care. In addition, health care professionals must determine if psychiatric consultation is appropriate and necessary. At a minimum, all health care professionals must be sensitive to potential suicidal ideation. Explicitly or tacitly discouraging a patient from expressing suicidal ideation can make it more difficult for a patient to cope with his or her thoughts and feelings.

---

[70]William Breitbart, "Cancer Pain and Suicide," in *Advances in Pain Research and Therapy*, ed. K. Foley, J. J. Bonica, and V. Ventafridda, vol. 16 (New York: Raven Press, 1990), 400-401.

[71]Ibid.

When a patient requests assisted suicide or euthanasia, a health care professional should explore the significance of the request, recognize the patient's suffering, and seek to discover the factors leading to the request. These factors may include insufficient symptom control, clinical depression, inadequate social support, concern about burdening family or others, a sense of hopelessness, spiritual despair, loss of self-esteem, or fear of abandonment. These issues should be addressed in a process that involves both family members and health care professionals.

Any response to a request for assisted suicide or euthanasia is morally weighty. A ready agreement to the request could confirm a patient's sense of despair and worthlessness. An attempt to ignore or evade the request may make a patient feel that his or her suffering is not taken seriously, adding to a sense of helplessness. Clinicians who hold diverse views about assisted suicide and euthanasia generally agree about the ways in which a physician or nurse should respond when a patient makes such a request. All concur that in most cases patients' concerns can be addressed in ways other than assisted suicide or euthanasia.[72]

A request for assisted suicide or euthanasia may arise from diverse causes, including inadequate symptom control, clinical depression, a lack of social or financial resources, concern about burdening family or others, spiritual crisis, hopelessness, loss of self esteem, or fear of abandonment. In many cases, multiple factors contribute to a patient's sense of despair. Physicians, nurses, social workers, and other health care professionals must be prepared to listen carefully and explore the meaning of the request. This interaction can identify the clinical treatment or psychosocial support the patient may need. The process of communication itself often helps the patient feel less alone and desperate.

Some of the factors leading to a patient's suffering and desire for suicide are clearly within the purview of medical practice. These can and must be addressed. As discussed throughout the report, many patients receive inadequate pain and symptom management. An ac-

---

[72]T. E. Quill, "Doctor, I Want to Die," *Journal of the American Medical Association* 270 (1993): 872. See also N. Coyle, "The Euthanasia and Physician-Assisted Suicide Debate: Issues for Nursing," *Oncology Nursing Forum* 19, no. 7 suppl. (1992): 45; J. Teno and J. Lynn, "Voluntary Active Euthanasia: The Individual Case and Public Policy," *Journal of the American Geriatrics Society* 39 (1991): 827-30; Breitbart, "Cancer Pain," 409-10.

ceptable level of pain relief can be provided to almost all patients. Furthermore, many terminally ill patients, especially those who consider actively ending their lives, are clinically depressed. Their depression, like that of others, generally responds to psychiatric treatment.

Interventions to increase a patient's functioning can also serve to reduce suffering and improve the quality of life. For example, an individual suffering from quadriplegia can benefit from rehabilitative therapy and from devices to enhance their mobility.[73] For some individuals suffering from amyotrophic lateral sclerosis (ALS), the ability to communicate may be most crucial and can be enhanced with technological assistance.[74] Treatment for symptoms such as severe nausea or difficulty breathing may also significantly improve the patient's quality of life.[75]

Other types of suffering are more difficult to address. Responding to a patient's personal and psychosocial needs can usually be accomplished best with the participation of family members and others close to the patient. Professional colleagues can also offer valuable assistance. A social worker can address psychosocial problems. A chaplain can respond to a patient undergoing a spiritual crisis. Nonetheless, referral to a social or spiritual "specialist" will rarely suffice to resolve a patient's concerns. The process of dying, or chronic illness, is complicated and profound. The patient's experience of suffering often has deeply personal meanings or sources.[76] Without the ongoing involvement of health care professionals and others close to the patient, the patient will feel abandoned.[77]

---

[73]D. R. Patterson et al., "When Life Support is Questioned Early in the Care of Patients with Cervical-Level Quadriplegia," *New England Journal of Medicine* 328 (1993): 506-9; Sharon S. Dittmar, *Rehabilitation Nursing: Process and Application* (St. Louis: C. V. Mosby, 1989).

[74]T. M. Sullivan, "The Language of Love," *Ladies' Home Journal*, March 1994, 24-28.

[75]See chapter 1.

[76]As Arthur Kleinman writes of those facing chronic illness: "In the long, oscillating course of chronic disorder, the sick, their relatives, and those who treat them become aware that the meanings communicated by illness can amplify or dampen symptoms, exaggerate or lessen disability, impede or facilitate treatment. ... However, these understandings often remain unexamined, silent emblems of a covert reality that is usually dealt with indirectly or not at all." *The Illness Narratives: Suffering, Healing, and the Human Condition* (New York: Basic Books, 1988), 9.

[77]As ethicist Paul Ramsey explains: "If the sting of death is sin, the sting of dying is solitude. What doctors should do in the presence of the dying is only a special case of what should be done to make a human presence felt to the dying. Desertion is more choking than death, and more feared. The chief problem of dying is how not to die

Marshaling personal and professional resources will often help patients even in the most difficult circumstances. In the words of a director of a supportive care program:

> Clearly defined goals, a time frame for assessing the effectiveness of a treatment measure, continuity of care, and working with the family as a unit all help to lessen the feelings of abandonment and hopelessness that frequently accompany requests for euthanasia or physician-assisted suicide.[78]

Even more so than with conventional medical interventions, attempts to address the concerns that lead a patient to request suicide assistance or euthanasia carry no guarantee of success. Medicine, and even an expanded program of supportive care, will not eliminate all suffering. Still, conscientious pain management and supportive care can do much to alleviate suffering. In most cases, they can help the patient achieve a resolution that he or she finds tolerable. In all cases, they manifest a commitment not to abandon the patient.

---

alone." *The Patient as Person* (New Haven: Yale University Press, 1970), 134. The importance of the personal and psychosocial support provided by health care professionals is discussed in M. A. Boyle and R. L. Ciuca, "Amyotrophic Lateral Sclerosis," *American Journal of Nursing* 1 (1975): 66-68.

[78]Coyle, "The Euthanasia and Physician-Assisted Suicide Debate," 45.

Appendices

Appendix A
Initial Assessment for Cancer Pain

From A. Jacox et al., *Management of Cancer Pain, Clinical Practice Guideline* no. 9, AHCPR pub. no. 94-0592 (Rockville, Md.: U. S. Department of Health and Human Services, Public Health Service, Agency for Health Care Policy and Research, March 1994), 25.

A. Assessment of pain intensity and character

1. **Onset and temporal pattern**—When did your pain start? How often does it occur? Has its intensity changed?
2. **Location**—Where is your pain? Is there more than one site?
3. **Description**—What does your pain feel like? What words would you use to describe your pain?
4. **Intensity**—On a scale of 0 to 10, with 0 being no pain and 10 being the worst pain you can imagine, how much does it hurt right now? How much does it hurt at its worst? How much does it hurt at its best?
5. **Aggravating and relieving factors**—What makes your pain better? What makes your pain worse?
6. **Previous treatment**—What types of treatments have you tried to relieve your pain? Were they and are they effective?
7. **Effect**—How does the pain affect physical and social function?

B. Psychosocial assessment

Psychosocial assessment should include the following:

1. Effect and understanding of the cancer diagnosis and cancer treatment on the patient and the caregiver.
2. The meaning of the pain to the patient and the family.
3. Significant past instances of pain and their effect on the patient.
4. The patient's typical coping responses to stress or pain.
5. The patient's knowledge of, curiosity about, preferences for, and expectations about pain management methods.
6. The patient's concerns about using controlled substances such as opioids, anxiolytics, or stimulants.
7. The economic effect of the pain and its treatment.
8. Changes in mood that have occurred as a result of the pain (e.g., depression, anxiety).

C. Physical and neurologic examination

1. Examine site of pain and evaluate common referral patterns.
2. Perform pertinent neurologic evaluation.
   - Head and neck pain—cranial nerve and fundoscopic evaluation.
   - Back and neck pain—motor and sensory function in limbs; rectal and urinary sphincter function.

D. Diagnostic evaluation

1. Evaluate recurrence or progression of disease or tissue injury related to cancer treatment.
   - Tumor markers and other blood tests.
   - Radiologic studies.
   - Neurophysiologic (e.g., electromyography) testing.
2. Perform appropriate radiologic studies and correlate normal and abnormal findings with physical and neurologic examination.
3. Recognize limitations of diagnostic studies.
   - Bone scan—false negatives in myeloma, lymphoma, previous radiotherapy sites.
   - CT scan—good definition of bone and soft tissue but difficult to image entire spine.
   - MRI scan—bone definition not as good as CT; better images of spine and brain.

Appendix B
Brief Pain Inventory (Short Form)

This form was developed by the Pain Research Group, Department of Neurology, University of Wisconsin-Madison, and is used with permission. It appears in A. Jacox et al., *Management of Cancer Pain, Clinical Practice Guideline* no. 9, AHCPR pub. no. 94-0592 (Rockville, Md.: U. S. Department of Health and Human Services, Public Health Service, Agency for Health Care Policy and Research, March 1994), 228-29.

Brief Pain Inventory (Short Form)

Study ID#_____   Hospital#_____

Do not write above this line

Date: _____/_____/_____

Time:_____

Name:_____ _____ _____
                          Last   First   Middle Initial

1) Throughout our lives, most of us have had pain from time to time (such as minor headaches, sprains, and toothaches). Have you had pain other than these everyday kinds of pain today?   1. Yes   2. No

2) On the diagram, shade in the areas where you feel pain. Put an X on the area that hurts the most.

3) Please rate your pain by circling the one number that best describes your pain at its **worst** in the past 24 hours.

0	1	2	3	4	5	6	7	8	9	10

No pain   Pain as bad as you can imagine

4) Please rate your pain by circling the one number that best describes your pain at its **least** in the past 24 hours.

0	1	2	3	4	5	6	7	8	9	10

No pain   Pain as bad as you can imagine

5) Please rate your pain by circling the one number that best describes your pain on the **average.**

0	1	2	3	4	5	6	7	8	9	10

No pain   Pain as bad as you can imagine

6) Please rate your pain by circling the one number that tells how much pain you have **right now.**

0 . 1 2 3 4 5 6 7 8 9 10
No   Pain as bad as
pain   you can imagine

7) What treatments or medications are you receiving for your pain?

---

8) In the past 24 hours, how much **relief** have pain treatments or medications provided? Please circle the one percentage that most shows how much relief you have received.

0% 10% 20% 30% 40% 50% 60% 70% 80% 90% 100%
No   Complete
relief   relief

9) Circle the one number that describes how, during the past 24 hours, **pain has interfered** with your:

A. General activity

0 1 2 3 4 5 6 7 8 9 10
Does not   Completely
interfere   interferes

B. Mood

0 1 2 3 4 5 6 7 8 9 10
Does not   Completely
interfere   interferes

C. Walking ability

0 1 2 3 4 5 6 7 8 9 10
Does not   Completely
interfere   interferes

D. Normal work (includes both work outside the home and housework)

0 1 2 3 4 5 6 7 8 9 10
Does not   Completely
interfere   interferes

E. Relations with other people

0 1 2 3 4 5 6 7 8 9 10
Does not   Completely
interfere   interferes

F. Sleep

0 1 2 3 4 5 6 7 8 9 10
Does not   Completely
interfere   interferes

G. Enjoyment of life

0 1 2 3 4 5 6 7 8 9 10
Does not   Completely
interfere   interferes

Source: Pain Research Group, Department of Neurology, University of Wisconsin-Madison. Used with permission. May be duplicated and used in clinical practice.

Appendix C
American Pain Society Quality Assurance Standards for Relief of Acute Pain and Cancer Pain

These standards were developed by the Committee on Quality Assurance Standards, American Pain Society (Mitchell B. Max, chair). They appear in *Proceedings of the VI World Congress on Pain*, ed. M. R. Bond, J. E. Charlton, and C. J. Woolf (New York: Elsevier Science Publishers, 1991), 185-89.

American Pain Society quality assurance standards for relief of acute pain and cancer pain

Committee on Quality Assurance Standards*, American Pain Society

Introduction

Undertreatment of acute pain and chronic cancer pain persists despite decades of efforts to provide clinicians with information about analgesics (NIH Consensus Conference, 1986; Donovan et al., 1987; Hill and Fields, 1989). To assure that pain is communicated and that treatment is rapidly adjusted to provide relief, traditional educational approaches must be complemented by interventions that more directly influence the routine behaviors of clinicians and patients (Soumerai and Avorn, 1984; Morgan, 1986; Hodes, 1989; Edwards, 1990; Max, 1990).

In the United States, virtually all health care facilities have 'quality assurance committees', composed of physicians, nurses, pharmacists, other clinicians and administrators. Each committee chooses a number of clinical objectives that they consider important to monitor. They examine 'process', that is, whether the appropriate personnel follow the proper procedures in dealing with the

clinical problem, and 'outcome', the result for the patient. Outside organizations, most notably the Joint Commission on Accreditation of Healthcare Organizations or JCAHO (O'Leary, 1987) make regular inspections of facilities to assess how well they are monitoring care. Because the economic viability of facilities often depends on successful accreditation, administrators provide strong incentives for professionals to comply.

To support individual clinicians who wish to make pain relief a targeted outcome in their facilities, as recommended by a recent NIH Consensus Conference (1986), the American Pain Society has developed the following draft standards with the informal advice of JCAHO staff. The standards will be disseminated through publication in medical and nursing journals, and mailings to hospitals. The standards focus on the treatment of acute pain and cancer pain because there is already a scientific consensus regarding treatment methods, particularly the use of analgesic drugs, but some facilities may also wish to examine treatment of chronic pain not due to cancer, or the outcomes of non-pharmacological treatments.

A number of other materials will be distributed with these standards to facilitate their use, such as the American Pain Society's pamphlet, *Principles of Analgesic Use for the Treatment of Acute Pain and Chronic Cancer Pain* (American Pain Society, 1990; Standard II); a brief questionnaire to assess patient's satisfaction with analgesic care (Standard IC), included in the Appendix; and a patient education brochure that declares the facility's commitment to responsive analgesic care (in preparation).

*Mitchell B. Max, National Institute of Dental Research, Bethesda, MD (chair); Marilee Donovan, Oregon Health Sciences University Hospitals, Portland, OR; Russell K. Portenoy, Memorial Sloan-Kettering Cancer Center, New York, NY; Charles S. Cleeland, University of Wisconsin, Madison, WI; L. Brian Ready, University of Washington, Seattle WA; Daniel B. Carr, Massachusetts General Hospital, Boston, MA; W. Thomas Edwards, Harborview Medical Center, Seattle, WA; Mary A. Simmonds, Pennsylvania State College of Medicine, Hershey, PA; and Wayne O. Evans, Rehabilitation Center for Pain, Indianapolis, IN; USA.

American Pain Society quality assurance standards for relief of acute pain and cancer pain

Preface (to be included with standards)

In the majority of patients with acute pain and chronic cancer pain, comfort can be achieved with the attentive use of analgesic medications. Historically, however, the outcomes of analgesic treatment have often not been satisfactory, largely because clinical care units have had no systems in place to assure that the occurrence of pain is recognized and that when pain persists, there is rapid feedback to modify treatment. These suggested standards are offered as one approach to developing such a system. Individual facilities may wish to modify these standards to suit their particular needs.

The guidelines are intended for hospitals and chronic care facilities in which only conventional analgesic methods are used (e.g., intermittent parenteral or oral analgesics) as well as those using the most modern technology for pain management. In either case, the quality of pain control will be enhanced by a dedicated pain management team, whose personnel acquire special training in pain relief. Newer, more aggressive methods of pain control, such as patient-controlled analgesic infusion, epidural opiate administration, and regional anesthetic techniques may provide better pain relief than intermittent parenteral analgesics in many patients, but carry their own risks. Should institutions choose to use these methods, they must be delivered by an organized team with frequent follow-up and titration, and adequate briefing of the primary caregivers. Such teams should be organized under one of the recognized medical departments of the facility. Specific standards for such methods, monitored by that department, might well augment the general guidelines articulated here.

I. Recognize and treat pain promptly

IA. Chart and display pain and relief (Process)

A measure of pain intensity and a measure of pain relief are recorded on the bedside vital sign chart or a similar record that facilitates regular review by members of the healthcare team and is incorporated in the patient's permanent record.

IA1. The intensity of pain/discomfort is assessed and documented on admission, after any known pain-producing procedure, with each new report of pain, and routinely, at regular intervals that depend upon the severity of pain. A simple, valid measure of intensity will be selected by each clinical unit. For children, age-appropriate pain intensity measures will be used.

IA2. The degree of pain relief is determined after each pain management intervention, once a sufficient time has elapsed for the treatment to reach peak effect (e.g., 1 hour for parenteral analgesics and 2 hours for oral analgesics). A simple, valid measure of pain relief will be selected by each clinical unit.

IB. Define pain/relief levels to trigger review (Process)

Each clinical unit will identify values for pain intensity rating and pain relief rating that will elicit a review of the current pain therapy, documentation of the proposed modifications in treatment, and subsequent review of its efficacy. This process of treatment review and follow-up should include participation by physicians and nurses involved in the patient's care. As the general quality of treatment improves, the clinical unit will upgrade this standard, to encourage a continuous process of improvement.

IC. Survey patient satisfaction (Outcome)

At regular intervals to be defined by the clinical unit and the quality assurance committee, each clinical unit will assess a randomly selected sample of patients who have had surgery within 72 hours, another acute pain condition, and/or have a diagnosis of cancer. Patients will be asked whether they have had pain during the current admission. Those who have experienced pain will then be asked:

(1) Current pain intensity.
(2) Intensity of the worst pain they experienced in the past 24 hours (or other interval selected by the clinical unit).
(3) Degree of relief obtained from pain management interventions.
(4) Satisfaction with responsiveness of the staff to their reports of pain.
(5) Satisfaction with relief provided.

II. Make information about analgesics readily available (Process)

Information about analgesics and other methods of pain management, including charts of relative potencies of analgesics, is situated on the unit in a way to aid writing and interpreting orders. Nurses and physicians can demonstrate the use of this material. Appropriate training to treat their patients' pain is available to health professionals and included in continuing education activities.

III. Promise patients attentive analgesic care (Process)

Patients are informed on admission, verbally and in a printed format, that effective pain relief is an important part of their treatment, that their com-

munication of unrelieved pain is essential, and that health professionals will respond quickly to their reports of pain. Pediatric patients and their parents will receive materials appropriate to the age of the patient.

IV. Define explicit policies for use of advanced analgesic technologies (Process)

Advanced pain control techniques, including intraspinal opioids, systemic or intraspinal patient-controlled opioid infusion (PCA) or continuous opioid infusion, local anesthetic infusion, and inhalational analgesia are governed by policy and standard procedures which define the acceptable level of monitoring of patients, and define appropriate roles and limits of practice for all groups of health care providers involved. Such policy includes definitions of physician accountability, nurse responsibility to patient and physician, and the role of pharmacy.

V. Monitor adherence to standards (Process)

VA. An interdisciplinary committee, including representation from physicians, nurses, and other appropriate disciplines (e.g., pharmacy) monitors compliance with the above standards, considers issues relevant to improving pain treatment, and makes recommendations to improve outcomes and their monitoring. Where a comprehensive pain management team exists, its activities are monitoring through the parent department's quality assurance body, which may also serve as the facility's quality assurance committee for pain relief. In a nursing home or very small hospital where an interdisciplinary pain management committee is not feasible, one or several individuals may fulfill this role.

VB. At least the chairperson of the committee has experience working with issues related to effective pain management.

VC. The committee meets at least every 3 months to review process and outcomes related to pain management.

VD. The committee interacts with clinical units to establish procedures for improving pain management where necessary, and reviews the results of these changes within 3 months of their implementation.

VE. The committee provides regular reports to administration and to the medical, nursing, and pharmacy staffs.

Example of patient outcome questionnaire (Standard IC)

(To be filled out by interviewer)

1. At any time during your care, have you needed treatment for pain?

    _____ Yes   _____ No

2. Have you experienced any pain in the past 24 hours?

    _____ Yes   _____ No

3. On this scale, how much discomfort or pain are you having right now? (Category, numerical, or visual analog scales may be used for questions 3 – 5.)

    _____ (Record rating)

4. On this scale, please indicate the worst pain you have had in the past 24 hours.

    _____ (Record rating)

5. On this scale, please indicate how much relief you generally obtained from the medication or other treatment you were given for pain.

    _____ (Record rating)

6. Select the phrase which indicates how satisfied you are with the way your nurses treated your pain.

    Very satisfied, satisfied, slightly satisfied, slightly dissatisfied, dissatisfied, very dissatisfied

7. Select the phrase which indicates how satisfied you are with the way your nurses treated your pain.

    Very satisfied, satisfied, slightly satisfied, slightly dissatisfied, dissatisfied, very dissatisfied

8. When you asked for pain medication, what was the longest time you had to wait to get it?

    _____ Record answer, or choose from: 15 minutes or less, 15 – 30 minutes, 30 – 60 minutes, more than one hour, never asked for pain medication.

9. Was there a time that the medication you were given for pain didn't help and you asked for something more or different to relieve the pain?

    _____ Yes   _____ No

    If you answer is yes, how long did it take before your doctor or nurse changed your treatment to a stronger or different medication and gave it to you?

    _____ Record answer, or choose from: 1 hour or less, 1 – 2 hours, 2 – 4 hours, 4 – 8 hours, 8 – 24 hours, more than 24 hours.

10. Early in your care, did your doctors or nurses discuss with you that we consider treatment of pain very important, and did they ask you to be sure to tell them when you have pain?

    _____ Yes   _____ No

11. Do you have any suggestions for how your pain management could be improved?

Acknowledgements

We would like to acknowledge the thoughtful contributions of many American Pain Society members to this project, particularly Ronald Dubner, Judith Spross, Christine Miaskowski, Margo McCaffery, Betty Ferrell and Donald Tyler.

References

American Pain Society (1990) Principles of analgesic use in the treatment of acute pain and chronic cancer pain. Clin. Pharmacy, 9: 601–611.

Donovan, M., Dillon, P. and McGuire, L. (1987) Incidence and characteristics of pain in a sample of medical-surgical inpatients. Pain, 30: 69–87.

Edwards, W.T. (1990) Optimizing opioid treatment of postoperative pain. J. Pain Symptom Manage., 5: S24–36.

Hill, C.S., Jr. and Fields, W.S. (Eds.) (1989) Drug Treatment of Cancer Pain in a Drug-Oriented Society. Raven Press, New York, NY.

Hodes, R.L. (1989) Cancer patients' needs and concerns when using narcotic analgesics. In C.S. Hill, Jr. and W.S. Fields (Eds.), Drug Treatment of Cancer Pain in a Drug-Oriented Society. Raven Press, New York, NY, pp. 91–99.

Max, M.B. (1990) Improving outcomes of analgesic treatment. Ann. Intern. Med., 113: 885–889.

Morgan, J.P. (1986) American opiophobia: customary underutilization of opioid analgesics. In B. Stimmel (Ed.), Controversies in Alcoholism and Substance Abuse. Haworth Press, New York, NY, pp. 163–173.

NIH Consensus Development Conference Statement (1986) The Integrated Approach to the Management of Pain. Bethesda, MD, National Institutes of Health.

O'Leary, D.S. (1987) The joint commission looks to the future. JAMA, 258: 951–952.

Soumerai, S.B. and Avorn, J. (1984) Efficacy and cost-containment in hospital pharmacotherapy: state of the art and future directions. Milbank Mem. Fund Quarterly; Health Society, 62: 447–474.

Appendix D
Detection and Diagnosis
of Depression

From Depression Guideline Panel, *Depression in Primary Care: Detection, Diagnosis, and Treatment*, Quick Reference Guide for Clinicians, no. 5, AHCPR pub. no. 93-0552 (Rockville, Md.: U. S. Department of Health and Human Services, Public Health Service, Agency for Health Care Policy and Research, April 1993), 2-9. Further information, including guidelines for treating major depression, may be found in this publication and in the Depression Guideline Panel's *Depression in Primary Care, Clinical Practice Guideline*, no. 5, vols. 1 and 2, AHCPR pub. nos. 93-0550 and 93-0551 (Rockville, Md.: U. S. Department of Health and Human Services, Public Health Service, Agency for Health Care Policy and Research, April 1993).

References in the Depression Guideline Panel's text are to American Psychiatric Association, *Diagnostic and Statistical Manual of Mental Disorders*, 3d rev. ed. (Washington: American Psychiatric Press, 1987).

The following step-wise process can assist primary care practitioners in detecting, diagnosing, and treating major depression.

1. Maintain a high index of suspicion and evaluate risk factors.

Surveys consistently show that 6 to 8 percent of all outpatients in primary care settings have major depressive disorder; women are at particular risk for depression. Although sadness is frequently a presenting sign of depression, not all patients complain of sadness, and many sad patients do not have major depression. Common complaints of patients in primary care settings with major depressive disorder include:

■ Pain—including headaches, abdominal pain, and other body aches.

■ Low energy—excessive tiredness, lack of energy or a reduced capacity for pleasure or enjoyment.

■ A mood of apathy, irritability, or even anxiety rather than, or in addition to, any overt sadness may be present.

■ Sexual complaints—problems with sexual functioning or desire.

The clinician should be doubly alert to the likelihood of depression in individuals under age 40.

Additional clinical clues that raise the likelihood of a major depressive disorder include:

■ Prior episodes of depression.

■ A family history of major depressive or bipolar disorder.

■ A personal or family history of suicide attempt(s).

■ Concurrent general medical illnesses.

■ Concurrent substance abuse.

■ Symptoms of fatigue, malaise, irritability, or sadness.

■ Recent stressful life events and lack of social supports. (Stress should not be used to "explain away" depression; stress may precipitate a depression in some cases.)

2. Detect depressive symptoms with a clinical interview.

Major depressive disorder is a syndrome consisting of a constellation of signs and symptoms that are not normal reactions to life's stress. A sad or depressed mood is only one of the several possible signs and symptoms of major depressive disorder. The clinician may find it useful to provide the patient with a written list of depressive symptoms (pages 3 and 4) and ask the patient to indicate any symptoms experienced. This patient self-report can increase the likelihood of detecting major depression.

Diagnosis

Diagnostic criteria for major depressive disorder.

For major depressive disorder, at least five of the following symptoms are present during the same time period, and at least the one of the first two symptoms must be present. In addition, symptoms must be present most of the day, nearly daily, for at least 2 weeks.

- **Depressed mood most of the day, nearly every day.**

- **Markedly diminished interest or pleasure in almost all activities most of the day, nearly every day (as indicated either by subjective account or observation by others of apathy most of the time).**

- Significant weight loss/gain.

- Insomnia/hypersomnia.

- Psychomotor agitation/retardation.

- Fatigue (loss of energy).

- Feelings of worthlessness (guilt).

- Impaired concentration (indecisiveness).

- Recurrent thoughts of death or suicide.

Source: American Psychiatric Association, 1987.

All depressed patients should be assessed for the risk of suicide by direct questioning about suicidal thinking, impulses, and personal history of suicide attempts. Patients are reassured by questions about suicidal thoughts and by education that suicidal thinking is a common symptom of the depression itself and not a sign that the patient is "crazy."

Table 1 lists the risk factors associated with completed suicide.

If suicide is a distinct risk (specific plans or significant risk factors exist), consult a mental health specialist immediately. The patient may need specialized care or hospitalization.

Table 1. Suicide risk factors

Psychosocial and clinical
Hopelessness
Caucasian race
Male gender
Advanced age
Living alone

History
Prior suicide attempts
Family history of suicide attempts
Family history of substance abuse

Diagnostic
General medical illnesses
Psychosis
Substance abuse

Bipolar illness. A small percentage of patients with major depressive disorder have bipolar illness. These patients experience mood cycles with discrete episodes of depression and mania. In between episodes, they may feel perfectly normal.

Diagnostic criteria for mania.

For mania, at least four of the following symptoms, including the first one listed, must be present for a period of at least 1 week.

- **A distinct period of abnormally and persistently elevated, expansive, or irritable mood.**

- Less need for sleep.

- Talkative or feeling pressure to keep talking.

- Distractibility.

- Flight of ideas.

- Increase in goal-directed activity (either socially, at work or school, or sexually) or psychomotor agitation.

- Inflated self-esteem or grandiosity.

- Excessive involvement in pleasurable activities which have a high potential for painful consequences (buying sprees, sexual indiscretions, or foolish business investments).

Source: American Psychiatric Association, 1987.

3. Diagnose the mood disorder using clinical history and interview.

Many patients are aware of only some symptoms and may minimize their disability. Interviewing someone who knows the individual well (a spouse, close friend, or relative) can be extremely valuable in obtaining an accurate picture of the patient's symptoms, degree of disability, and course of illness.

Figure 1. Differential diagnosis of primary mood disorders

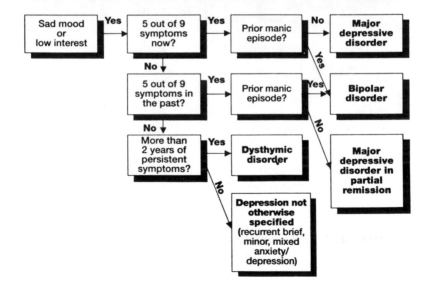

Practitioners should always ask about prior manic episodes, since bipolar disorder, if present, requires a different treatment approach.

Figure 1 shows the diagnostic decisions needed to arrive at a diagnosis of a primary mood disorder.

4. Evaluate patients with a complete medical history and physical examination.

The patient's initial complaints should be evaluated thoroughly with a medical review of systems and a physical examination. If no cause or associated factors can be found for the initial presenting medical complaint, diagnose the patient for a primary mood syndrome.

5. Identify and treat potential known causes (if present) of mood disorder.

Approximately 10-15 percent or more of major depressive conditions are caused by general medical

Figure 2. Conditions associated with mood symptoms or major depressive episodes

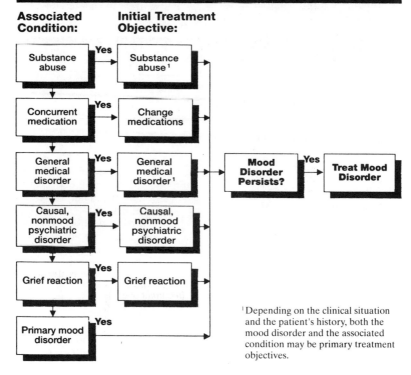

[1] Depending on the clinical situation and the patient's history, both the mood disorder and the associated condition may be primary treatment objectives.

illnesses or other conditions (see Figure 2). Generally, the principle is to treat the associated condition first. If the depression persists after treatment of the associated condition, major depressive disorder should be diagnosed and treated. Potential associated conditions include:

■ **Substance abuse.** Too much alcohol, use of illicit drugs, or abuse of prescription medicines can cause or complicate a major depressive episode. In most cases, once the substance has been discontinued, the depression lifts (Figure 3).

■ **Concurrent medication.** Depression may be an idiosyncratic side effect of many medications. However, the clinician should be aware that this effect is uncommon and usually occurs within days to weeks of starting the medication. Current evidence clearly implicates only reserpine, glucocorticoids, and anabolic steroids with the de novo development of depression as a potential side effect of the drug. Changing to a different medication often relieves the depression (Figure 4).

■ **General medical disorders.** Depression can occur in the presence of another general medical condition (Figure 4) (most commonly, autoimmune, neurologic, metabolic, infectious, oncologic, and endocrine disorders, among others). There are several possibilities in such cases:

The general medical disorder biologically causes or triggers a depression; for example, hypothyroidism can be accompanied by depressive symptoms. In this case, treat the general medical disorder first.

The general medical disorder psychologically results in depression; for example, a patient with cancer may become clinically depressed as a reaction to the prognosis, pain, or incapacity, although most patients with cancer do not suffer a major depressive episode. In this case, treat the depression as an independent disorder.

The general medical disorder and the mood disorder are not causally related. In this case, treat the depression.

■ **Other causal nonmood psychiatric disorders.** These generally include eating disorders, obsessive-compulsive disorder, and some cases of panic disorder (Figure 3).

When generalized anxiety disorder co-exists with major depression, treatment should be directed toward the major depression first.

If panic disorder is present only during major depressive episodes, the major depression is treated first.

If panic disorder and major depression are both present and the panic disorder has been present without episodes of major depression in the past, the clinician must judge which is the most significant condition (e.g., by family history, the level of current disability attributable to each, and the prior course of illness) and treat that condition

Figure 3. Relationship between major depressive and other current psychiatric disorders

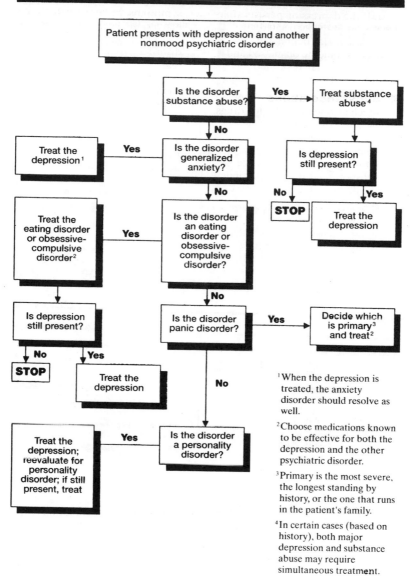

Patient presents with depression and another nonmood psychiatric disorder

Is the disorder substance abuse? — **Yes** → Treat substance abuse [4]

No

Treat the depression [1] ← **Yes** — Is the disorder generalized anxiety?

Is depression still present?

No

No → **STOP**   **Yes** → Treat the depression

Treat the eating disorder or obsessive-compulsive disorder [2] ← **Yes** — Is the disorder an eating disorder or obsessive-compulsive disorder?

No

Is depression still present?

Is the disorder panic disorder? — **Yes** → Decide which is primary [3] and treat [2]

No → **STOP**   **Yes** → Treat the depression

No

Treat the depression; reevaluate for personality disorder; if still present, treat ← **Yes** — Is the disorder a personality disorder?

[1] When the depression is treated, the anxiety disorder should resolve as well.

[2] Choose medications known to be effective for both the depression and the other psychiatric disorder.

[3] Primary is the most severe, the longest standing by history, or the one that runs in the patient's family.

[4] In certain cases (based on history), both major depression and substance abuse may require simultaneous treatment.

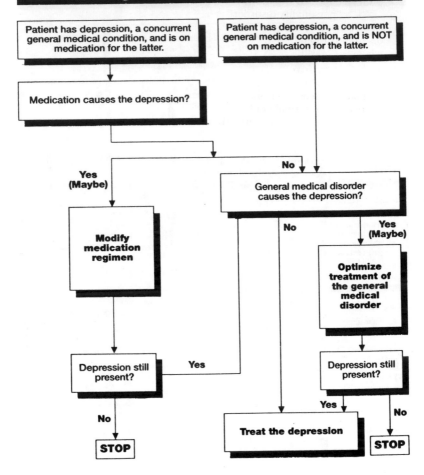

Figure 4. Relationship between major depressive and other current general medical disorders

Note: In some clinical situations, treatment of the depression (e.g., if severe, incapacitating, or life-threatening) cannot be delayed until treatment for the general medical disorder has been optimized.

first. (Some medications have proven effective for both disorders and, therefore, may be preferred in such situations.)

If a "personality disorder" is suspected, the major depressive disorder is treated first, whenever feasible.

■ **Grief reaction.** It is important to differentiate a normal grief reaction from depression. A normal grief reaction persists for 2 to 6 months and improves steadily without specific treatment. Most grief reactions do not meet criteria for a major depressive episode. Grief reactions are usually seen by patients as normal and appropriate. While unpleasant, they rarely cause significant and prolonged impairment in work or other functions. Some individuals experience symptoms of depression along with the grief reaction. If the major depressive episode persists for more than 2 months after the loss, a major depressive disorder should be diagnosed and treated.

6. Reevaluate for mood disorders.

If the depression persists after treatment of the associated psychiatric, general medical, or substance abuse disorders, the depression should be diagnosed and treated.

Appendix E
Questions to Ask In the Assessment of Depressive Symptoms for Severely Ill Patients

This list of questions was formulated by Jimmie C. Holland, M.D., who served as a consultant to the Task Force. The process of evaluating clinical depression in cancer patients is discussed in A. J. Roth and J. C. Holland, "Treatment of Depression in Cancer Patients," *Primary Care in Cancer* 14 (1994): 24-29.

Mood

- How well are you coping? Well? Poorly?   (Well being)
- How are your spirits? Down? Blue? Depressed? Sad? Do you cry sometimes? How often? Only alone?   (Mood)
- Are there things you still enjoy doing or have you lost pleasure in the things you used to do?   (Anedonia)
- How does the future look to you? Bright? Black?   (Hopelessness)
- Do you feel you can change things or are they out of control?   (Helplessness)
- Do you worry about being a burden? Feel others might be better off without you?   (Worthlessness, guilt)

Physical Symptoms

(Evaluate in the context of illness-related symptoms.)

- Do you have pain which isn't controlled?   (Pain)
- How much time do you spend in bed? Weak? Fatigue easily? Rested by sleep?   (Fatigue)
- How are you sleeping? Trouble going to sleep? Awake early? Often?   (Insomnia)
- How is your appetite? Food tastes good? Weight loss or gain?   (Appetite)

- How is your interest in sex? Extent of sexual activity?
  Concerned about partner? (Libido)
- Do you think or move more slowly? (Psychomotor slowing)

Suicidal Risk

(Open with a statement acknowledging the normality of suicidal thoughts for those with the patient's illness; asking about these thoughts does not enhance risk.)

- Many patients with your illness have passing
  thoughts about suicide, such as "I might do
  something if it gets bad enough." Have you (Acknowledge
  ever had thoughts like that? normality)
- Do you have thoughts of suicide? How? Plan? (Level of risk)
- Have you ever had a psychiatric disorder,
  depression, or made a suicide attempt? (Prior history)
- Have you had a problem with alcohol or drugs? (Substance abuse)
- Have you lost anyone close to you recently? (Bereavement)

Appendix F
Requests for Euthanasia and Assisted Suicide: Nursing Management Principles

From N. Coyle, "The Euthanasia and Physician-Assisted Suicide Debate: Issues for Nursing," *Oncology Nursing Forum* 19, no. 7 suppl. (1992): 45.

- Establish a rapport with the patient.
- Know the issues for the individual patient.
  - Inadequate symptom control
  - Depression, hopelessness, spiritual despair
  - Being a burden on the family
  - Altered quality of life and unacceptable limitations
  - Has lived a full life and wants to die while still in control
- Address the issues.
- Do not act independently; involve colleagues from other disciplines.
- Address suicide vulnerability factors.
- Assess family status and adequacy of support resources.
- Know the law.

Reprinted from the *Oncology Nursing Forum* with permission from the Oncology Nursing Press, Inc.

Appendix G
Additional Resources

Academy of Hospice Physicians
500 Dr. M. L. King Street N., Suite 200
St. Petersburg, FL 33705
(813) 823-8899

Agency for Health Care Policy and Research (AHCPR)
Executive Office Center, Suite 501
2101 East Jefferson Street
Rockville, MD 20852
(800) 358-9295 to order publications

Agency of the Department of Health and Human Services that has produced separate guides for patients and clinicians on a number of topics, including acute pain management, cancer pain management, and depression. These are available free of charge.

Acute pain management: *Pain Control After Surgery: A Patient's Guide, Clinical Practice Guideline on Acute Pain Management, Quick Reference Guide on Acute Pain Management in Adults,* and *Quick Reference Guide on Acute Pain Management in Infants, Children, and Adolescents.*

Cancer pain management: *Managing Cancer Pain* (Patient Guide), *Clinical Practice Guideline on Management of Cancer Pain,* and *Quick Reference Guide on Management of Cancer Pain: Adults.*

Depression: *Depression Is a Treatable Illness: A Patient's Guide, Clinical Practice Guideline on Depression in Primary Care* (vols. 1 and 2), and *Quick Reference Guide on Depression in Primary Care: Detection, Diagnosis, and Treatment.*

Alzheimer's Association
919 N. Michigan Avenue, Suite 1000
Chicago, IL 60611-1676
(800) 272-3900 or (312) 335-8700

American Cancer Society
1599 Clifton Road, N.E.
Atlanta, GA 30329-4251
(800) ACS-2345

Provides information about cancer, treatment, and services to patients and families, as well as health care professionals. Together with the National Cancer Institute, publishes *Questions and Answers About Pain Control: A Guide for People with Cancer and Their Families*.

American Chronic Pain Association
P.O. Box 850
Rocklin, CA 95677-0850
(916) 632-0922

American Pain Society
5700 Old Orchard Road, First Floor
Skokie, IL 60077-1057
(708) 966-5595

Publishes *Principles of Analgesic Use in the Treatment of Acute Pain and Cancer Pain* and a membership directory of health care professionals and institutions, and conducts educational programs.

American Society of Clinical Oncology
435 N. Michigan Avenue, Suite 1717
Chicago, IL 60611-4067
(312) 644-0828

Conducts educational programs for physicians. The Society's "Cancer Pain Assessment and Treatment Curriculum Guidelines" appear in *Journal of Clinical Oncology* 10 (1992): 1976-82.

American Spinal Injury Association
355 E. Superior, Room 1436
Chicago, IL 60611
(312) 908-6207

A source of information for health care professionals.

Amyotrophic Lateral Sclerosis (ALS) Association
21021 Ventura Boulevard, Suite 321
Woodland Hills, CA 91364-2206
(800) 782-4747 or (818) 340-7500

Provides education, information, and referral services to assist ALS patients and their families, and information for health care professionals. Publications include *Managing ALS* guides for patients and family members.

Arthritis Foundation
1314 Spring Street, NW
Atlanta, GA 30309
(404) 872-7100

Cancer Care
1180 Avenue of the Americas, Second Floor
New York, NY 10036
(212) 221-3300

Provides support services, counseling, and information for cancer patients and families.

Centers for Disease Control (CDC), National AIDS Hotline
(800) 342-2437; Spanish (800) 344-7432; TDD (800) 243-7889

A source of information about HIV/AIDS and support services.

Commission on Accreditation of Rehabilitation Facilities
101 N. Wilmot Road, Suite 500
Tucson, AZ 85711
(602) 748-1212 (voice or TDD)

Provides lists of accredited facilities and programs.

Gay Men's Health Crisis
129 West 20th Street
New York, NY 10011-0022
(212) 807-6655

Provides support services and legal advice for people with AIDS.

International Association for the Study of Pain (IASP)
909 NE 43rd Street, Suite 306
Seattle, WA 98105
(206) 547-6409

Publishes *Core Curriculum for Professional Education in Pain*.

International Hospice Institute
1275 K Street, NW, 10th Fl.
Washington, D. C. 20005
(202) 842-1600

Mayday Fund
30 Rockefeller Plaza, 55th Floor
New York, NY 10112
(212) 649-5800

A private foundation that provides grants and executes programs
to reduce the human problems associated with pain and its
consequences.

Memorial Sloan-Kettering Cancer Center
1275 York Avenue
New York, NY 10021
(212) 639-2000
Pain Hotline (212) 639-7918

Hospital and research institution that is a WHO Collaborating
Center for Cancer Pain Research and Education. Operates Network project that trains educators and clinicicans nationwide in
palliative care.

Muscular Dystrophy Association
New York Metropolitan Chapter:
10 E. 40th Street, Suite 4105
New York, NY 10016
(212) 679-6215

National Office:
3300 E. Sunrise Drive
Tucson, AZ 85718
(602) 529-2000

National Cancer Institute, Cancer Information Service
Office of Cancer Communications, Building 31, Room 10A24
Bethesda, MD 20892
(800) 4CANCER

Provides information for patients and families, health care professionals, and the public about pain control and other topics related to cancer.

National Chronic Pain Outreach Association
7979 Old Georgetown Road, Suite 100
Bethesda, MD 20814-2429
(301) 652-4948; fax (301) 907-0745

Offers information and pamphlets for patients, information about chronic pain support groups, and referrals to pain management specialists and clinics.

National Coalition for Cancer Survivorship
1010 Wayne Avenue, 5th Floor
Silver Spring, MD 20910-9796
(301) 650-8868

Publications include *Teamwork: The Cancer Patient's Guide to Talking with Your Doctor*, and *Charting the Journey: An Almanac of Practical Resources for Cancer Survivors*.

National Headache Foundation
5252 North Western Avenue
Chicago, IL 60625
(800) 843-2256 or (312) 878-7715

National Hospice Association
1901 N. Moore Street, Suite 901
Arlington, VA 22209
(800) 658-8898

Offers information and referral services.

National Multiple Sclerosis Society
733 Third Avenue
New York, NY 10017
(800) LEARNMS

National Spinal Cord Injury Association
600 W. Cummings Park, Suite 2000
Woburn, MA 01801
(617) 935-2722

National Spinal Cord Injury Hotline
(800) 526-3456

Offers information about spinal cord injury and living with spinal cord injury, as well as referral services and access to support groups.

Oncology Nursing Society
501 Holiday Drive
Pittsburgh, PA 15220
(412) 921-7373

Publications include *Cancer Related Resources in the U. S.* and *ONS Position Paper on Cancer Pain*.

Rehabilitation Nursing Foundation, Association of Rehabilitation Nurses
5700 Old Orchard Road, First Floor
Skokie, IL 60077-1057
(708) 966-3433

Publishes *The Specialty Practice of Rehabilitation Nursing: A Core Curriculum*.

United Cerebral Palsy Foundation Association
1522 K Street, NW, Suite 1112
Washington, DC 20005
(800) 872-5827

Offers a referral service and information about interventions, patient and family support, assisted technology, and employment.

Washington State Medical Association
2033 Sixth Avenue, #1100
Seattle, WA 98121
(206) 441-9762

Publishes *Pain Management and Care of the Terminal Patient*, a handbook for health care professionals.

Wisconsin Cancer Pain Initiative
3675 Medical Science Center
University of Wisconsin Medical School
1300 University Avenue
Madison, WI 53706
(608) 262-0978

> Pamphlets for patients include *Cancer Pain Can Be Relieved*, *Children's Cancer Pain Can Be Relieved*, and *Jeff Asks About Cancer Pain* (for adolescents). Also publishes a *Handbook of Cancer Pain Management* for health care professionals.

World Health Organization
WHO Publications Center USA
49 Sheridan Avenue
Albany, NY 12210
(518) 436-9686

> Publishes *Cancer Pain Relief* (1986) and *Cancer Pain Relief and Palliative Care* (1990).

Other Publications

Bonica, John J., ed., *The Management of Pain*, 2d ed. (Philadelphia: Lea and Febiger, 1990). A comprehensive two-volume work for health care professionals.

Cowles, Jane, *Pain Relief: How to Say No to Acute, Chronic, and Cancer Pain* (New York: MasterMedia, 1993). A comprehensive and accessible guide for patients; includes extensive lists of resources.

Dittmar, Sharon S., *Rehabilitation Nursing: Process and Application* (St. Louis: C. V. Mosby, 1989). Includes as an appendix a list of "Organizations for the Disabled."

Doyle, Derek, Geoffrey W. C. Hanks, and Neil MacDonald, eds., *Oxford Textbook of Palliative Medicine* (New York: Oxford University Press, 1993).

Holland, Jimmie C. and Julia H. Rowland, eds., *Handbook of Psychooncology* (New York: Oxford University Press, 1989).